D0340066

PRAISE FOR

The Setup: A True Story of Dirty Cops, Soccer Moms, and Reality TV

"Journalist Pete Crooks has very carefully reported a tale of people who believed that reality television was the fastest pathway to the fame they so desperately wanted. In many ways, this book is a cautionary tale to all those who believe fame is so important to obtain... You will be given a unique insight into a house of cards constructed to lead to media fame—and to discover more sinister behavior that was occurring just behind the curtain, when the cameras weren't shooting."

—JOE KENDA, retired police detective, subject of Discovery Television's *Homicide Hunter: Lieutenant Joe Kenda*

"I am an incurable reader of thrillers—and *The Setup* is most certainly a riveting real-life thriller. But the book is also much more than that: It's an inside-out look at the manipulative allure of reality television and a telling tale about what people will do for fifteen minutes of fame. This deeply layered crime and corruption story is the ultimate 'truth is stranger than fiction' scenario for a celebrity-obsessed culture. Once I started reading, I could not put *The Setup* down."

—LOUISE FLETCHER, Academy Award–winning actress, *One Flew Over the Cuckoo's Nest*

"I ate this book up. A true crime story about a delusional suburban detective trying to sell a reality show about soccer moms? Yes, you are going to laugh *a lot*, but because Crooks treats his subjects respectfully and like the fallible humans we all are, the absurdity isn't mean spirited. Only a true noir fan could have done such a bang-up job."

—BETH LISICK, *New York Times* bestselling author,
Everybody into the Pool

"*The Setup* takes you on a rambunctious ride-along through some ugly terrain. Not the *faux* paradise of the Bay Area's affluent suburbs, but the delusional, desperate, duplicitous, and thoroughly despicable lives of miscreants who will do *anything* for a shot at fame—as long as it's televised. Pete Crooks' wild tale is a valuable cultural exposé, detailing how America's cult of celebrity can actually breed sociopathic criminals."

—EDDIE MULLER, author, *Dark City: The Lost World of Film Noir*
and founder of the Film Noir Foundation

The Setup

A TRUE STORY of Dirty Cops, Soccer Moms, and Reality TV

PETE CROOKS

BENBELLA BOOKS, INC.
Dallas, Texas

BenBella Books, Inc.
10300 N. Central Expressway
Suite #530
Dallas, TX 75231
www.benbellabooks.com
Send feedback to feedback@benbellabooks.com.

Printed in the United States of America
10 9 8 7 6 5 4 3 2 1

Library of Congress Cataloging-in-Publication Data

Crooks, Pete.
The setup : a true story of dirty cops, soccer moms, and reality TV / by Pete Crooks.
pages cm
Includes bibliographical references and index.
ISBN 978-1-940363-31-8 (trade cloth : alk. paper) — ISBN 978-1-940363-55-4 (electronic) 1. Butler, Chris (Private investigator) 2. Private investigators—California. 3. Women private investigators—Press coverage—California. 4. Police corruption—California. 5. Criminal investigation—Corrupt practices—California. 6. Reality television programs—California. I. Title.
HV8083.B87C76 2015
363.28'9092—dc23

2014027929

Editing by Erin Kelley
Copyediting by Francesca Drago
Proofreading by Lisa Story and Harrison Flanders
Cover design by Pete Garceau
Text design and composition by John Reinhardt Book Design
Printed by Lake Book Manufacturing

Distributed by Perseus Distribution
www.perseusdistribution.com
To place orders through Perseus Distribution:
Tel: (800) 343-4499
Fax: (800) 351-5073
Email: orderentry@perseusbooks.com

This book is dedicated to everyone who hates being lied to.

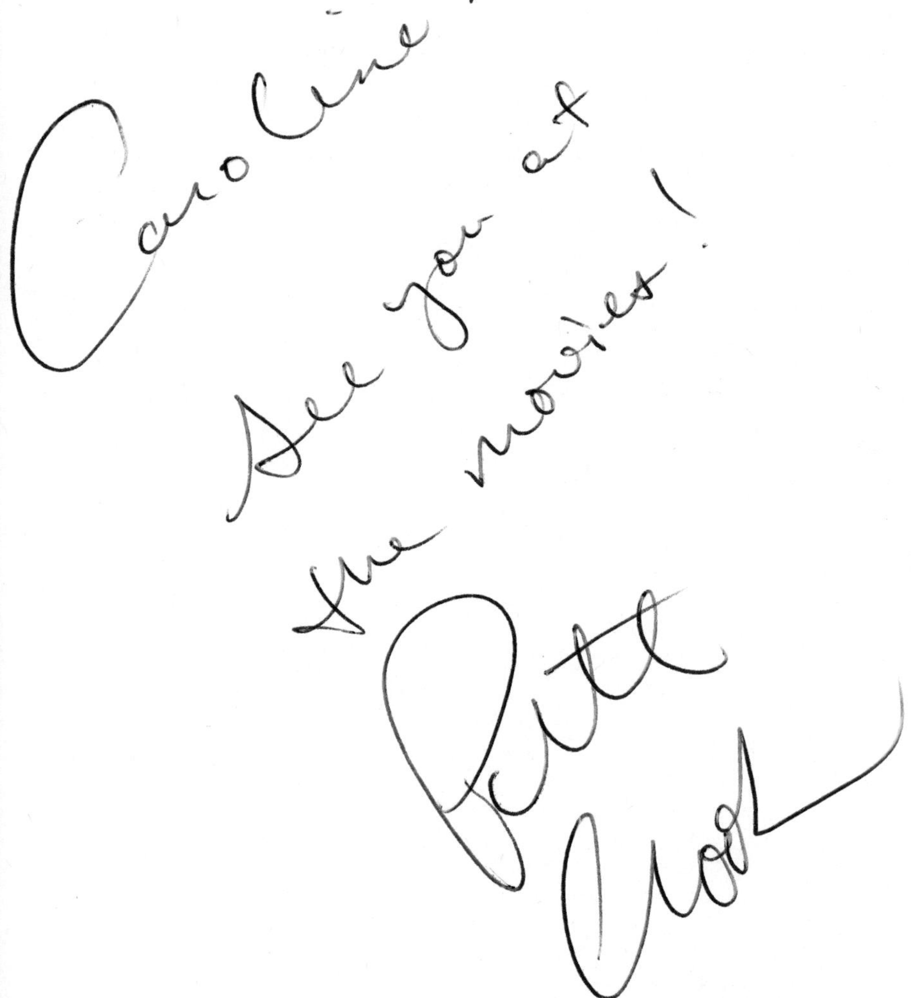

CONTENTS

Part Three: The Investigation

Part Four: A Bright White Spotlight

INTRODUCTION

FAME IS A VERY CURIOUS THING.

Many of those who have it wish they didn't. Many of those who desire it have no real understanding of what it means. But there are a very few who desire fame at any cost. Those few will lie, cheat, steal, sell narcotics, whatever they think they must do, with no consideration of the consequences. Fame is what they seek. They will have it no matter what.

Journalist Pete Crooks has very carefully reported a tale of people who believed that reality television was the fastest pathway to the fame they so desperately wanted. In many ways, this book is a cautionary tale to all those who believe fame is so important to obtain.

You, the reader, will be taken along on Crooks' wild ride covering the bizarre story of reality TV's "PI Moms," and observe as Crooks transforms from a writer of pop culture profiles into, as he puts it, an "accidental investigative reporter." You will be given a unique insight into a house of cards constructed to lead to media fame—and discover the more sinister behavior that was occurring just behind the curtain, when the cameras weren't shooting.

As an experienced criminal investigator, I have seen this behavior on more occasions than I care to recall. During my years as a homicide detective in Colorado Springs, Colorado, I have interviewed all forms of liars—from simple charlatans to sociopathic killers. There are those among us who possess a certain moral flexibility that permits one awful thing to happen after another to reach the desired outcome.

As a result of my career, I was relentlessly pursued by television producers, and I finally agreed to do a show based on some of the 387 homicide cases that came across my desk. I am truly amazed, but *Homicide Hunter: Lieutenant Joe Kenda* has done very well on the Investigation Discovery network. As a result, I have accidentally achieved a small degree of fame. Which is meaningless to me.

But for the people in *The Setup: A True Story of Dirty Cops, Soccer Moms, and Reality TV*, the desire to achieve fame overcame their judgment, their common sense, and in some cases, led to conspiratorial and criminal behavior.

I think you, the reader, will find the story fascinating.

—Joe Kenda
Colorado Springs police detective, retired
Subject of the Investigation Discovery show *Homicide Hunter: Lieutenant Joe Kenda*

PART ONE
THE RIDE-ALONG

1

Have We Got a Story for You

THE BIGGEST STORY in my career as a journalist started as a puff piece.

When the story showed up—for me, at least—I was working as senior editor for *Diablo*, a monthly lifestyle magazine that covers dining, shopping, and society events in the suburban towns of the San Francisco Bay Area. *Diablo* is big and glossy and focuses on lifestyle stories in a very affluent area. It's a very cheerful magazine.

My beat has always had a heavy emphasis on entertainment. I write most of the magazine's pop culture pieces and guides to the local arts scene. Any story about a local personality chasing the contemporary American Dream of celebrity is likely to fall on my desk.

And that's exactly what happened on August 23, 2010.

A Beverly Hills–based publicist contacted me about an East Bay client—a retired cop named Chris Butler. Butler ran a private investigation company out of the suburban city of Concord, California, and he had an interesting angle to his business. Butler staffed his PI firm exclusively with soccer moms.

I'm a huge fan of detective novels and film noir, so I was immediately interested, imagining myself tagging along with some private eyes on a stakeout. The story was both voyeuristic and empowering—I'd write about these suburban moms catching unfaithful husbands and deadbeat dads, insurance frauds and workplace injury liars. Thanks to their mandatory martial arts training, the PI Moms could even employ the occasional chokehold or knee to the nuts, if the guy was really asking for it.

The piece was writing itself!

Clearly, these PI Moms didn't need *Diablo* to turn them into a media sensation. By the time I got the pitch, they already had plenty of press. From March through July 2010, Butler and his PI Moms had enjoyed a tsunami of national media hype, with publicity from *People* magazine, the *Today* show, and Fox News. The PI Moms' biggest media conquest had been the *Dr. Phil* show, which had invested an hour in Butler and his sexy, skilled investigators.

Regional lifestyle magazines like *Diablo* love to celebrate any kid from the neighborhood who has made it big. *Diablo*'s area of coverage claims Tom Hanks and Green Day as backyard celebrities, as well as Markie Post from the 1980s sitcom *Night Court*.

The PI Moms pitch landed squarely in our celebrity sweet spot. In addition to the celebrity hook, the story was a great fit for *Diablo*'s readership demographic: East Bay women in the same age range as the PI Moms.

And then the story got even better.

The publicist told me that I was the first to know that the PI Moms were soon to be featured in their own reality show. In the coming months, Americans would follow these East Bay mommy snoops every Tuesday night on the Lifetime cable network. Water-cooler conversations and message-board debates about the PI Moms were sure to follow.

Real Housewives, PI? I thought. *That sounds like a hit.*

Finally, the publicist offered more than just an interview. He said I could interview the PI Moms while riding along on an actual investigation. I was welcome to tag along with a couple of lady gumshoes on a stakeout, and write all about what happened.

I told the publicist I was in.

2
The King of Stings

ONE DAY AFTER MY CALL with the publicist for the PI Moms, I received a call from Chris Butler, the man in charge of the operation.

Butler spoke in a cool monotone, heavy on the been-there, done-that authority. He told me a bit about his background, which was not too far off from the bios of renegade cops from the movies—Dirty Harry Callahan and *Lethal Weapon*'s Martin Riggs. Butler told me he was a former SWAT cop from Antioch, California, and that his police career was cut short when the squares behind the desk couldn't deal with his envelope-pushing techniques for hooking criminals.

The bio section of Butler's then-active website, Uncover-Truth.com, summed up his career like this:

> [Butler's] creative, cutting-edge methods of investigating and arresting criminals, coupled with an intense work ethic, was [*sic*] lauded by prosecutors as extremely effective. Law enforcement administration often had trouble understanding his tactics and drive, as they were well above the standards of routine performance.

Tired of being hassled by The Man, Butler went independent and acquired a PI firm from a retired FBI agent who had been called back

Butler's website promoted his PI abilities and his national media exposure.

into government service. Butler told me that, while building his business, he discovered an invaluable (but previously untapped) gold mine of a recruiting pool for private investigators: suburban soccer moms.

"At first, I hired former and off-duty law enforcement officers, all men, to work on assignments. They were too often competitive, impatient, and difficult to deal with," said Butler. "Then I hired a mom, and she was the best investigator I had worked with. She was patient and worked well with the other investigators, and she could multitask better than any of my employees, because moms are always multitasking."

Moms, Butler realized, are natural investigators. Moms have built-in bullshit detectors and a sixth sense for the truth.

Butler said a lightbulb went on, and he started hiring moms exclusively. Instantly, he claimed, the quality of his work product skyrocketed.

Butler's rap, though catchy, had an infomercial tone. I started picturing ShamWows and Magic Bullet blenders while Butler talked up his newfound celebrity status, acquired from his spring 2010 trifecta of national media stories about the PI Moms.

"After the *Today* segment aired, I had Al Roker calling me from his dressing room, saying, 'I have a production company, let's talk about a reality show,'" Butler claimed. "After we were on *Dr. Phil*, the phones in our office started to melt!"

Butler said that after *Dr. Phil* pimped the PI Moms, women from all corners of the country wanted to come out to Concord, California, to enter the official PI Mom training program. Interest was so hot that Butler envisioned an opportunity to franchise his brand and create PI Mom outlets from coast to coast.

Kind of like Curves, but for catching cheating husbands.

All the attention had led Electus, a company run by former NBC Entertainment chairman Ben Silverman, to produce a *PI Moms* reality show for Lifetime Television, a subsidiary of A&E Networks. Once the Lifetime show hit the airwaves, Butler told me the show's success was a slam dunk, because he had the goods.

"Lifetime bought the show for the most money it had ever offered for a reality series," Butler bragged—an absurd claim, I would realize later, when considering that Lifetime had previously purchased the proven hit *Project Runway* from the Bravo channel.

Butler's business ambitions and the sizzle of a reality show were important threads in the story I was already writing in my head, but I was equally interested in the cases that Butler and the Moms were investigating. I asked about the ride-along case the PR agent had promised me, quizzing Butler about what kind of investigation I might be tagging along on.

Butler described one of his favorite types of cases: the undercover sting. After the call, I found that his website offered detailed definitions of setups, as well as a general outline of how Butler's clandestine operations were crafted. The website stated:

> When all other investigative methods have failed, or if your problem requires a more proactive approach, an undercover sting may be the last, or only, effective strategy remaining . . . An undercover sting is an intricate illusion created to fool a Subject into thinking that the circumstances that they find themselves in are real.

Which, in Butler-speak, means: Butler & Associates Private Investigations can help you trick or deceive someone. The website went on to wax philosophical about stings:

> The illusion created by this designed coincidence is crafted to weaken the professional (or protective) façade we all erect to effectively hide our true base

> desires. The end product of the undercover sting often results in hard evidence that can be used to criminally prosecute or introduce a means of leverage to a preexisting situation.

Translation: If a client were to hire Butler for a sting, Butler could make a significant other or professional adversary believe an illusion was real. Which could really help the client mess up someone's situation, if need be.

The website also offered a disclaimer:

> It is important to note that our personnel NEVER induce a Subject into engaging in activity; we simply create the illusion of a scenario, within which the Subject is free to act as he or she pleases. Our investigators are there to observe, record, and report. Drug dealers, drunk drivers, scam artists, pedophiles, perjurers, thieves . . . all have been caught as a result of our designed coincidences.

Translation: Don't worry! Undercover stings are never illegal, and Butler & Associates only stings the worst types of subjects: pedos and grifters and losers who drive through school zones while drinking from an open container.

As Butler proudly described his sting success rate, I felt a couple of tremors in my moral compass. Stinging people and setting them up—isn't that kind of shady? *Diablo*'s vibe has always been Stay Classy, East Bay.

The sting Butler wanted to take me on was an old classic; noir buffs will recognize it as the kind Dan Duryea pulled on Edward G. Robinson in *Scarlet Street*.

Butler was planning to set up a horny husband.

The PI pooh-bah explained that he and the PI Moms had a female client who thought her husband might be secretly seeing other women.

"This guy has been frequenting a dating website called MillionaireMatch.com," Butler explained. The horny husband's online indiscretions made him a mark, a sucker susceptible to a scam in which he could be easily duped into making a date with a mystery woman who didn't exist.

Butler told me that he had created his own MillionaireMatch account, and contacted the husband, posing as an available MILF.

Butler described sending the husband pictures of one of the PI Moms to test what virtual eye contact (and a hint of cleavage) would do to the unsuspecting man's better judgment. Butler was now ready to lure the man in, and ask the dope for a date.

If the guy fell for the trap, Butler would send in a PI Mom for a flirt-and-tease meeting in a Starbucks or wine bar. Butler would be parked nearby to provide protection—and of course, to secretly videotape the meeting. He hoped I could be sitting in a van with a team of two PI Moms, all of us observing the operation.

I asked Butler what would happen if the husband didn't take the bait and ignored or deleted his online come-hithers.

"Then we would move to Phase Two of the sting," Butler explained, "in which I assign a decoy to approach him in an unexpected place, like his gym."

I asked Butler for a further explanation of the decoy assignment. Butler said the decoy is a woman, not a PI Mom but a sexy special agent whose job title seemed to be Professional Seductress. Butler told me about a woman whose day job was working late nights in the San Francisco underground club scene, and who was 100 percent smoking hot.

I thought of Linda Fiorentino in *The Last Seduction*, but in workout clothes.

"This girl is a knockout, Pete," he told me. "A *very* sexy girl. She approaches the Subject, she flirts with him, and we observe how he reacts."

I imagined myself at the gym, being approached by Linda Fiorentino.

Maybe she would wear a combo of Victoria's Secret and Lululemon, I thought. *Maybe she would start doing stretches in front of me, while mentioning how much she liked my receding hairline.*

Even in my own imagining, I worried that I might not excuse myself from the decoy to go call my wife.

"Gotta tell you, Chris, I'm not crazy about this scenario," I said. "If you didn't put the girl there, who knows if the guy would be cheating?"

Butler said that some of his clients just wanted to see what their partner would do, if tempted with forbidden fruit.

"I get it, Chris," I said. "But I really don't want to write about you baiting some dude with a hottie."

The King of Stings seemed concerned that I hadn't instantly jumped at the chance to trick an unsuspecting schlub into thinking that a voluptuous maiden wanted to jump his Under Armours.

"I totally understand your position, and the position of your magazine," Butler conceded, attempting to correct the coarseness of his swing-and-a-miss.

To Butler's delight, I invited him to keep trying. "If you were following someone who happened to be actually cheating, I'd be OK with that," I said.

Fortunately, Butler responded, his firm was so busy with cases that it would be no problem to find a case that suited my sensitive ethics. He said he would get back to me shortly, and the very next day, Butler emailed me to tell me about an entirely different case, one that just happened to fulfill all of my ethical requirements. I was so wrapped up in the story that the coincidences lining up seemed like they were just that, coincidences.

Butler explained that his client, a wealthy fifty-three-year-old widow, had recently gotten engaged to a much younger man. As the couple's wedding date approached, the client began to wonder if there was funny business happening during her boyfriend's long trips to the gym. The suspicious behavior seemed to occur every other Saturday, when the widow had to spend her days at work.

Butler explained the PI Moms had been working with the client for a while, helping her soberly collect information about the situation before she went through with the wedding.

"The PI Moms have been coaching her to avoid questioning him, as this tends to alert the cheating party to the fact that their partner may be suspicious," Butler wrote. "The PI Moms are also coaching her to avoid confronting him after she learns the truth; an anti-*Cheaters* TV show approach."

I hadn't ever seen *Cheaters*, but somehow knew exactly what it was: a late-night reality show about cheating spouses getting caught on camera, looking like sensationally stupid douche bags.

Butler assured me that his case wouldn't be anything like that.

Butler said the next Saturday that the widow had to work happened to be September 11, and the Moms planned to tail the fiancé that day.

Butler told me that his client was a big fan of *Diablo*, so she agreed to let me write about her case, with the caveat that I would not reveal her name or any identifying details about her or her fiancé.

That way, her neighbors, who also subscribed to *Diablo*, wouldn't gossip.

On Thursday, September 9—two days before the ride-along—I visited Butler's office for the first time, located at 1000 Detroit Avenue in Concord.

Butler's workplace did not measure up to the flashy impression I had formed during the Beverly Hills publicist's pitch. I expected swankier digs for a business that had received so many accolades in national media stories.

The office was located in a storage warehouse in an industrial area of Concord. Unit J, Butler's space, was toward the back of the warehouse's parking lot. The nondescript location just didn't seem like a place for a guy with a big TV show in the works to be running his business from.

I have a habit of using TV and movies as a reference filter in my life, having spent so much of my life watching screens. The thought that came to mind—*Jim Rockford worked out of a rusty mobile home on* The Rockford Files—made Butler's Unit J seem less seedy.

Unit J's exterior windows and door were blacked out with some kind of reflective material, so anyone standing outside could not see in. There was no sign or lettering on the door to suggest that the space was an office of any kind. Standing in front of the door, I looked up, and noticed a security camera positioned above the upper right corner, pointing down at me.

I looked at my reflection in the door's shiny darkness, and I thought of the scene from the film *This Is Spinal Tap*, when the band stares dumbfounded at its all-black album cover for the first time. Guitarist Nigel Tufnel looks at his reflection in the cover and asks, "How much more black could it be? The answer is none. None more black."

None more black. The line made me laugh.

Instantly, I felt self-conscious and a bit foolish, realizing that Butler and the PI Moms might be a few feet away on the other side of the door, watching me through the one-way window or via the security camera.

I stopped laughing and rang the bell. The door opened immediately.

3

Let's Go for a Ride-Along

UNIT J'S FRONT DOOR was not opened by Chris Butler, or by one of the PI Moms.

The person who opened the door to Butler's world was Carl Marino. Marino, forty, was clean-cut and gym-fit, with sea-green eyes and Macy's-model looks. He welcomed me into the office.

As I stepped inside, I noticed that the narrow hallways of Butler's office space were decorated with photos of classic TV detectives from the 1970s and '80s: *Columbo; Magnum, PI; Moonlighting*; and, of course, *Charlie's Angels*. Extra-cheesy fare like *Remington Steele* and *Scarecrow and Mrs. King* were also displayed; there may have been a *Riptide*.

The Rockford Files was noticeably absent.

Chris Butler approached from the bowels of the warehouse. Butler was on the pudgy side of stocky, maybe even steroid-puffy. He wore a neatly trimmed goatee and sported silver hair that looked as though it had been purchased from a midrange supplier. He was dressed in tight designer jeans, expensive boots, and a tight black t-shirt with the word "Clout" embossed in biker font. The PI's overall look was carefully considered—Butler was projecting metrosexual *Sons of Anarchy*.

We shook hands and Butler gave me a DVD, a burned copy of his *Dr. Phil* appearance.

Chris Butler poses in his office, next to his wall of TV detective photos.
Photo by Sherry LaVars.

"You're going to want to watch this," Butler told me.

I could tell he expected me to be impressed, like he was doing my regional magazine a favor after dancing on the national stage with Dr. Phil McGraw.

Then again, our magazine has a lot of wealthy female readers, some of whom may have cheating husbands. A feature article would be a perfect way for Butler to drum up some new business to pay the bills.

Butler led me to the center of the office, where two women (real PI Moms!) were seated at a conference table. Two more Moms appeared from the back of the office and told Butler they were going out on a case. Carl Marino stayed near the front door, and sat down at his desk, presumably to get back to his own work, whatever that was.

I introduced myself to the two PI Moms at the conference table, Charmagne Peters and Denise Antoon, friendly fortysomethings who I recognized from the *People* magazine story.

Charmagne raved about a recent feature I had written about actor Will Forte, who grew up in the East Bay before making it big on *Saturday Night Live*. When Forte's *MacGruber* movie was ready to hit multiplexes,

Diablo put him on the cover in an Indiana Jones jacket with copy reading, "Will Forte Blows Up."

"It was a *great* article," said Charmagne, who was in the same graduating high school class as Will Forte.

Denise, who lived in the East Bay burb of Dublin, had a BA in criminal justice and a law degree. She came to work for Butler after years as an expert jury selector. She had worked on the Scott Peterson case, one of California's most sensational murder trials post-OJ.

Charmagne seemed to be the template of PI Mom transformation, from soccer mom to super sleuth. The mother of two lived in the affluent town of Orinda, and had previously been a client of Butler & Associates. Charmagne told me she had hired Butler to investigate her teenage nephew, a young man with psychological problems, who she believed was having paranoid delusions about being followed. The teenager's behavior, as Charmagne described it, was so intense and erratic that his entire family was in a desperate panic.

Fortunately, Butler and the PI Moms had been able to prove that the nephew's parallax view was askew. In the end, the nephew's parents realized their kid was not being followed or phone-tapped, and that strong medication was the most effective way to make the black helicopters disappear.

Charmagne said she had been so impressed by Chris Butler and the PI Moms' quality of work and concern for the young man, she decided to take the plunge and become an investigator. She came in a concerned client, and transformed into a grown-up Nancy Drew with a minivan.

As I was chatting with the moms, I noticed that Butler was reading and sending text messages rather than engaging in the conversation. Much later, I would discover that Butler was being pinged by Carl Marino, who was sitting just a few feet away.

When Butler wasn't tapping texts to Marino, he was glancing at a panel of screens near Marino's desk. The screens displayed closed-circuit feeds from several security cameras, including the one I had noticed above the front door.

I could see my car parked in the lot on one screen. A white Mercedes pulled into the adjacent spot. Butler saw the sedan as well, which prompted him to interrupt my conversation with Denise and Charmagne.

"Pete, I invited my client, who I described to you in the email, to come and meet you today and talk about her case," Butler told me.

On one of the screens, we watched a woman step out of her Mercedes, walk to the front door, and buzz the bell. Carl Marino let her in.

Butler introduced me to Sharon the Client, a petite, pretty blonde in her early fifties. This was the woman he had described in the email. Sharon the Client was dressed fancy-casual. Her blouse was decorated with impressive, intricate beading, which matched her earrings. Her white jeans looked more Nordstrom than Old Navy.

Sharon the Client shook my hand and told me how much she enjoyed *Diablo* magazine before explaining why she was hiring the PI Moms. Sharon told me she was engaged to a man named Al, a fun guy who she met a few years after her longtime husband passed away unexpectedly. Sharon had been dipping her toe in the dating pool when she met Al during happy hour at a now-defunct cocktail lounge, Bing Crosby's.

Al swept Sharon the Client off her feet, which she feared may have been too easy due to her naivety—she had been with her late husband since high school. Smooth-Talking Al quickly proposed, then moved into Sharon's home in the affluent suburb of Lafayette.

Sharon told me that she had wanted her daughter, currently in high school, to enter college before getting married again, so no wedding date was set yet. As the engagement progressed, Sharon started to notice troubling behavior from her fiancé.

"Al takes these longs trips to the gym. He's gone for hours and hours," she told me, her voice quivering. "He came back once and I checked his gym bag, and his workout clothes were in there neatly folded like he hadn't worked out at all."

Butler chimed in a few words of tough-guy wisdom.

"In my experience, if you suspect there's a problem, there probably is," Butler said. "I'd say it's true 95 percent of the time. That's why we've been working with Sharon to help her with the situation. If her fiancé is fooling around, we will be able to help her get her ducks in a row."

Sharon the Client began to cry. I felt badly for her. I had come to Butler's office expecting to make some small talk with the PI Moms, and did not expect to witness a client baring her soul.

"I just need to know if something is going on," Sharon the Client sniffled. "I need to know before I marry him."

The PI Moms sprang into action. Charmagne grabbed a box of Kleenex while Denise asked Sharon if she would like a hug. Sharon the Client nodded sadly and dabbed at her tears with the tissue.

"I'm so glad they're moms," Sharon the Client told me softly. "They understand what I'm going through."

Two days later was Saturday, September 11: the day of the ride-along.

I returned to Butler's office to tag along with Charmagne and Denise, and to find out if Smooth-Talking Al was up to no good. I was told to arrive at 11 AM for some prep time, as the surveillance was scheduled to begin at high noon.

Butler, wearing another outfit of black t-shirt, jeans, and boots, was tinkering with a brightly painted Harley Davidson in the garage half of his warehouse space. Butler was irritated that one of the motorcycle's mirrors was broken.

"Damn it," Butler spat. "I loaned this to some law enforcement contacts to use for an undercover drug case. If they are going to break something, they need to fix it before they return it."

I hadn't noticed that the garage, adjacent to Unit J, was part of Butler's office during my first visit. The garage was filled with tools, toys, and vehicles. Along with the motorcycle, there was a four-door Cadillac that Butler claimed was outfitted with a bunch of hidden cameras.

The garage also housed a pristine vintage Volkswagen Beetle, which Butler told me he wanted to sell for at least $30,000—because he had restored it to be an exact replica of "Herbie" in the 1968 Disney movie, *The Love Bug*.

After the tour, I met Charmagne and Denise in the parking lot. They were loading bottled waters and trail mix into a silver Honda minivan. Charmagne made an announcement before we piled into her van.

"Now, I know I'm being a mom here," Charmagne said, "but if anyone needs to take a bathroom break, do it now. We could be stuck in the van for a while."

Butler's office was in a nondescript warehouse facility in Concord, CA. *Photo by Pete Crooks.*

An hour later, I was camped out in the back of the minivan, on patrol with the PI Moms.

We were parked in a quiet, shaded neighborhood of million-dollar homes, waiting for Sharon the Client's white Mercedes to drive past. Al's MO was to head to the gym at noon every Saturday and, at two minutes past noon, the Mercedes appeared with Al behind the wheel. The car sped down a hill, and Charmagne started to follow in her minivan. The first light we hit turned red, and the Benz disappeared around a bend.

"Shit," said Charmagne. "Don't put this in your article," she said and gunned the minivan through the red light. We caught up to the Mercedes, a mile up the road, and stayed one car length's distance behind it, all the way to the parking lot of a 24 Hour Fitness club.

Al, dressed in a t-shirt and sweats, got out of the Mercedes and walked very slowly toward the gym. Denise scrambled into the back of the van with a video camera to record his casual stroll.

Al certainly appeared to be headed for a workout. And, given his ridiculously muscled physique, my guess was that Al spent considerable time lifting weights and taking steroids.

Al's blond hair was crew cut, and he was considerably younger than the woman who started crying in front of me two days before. I silently hoped the surveillance would give Sharon the Client enough evidence to dump her fiancé; this guy had to be a gold digger. Al strutted into the gym.

"Now, we wait," said Denise. "This might take awhile. Sometimes our day is spent sitting here, just staring at a door."

Not this time. After fewer than ten minutes, Al came back outside, sporting Tommy Bahamas duds.

"Oh, don't we look pretty," said Charmagne. The game was on; we had a cheater in our sights. Denise trained the video camera at the possible lothario, and Al loped back to the Mercedes. He tossed his gym bag in the backseat, and drove away.

Charmagne fired up her van and slipped into traffic behind Sharon the Client's Mercedes. We followed Al to a freeway, where he headed south toward the ritzy town of Danville, and its even ritzier gated community of Blackhawk. Having covered events in Blackhawk on many occasions, I asked the PI Moms what might happen if that was indeed where the Subject was headed, and we got stuck at a gate guarded by some surly security.

"The guards at the gate can be strict," I told Charmagne. "If this dude is going to see someone in Blackhawk, he'll get through the gate if he's on the guest list. But we won't."

Charmagne saw my point, but mentioned that Butler had friends who worked Blackhawk security, so it should not be a problem. Still, she called Butler on her cell phone and told him that Al was wearing Tommy Bahamas and might be headed into the gated community.

Butler responded by biting Charmagne's head off.

I could hear his voice coming through Charmagne's phone, sounding like a furious adult's in a *Peanuts* special, lecturing the PI Mom about the rules of surveillance.

"Has he driven into Blackhawk?" Butler asked Charmagne, who replied that Al had not yet entered the gated community.

"You know that your job is not to assume what he is going to do," Butler barked. "Your job is to observe what he does do."

Charmagne hung up the cell phone, looked at Denise, and rolled her eyes.

About a minute later, the Mercedes pulled up to the security gate at Blackhawk. The guard checked the guest list and let Al right through. We were the next car in line, and Charmagne pulled up to the guard station in the minivan.

"Good afternoon," said the guard, holding the clipboarded guest list like a VIP nightclub bouncer. "Who are you here to see?"

Charmagne totally choked. "I, uh... Can we just turn around?" she asked. The guard nodded and waved a U-turn motion around his station.

We flipped the U, drove twenty yards away from Blackhawk, pulled off to the side of the road, and waited.

I questioned Butler's "don't assume, just observe" instructions, because my investigative instincts had been entirely prescient: Al had, in fact, gone into Blackhawk, and we were stuck outside the gate.

Now the Subject was out of sight, doing fuck knows what. And for who knows how long.

"If he's hooking up at someone's house, he could be in there for hours," I said to Charmagne and Denise. "And if we're out here, we won't know what's going on."

But just a few minutes later, the white Mercedes appeared and rolled past the security guard, and then right past Charmagne's minivan. As the car passed the van, I got a quick look through the passenger seat window. A female brunette, wearing giant Jackie O sunglasses, now accompanied Smooth-Talking Al.

Denise made a call to Chris Butler with a status update, so Butler could keep Sharon the Client informed of Al's activities throughout the surveillance. Charmagne pulled her van back onto the road, and followed the Mercedes at a distance of one car length.

We trailed Al onto a northbound freeway; I started asking the PI Moms where they thought the muscle-headed horndog might be taking his

Mystery Date. I fired away questions like a pestering child—an overgrown Red Chief from the O. Henry story.

"Where do you think he is going?" I asked, "Does he have the nerve to take his side dish to downtown Walnut Creek, so close to his fiancée's house? Does he even care if he gets seen with this woman?"

"We aren't supposed to assume anything," said Denise, parroting Butler. "Our job is simply to observe and report those observations."

The Mercedes stayed on the freeway, passed Walnut Creek, and headed for the Benicia-Martinez Bridge. I had been right about Blackhawk, so I continued to make predictions.

"Looks like we're going to wine country," I predicted. "The way that guy was dressed, he's taking his date up to Napa for a little tasting."

"Never assume, just observe," Charmagne and Denise repeated, in unison.

My prediction about Napa turned out to be dead-on, which made me wonder if I should open my own PI business.

Al and Mystery Date drove to the Napa Premium Outlets, a *Diablo*-friendly destination of designer discount stores. Al parked, got out of the Mercedes, and opened the door for his Mystery Date: a twentysomething, wearing a green dress that exposed copious cleavage.

"Are you getting this?" Charmagne asked her PI partner.

"Got it," Denise acknowledged, pointing her large video camera through the windshield.

Al and Mystery Date kissed, right next to the Mercedes, confirming all the fears that caused Sharon the Client to start crying in front of me in Butler's office.

"Got that as well," said Denise, who videotaped the kiss, and kept the tape running as the couple walked arm in arm into a jewelry store that advertised 80 percent discounts.

After a few minutes, the couple came out of the discount jewelers, with Mystery Date carrying a purple gift bag. They strolled through the mall to the Coach store.

Charmagne called Butler to check in and confirm that Al was, in fact, a cheating douche bag. We had already logged nearly three hours of surveillance and prep time, and Sharon the Client had booked the minimum requirement of four hours, for a fee of somewhere around $1,000.

Since Al had obviously lied about spending the day at the gym, I assumed we would head back to the East Bay, let Sharon the Client see the video of her lunkhead fiancé on a date with a floozy, and let the poor lady pull the plug on the engagement.

But first I wanted some lunch. I had not eaten anything all day, and it was almost 3 PM. I was getting a headache and the smell of the vinyl seats in Charmagne's minivan wasn't helping.

Instead of instructing his PI Moms to head home (or to the nearest In-N-Out Burger), Butler said that Sharon the Client insisted we continue following her fiancé. Sharon had even approved a backup team of investigators to join the surveillance party. Charmagne told me the backup PIs were driving to Napa from their home in San Francisco.

"What the hell do you need another team for?" I asked the PI Moms. "You've got video of the guy out on a date. Case closed. Let's get lunch."

Charmagne and Denise told me Sharon the Client wanted more dirt, a demand that fell under the company's customer-is-always-right policy. I suspected that the second team was a way for Butler to run up Sharon the Client's bill, taking advantage of her emotional distress.

Minutes later, the backup team arrived, driving a newish Mustang GT. A couple got out of the muscle car, looking as if they were stepping out of a Guess ad. I recognized Carl Marino, the guy who had opened the door at Butler's office two days before. He was with a slim brunette, who turned out to be his newlywed bride. Ilona Marino (née Gugan) had married Carl exactly two weeks prior to my ride-along. Chris Butler attended the wedding but the PI Moms did not.

Carl Marino approached the minivan. Charmagne showed Marino a picture of the man we had been following and described the brunette's big tits. Marino barely glanced at the Subject's photo, but did lean in the driver's side window to look at me and give a cool-guy nod.

I thought Butler only hired moms, I thought to myself. *What's up with Mr. Macy's Model?*

The Marinos headed back to the Mustang and zoomed off into the afternoon. Then, Al and Mystery Date came out of the Coach store, carrying another gift bag. Al opened the door for his date and gave her another kiss, which Denise documented on video.

The couple drove down a Napa highway and pulled into the parking lot of a popular wine-country restaurant called Rutherford Grill.

They parked and walked arm-in-arm toward the restaurant, stopping point-blank in front of Charmagne's minivan to smooch some more, apparently unaware that the woman in the passenger seat was pointing a giant, handheld video camera at them. They sauntered into the restaurant.

I hoped Al and Mystery Date would have a long, leisurely lunch; at least long enough for me to order an appetizer.

Once Al and Mystery Date entered the restaurant's outdoor patio area, Charmagne, Denise, and I piled out of the minivan and stealthily followed the couple. Rutherford Grill was packed, and Al and Mystery Date had taken a spot at a patio table for quick service. There was a forty-five-minute wait in the restaurant, and the only open seats on the patio were at the same table, an eight-top, located right next to the bar.

"That sucks," I said to Charmagne, nodding at the empty seats at their table. "I am starving."

"They have no idea we're watching them," said Charmagne. "We do this kind of thing all the time." She marched right over to the table and sat down with Al and Mystery Date. Denise and I joined her.

I sat down across from Mystery Date, smiled, and said hello. The midtwenties brunette reminded me of the actress Megan Fox—if Megan Fox's entire right arm was a tattooed sleeve.

Charmagne sat down and put a large leather purse on the table. The purse had a cell phone case, which housed a small video camera, attached to its exterior. Since Al and Mystery Date were in a public place, it was legal to record video of them. Recording their conversation without permission, however, was illegal—a misdemeanor and a civil rights violation.

I was sitting so close to the couple that I could hear every groan-inducing line Al was trying.

Smooth-Talking Al: You look beautiful today. Did I tell you that already?

Mystery Date: You did. Ugh, I'm sweating.

Al: I'd like to lick all that sweat off of you.

Mystery Date: I'd like that, too. I want to go horseback riding tomorrow at my friend's stables out past Tassajara.

Al: Is that near where we got that hotel room that time? That was a wild night.

Smooth. Talking. Al.

Al sipped a beer and Mystery Date ordered an appetizer of artichoke dip and a grilled artichoke entrée. Charmagne, Denise, and I ordered hamburgers and a *Flintstones*-sized plate of ribs, which we scarfed down as Al and Mystery Date flirted and lingered. We paid our check and hustled back to the minivan.

Al and Mystery Date came out a few minutes later, again stopping right in front of the van to kiss, then got into the Mercedes and drove to the acclaimed Peju winery off Highway 29. Charmagne called the Marinos and gave them the location.

Minutes later, the Marinos pulled the Mustang into the parking lot and went inside the winery. Charmagne, Denise, and I stayed in the van.

Al and Mystery Date were inside the tasting room for about an hour, during which time Charmagne received text messages from the Marinos, which she read aloud:

TEXT 1: Made contact with subject
TEXT 2: We r talking to them and taking pics 2gether
TEXT 3: They r drunk
TEXT 4: Just invited us back to their hotel!!

Charmagne called Butler again, who reported that Sharon the Client was furious and wanted to see her fiancé and Mystery Date for herself. Butler told Charmagne that he and Sharon were already en route, headed to Napa.

This struck me as an extraordinarily strange decision, as well as a complete contradiction to everything Butler told me about not confronting the cheater. The point of the infidelity surveillance was supposed to provide Sharon the Client with information that she could use to her advantage. There was no need to risk a potential confrontation with the emotional client, her horndog fiancé, and his much younger mistress.

"That's a horrible idea," I told the PI Moms, imagining a revenge-fueled climax from any of a thousand old noir movies. "What happens if she seems him with this younger woman and pulls a pearl-handled pistol out of her purse and starts shooting?"

Charmagne nodded, but said it was too late: Butler and Sharon the Client were on their way.

Denise fired up the video camera as Al, Mystery Date, and the Marinos came out of the winery. The foursome exchanged hugs and kisses before heading to their cars.

Al and Mystery Date appeared to be buzzed. Al groped at his date before opening the passenger door of the Mercedes.

"Get a room, you two!" yelled Carl Marino, across the parking lot.

"You know we have one!" Smooth-Talking Al yelled back, cackling.

Charmagne started up the minivan, and we pulled right behind Al and Mystery Date, who took advantage of every red light to make out. Al even campaigned for a blow job, clumsily pushing Mystery Date's head down toward his lap before the light turned green.

Just south of Napa, the Mercedes pulled into the Holiday Inn Express. Charmagne parked across the street, and Denise videotaped the couple moving the shopping bags they had acquired from the Napa Premium Outlets into the trunk. Then Al and Mystery Date headed toward the hotel.

Butler and Sharon the Client arrived soon after, accompanied by a female intern from Butler & Associates. Butler approached Charmagne's van and got an update about the gifts. Sharon was fuming and demanded to examine the trunk of the Mercedes.

"I want to see what he bought her," screamed Sharon the Client. "I want to look in the trunk of my own fucking car!"

Denise suggested that Butler let his client check the trunk of her Benz. Butler had a better idea. Like a flag-football quarterback, he sketched out a plan on his palm, showing the team how he would drive away with Sharon the Client's car. Sharon gave Butler her spare key, and Butler hustled over to the Mercedes and drove away.

The intern and Sharon the Client followed in Butler's Chrysler 3000. Charmagne, Denise, and I trailed behind them in the minivan. The caravan pulled into a parking lot less than a mile down Highway 29.

Sharon the Client jumped out of Butler's car, opened the trunk of her Mercedes, and found an empty jewelry box and a Coach bag. She went from furious to heartbroken, shrieked through tears, then collapsed into the spacious trunk. Butler and the Moms tried to comfort her.

Awkward.

I excused myself and headed for a Starbucks in the shopping center.

As I waited in line at the coffee shop, I tried to evaluate what I had just witnessed.

Sharon the Client now knew that her fiancé had been lying to her. She had to imagine that Al and Mystery Date were, at that very moment, gleefully sportfucking at the Holiday Inn Express, just a few hundred yards up the highway.

That couldn't feel very good.

But what really confused me was Butler's plan to take the Mercedes and leave Al and Mystery Date without a ride back to the East Bay. What was Al going to do when he came out of the hotel and realized the car was missing? Would he report it stolen? If so, would he say it was stolen from wine country, or from the East Bay, where he was supposed to be working out this entire time? So many plot holes!

A more serious concern was how Al would react if he realized he had been set up by his fiancée. My eyeball estimate of the guy was that he was a steroid user. Once he realized she had him followed—and humiliated him in front of his mistress with the stolen car snafu—who's to say he wouldn't blow up with 'roid rage and bash in her head with a barbell?

I suspended this internal Q&A when the barista announced that my latte was ready. I walked back to the parking lot where Butler and the PI Moms—and a somewhat subdued Sharon the Client—were waiting for me.

While this melodrama was unfolding, Carl and Ilona Marino were returning Chris Butler's black Mustang GT to the parking lot of Butler's office back in Concord. The Mustang was one of Butler's favorite toys, tricked out by a ton of horsepower, racing stripes, hood locks, and a killer stereo full of hard-rock music.

Butler had purchased the vehicle with the investment capital of a former client. In fact, with the savings of the woman who originally came up with the concept of "PI Moms," i.e., caring, sympathetic, and savvy women who could help keep other women from being exploited by manipulative men.

Butler had the Marinos drive the Mustang up to Napa that day not because Sharon the Client needed a second team of investigators, but because he wanted the couple to be featured in the *Diablo* article. Carl Marino clearly wanted to get some press for his part in the ride-along, as demonstrated by the texts he had sent to Butler throughout the day:

TEXT 1: Hope Charmagne is talking us up... Ilona had her game face on.
TEXT 2: It was a good day. Talk us up. ☺
TEXT 3: I officially love that car.

I would find out much later that Butler and Marino hoped that once the *PI Moms* show was a hit on Lifetime, they could spin off a series featuring Carl and Ilona opening a satellite private investigations office in Los Angeles, this one staffed by hungry actors instead of soccer moms. The actors would go to auditions by day and work cases at night.

Butler and Marino imagined that the show would be called *The Real Mr. and Mrs. Smith*, a riff on the hit action movie starring real-life couple-to-be Brad Pitt and Angelina Jolie. At Carl and Ilona's wedding two weeks before my ride-along, the couple made sure Butler was seated next to a young filmmaker who had cast Carl in his first acting role, a low-budget thriller called *Sedona's Rule*. Butler spent the wedding dinner pitching the filmmaker about shooting *The Real Mr. and Mrs. Smith* pilot.

Back in wine country, Chris Butler gave instructions to his team about how the last hour of my ride-along would play out. He said he would drive Sharon the Client back to her home and make sure she was emotionally stable after the day's traumatic revelations.

He instructed the PI Moms to take the minivan back to his office and upload all the video information to his office hard drive. He also told his intern, Tracy, to drive his Chrysler 3000 back to the office, and all three women to await his return for a debriefing on the day's events.

I was free to go back to business as usual, after being adhered to Charmagne's vinyl minivan seat for nearly ten hours. That Saturday night, business as usual meant taking society pictures at a fundraiser for a local nonprofit, the Ruth Bancroft Dry Gardens of Walnut Creek.

I told Butler I would check in with him again soon about the story.

As exciting as the ride-along had been, I still needed information about the Lifetime show, including an airdate so *Diablo* could schedule the story. I was curious about what kind of logistics and infrastructure would be required to film the wild events I had witnessed for a reality show.

Charmagne drove me and Denise back to the office. When we parked in front of Unit J, part of me was sorry to have the adventure come to an end. I had enjoyed the PI Moms' company and stories all day long, as weird and wild as the experience had been.

When we reached Butler's warehouse, Charmagne rigged up the hidden purse camera to a monitor so we could watch a bit of the footage shot at Rutherford Grill, which did not seem quite as a lurid without the talk of sweat-licking and horseback riding and hotel room hookups.

"It's too bad you didn't get video of him coming out and seeing that the car was gone," I said to Charmagne and Denise. "*That* would have been the money shot."

4

The Dr. Phil *Sizzle Reel*

IF THERE WAS ONE MEDIA APPEARANCE, more than any other, that helped land a reality show deal for Butler, it was *Dr. Phil*.

The *Dr. Phil* episode featuring Butler and the PI Moms aired in June 2010, and the program served as a sensational sizzle reel for Butler's business—which is exactly why he handed me a burned copy of the show when I visited his office to begin reporting this story.

I went home that night and popped the disc in to watch with my wife, Tamara, and my father-in-law, Jaap. "That's the private investigator I met today," I told my family, seeing Butler on screen with Dr. Phil McGraw. "He's a really interesting guy."

Dr. Phil introduced the PI Moms to his viewers as "gun-packing, hard-hitting, undercover PIs," then paused for an applause break. The studio audience ate it up.

Butler was in fine form on *Dr. Phil*. The PI was cool and authoritative, talking about his intense six-month training program that all PI Moms had to endure before going out into the field.

"We hit them with everything during that six-month period," Butler claimed. "If they don't make it, they wash out. And the wash-out rate is very high."

Charmagne and Denise, and a third PI named Michelle Allen, all sat on stage with Butler and Dr. Phil, talking about their busy lives, balancing their kids' baseball practices with bad guy surveillance details.

"We are cross-trained in everything," Charmagne claimed. "One of the assets of being a mom is that we are multitaskers. We always have our heads above water."

Dr. Phil also sent cameras to Concord to film the PI Moms taking a self-defense training class at the UFC Gym. The footage screamed: Gun-packing! Hard-Hitting! Undercover Moms!

"I think this is really interesting!" a grinning Dr. Phil told his audience before tossing to a commercial.

The bulk of the hour-long episode featured Butler and the PI Moms on the case, or, catching men being naughty. There were three cases featured: an infidelity surveillance, a business scam setup, and a hidden camera sting.

In the first case, Butler described sending a team of investigators off to Hawaii, at the behest of the client, to see what her husband would do if tempted with some cheater elixir. Butler produced video evidence of the husband (whose image was fogged) kissing a blonde decoy named Sharon Taylor, who would later be cast on the *PI Moms* show.

Butler's client appeared as well, wearing a wig, and told Dr. Phil how upset she had been when she first saw the footage.

"I needed to know that it wasn't just in my head," said the client, "Laura." "He wasn't just cheating on me; he was cheating on his kids. He was cheating on all of us."

The second case sent the PI Moms chasing after an unlicensed private investigator who had been advertising services on Craigslist. The Moms met with the man outside a Starbucks and got him to offer surveillance work, which is against the law to do in California without a state-issued PI license. As soon as the PI Mom handed over a check for $1,500, Butler appeared with a local police officer. The *Dr. Phil* camera crews filmed the unlicensed PI being issued a citation and receiving a lecture from Butler about the rules of private investigation.

"You've committed a misdemeanor," Butler told the unlicensed PI, who looked dumbfounded. "Had you lied, and said you had a license, you would have committed a felony."

The unlicensed PI turned out to be a former high-tech worker who had been downsized during the recession. He had been unemployed for a full year and was grasping at straws for income. He claimed he had no idea he had been breaking any laws by offering PI services without a license.

"That's in violation of state law, 'cuz you gotta have a license and there's gotta be something like six thousand hours of supervised training (to be a licensed investigator)," Dr. Phil told his audience. "There's a lot that goes into this, so we don't have a bunch of untrained yay-hoos getting in trouble, or doing something they shouldn't be doing."

Dr. Phil had a good point.

The show's final case was the most interesting, or at least, the most titillating. Butler told Dr. Phil that a biotech company had hired him to see where a certain employee was spending his lunch hours. Butler had obtained a copy of the employee's cell phone records and found a phone number that also showed up in the "erotic services" section of Craigslist.

Then, Butler sent an undercover male decoy—carrying a hidden camera briefcase—to get an erotic service massage at a hotel in San Ramon. As soon as the masseuse touched the decoy's dick, she was officially a prostitute, which would apparently have been valuable information to the biotech company that had hired Butler & Associates.

This case provoked giggles from the *Dr. Phil* studio audience, but confused my father-in-law, who is Dutch, and believes prostitution and drugs should be legal.

"I don't understand why they are investigating the prostitute," said my father-in-law. "She's just doing her job. They were hired to investigate the biotech employee."

Jaap had a good point.

The show's final segment featured Chuck Latting, the retired FBI agent and former Marine captain who had handed over his private investigation business to Butler in the late 1990s. Latting was presented as an advisor to the investigators, and he often teleconference with the PI Moms about cases.

Dr. Phil showed video of such a call, with Latting's disembodied voice coming through a speakerphone as the PI Moms sat around a conference table, beaming.

"Hey, Charlie!" the PI Moms said to the speakerphone. Just like on *Charlie's Angels*! Cue studio audience applause.

As the episode ended, Dr. Phil gave a shout-out to Butler's contact information on his website, DrPhil.com, so any of the millions of viewers watching the syndicated show could learn more about the PI Moms and their fearless leader.

The *Dr. Phil* episode was a perfect *PI Moms* sizzle reel, served up on a syndicated silver platter. Within a few weeks, Butler had his coveted reality show deal.

The *Dr. Phil* episode wasn't Butler's first sizzle reel.

Using investment capital from family members (as well as from the former client whose finances bought Butler's Mustang), Butler produced a couple of clip reels on his own. One of these was called *Investigating Butler*, which focused on the man himself and his many methods of investigation.

Investigating Butler contained testimonials from Chris Butler and some of his staff. Carl Marino was in the video, pretending to be a jewel thief who was apprehended by Butler in some phonied-up footage.

Marino has claimed he was cast the moment he walked into Butler's office in January 2009, after answering Butler's Craigslist ad for an undercover decoy. In Marino's telling, Butler hired Marino on the spot as an investigator, both in the field and on camera.

Other footage in the sizzle reel wasn't staged, but taken from actual investigations, such as the case that brought Charmagne Peters into Butler's business. Charmagne had told me that she hired Butler to spy on a mentally unstable nephew, which wasn't true.

I found out through sources and law enforcement reports that Charmagne had actually hired Butler to sting her then-husband to see if he would fall for a decoy sting. The husband bit the bait and was caught on tape kissing Sharon Taylor, the same blonde decoy seen smooching another husband in Hawaii on *Dr. Phil*.

Because he got such great footage of the sting on Charmagne's husband, Butler made sure to edit it into his sizzle reel, so he could show prospective reality show producers what he was capable of.

On September 22, 2010, I had another encounter with the PI Moms. This time, I met them at the UFC Gym in Concord, just a few minutes' drive from Butler's warehouse office.

The UFC Gym is the first in a proposed franchise of workout centers under the Ultimate Fighting Championship brand. It's a sprawling, two-story complex in a shopping mall retail space. Butler and the PI Moms started each weekday with a ninety-minute workout; their memberships were comped by UFC Gym in exchange for product placement.

According to Butler's website, UFC Gym was "the official self-defense and mixed martial arts instructional sponsor of Butler & Associates Private Investigations."

I arrived at 10 AM to work out with the PI Moms, who were scheduled to take a self-defense class from a mixed martial arts (MMA) instructor. When I arrived in the lobby of the gym, Charmagne ran to greet me.

She led me upstairs, where a group of PI Moms were gathered in a large caged room filled with a maze of heavy punching bags. I said hello to Denise, and recognized Ilona Marino from my ride-along two weeks before. There were several other women in the room, one of whom I recognized from a *People* magazine story from March 2010. The PI Moms were all dressed head-to-toe in UFC workout gear and gathered round their MMA *sabumnim* (instructor).

The *sabumnim* was a man named Marc Fickett, who was advertised on Butler's website as "the official MMA lead trainer for the Butler & Associates investigative staff."

Fickett had us run a few laps around the room before starting our self-defense. He showed the Moms how to react to an attacker by driving an open palm into the person's nose with one hand and then swinging the other palm into the attacker's eardrum. Apparently the open-palm plan works better than a closed-fist punch, not only by reducing injuries to the hand but also assault lawsuits from the person being hit. The closed fist is litigiously riskier, because it gives the appearance of assault more than self-defense.

"Smack the nose! Slap the eardrum!" commanded the *sabumnim*, as the PI Moms and I practiced the technique on the heavy hanging bags.

Sweep the leg! I thought, my movie brain recalling *The Karate Kid*.

The PI Moms and I continued to practice open-palm smacks, then ran some more laps around the room, at which point I was sweating like Albert Brooks in *Broadcast News*. I was easily the most out-of-shape person in the class, and excused myself to find a water fountain.

During my time-out, I spotted Chris Butler approaching me from across the gym. I shook his hand and asked some lingering questions I had about the ride-along. Charmagne had given me a call a few days after to tell me that Sharon the Client had kicked her cheating fiancé out on his ass after witnessing the lurid incidents in wine country.

Butler told me that Sharon the Client was relieved to be free of the relationship and was grateful for all Butler and the PI Moms had done. I still had some issues with Butler's methods, the strangest of which was how the PI had driven the cheating fiancé's car away from the Holiday Inn Express. I asked Butler how the fiancé explained the missing car to Sharon the Client.

"Oh, that," Butler said. "He called (Sharon the Client) the next morning and told her he got drunk with his buddies and slept on a couch. She said, 'I had you followed, and I know everything you were up to. I'm putting your stuff in a box on the driveway, and I'm going over to a friend's house at two PM. You can come by after that and pick it up, and I want you out of here.'"

I still didn't understand how the guy got home from wine country, or what he told his mistress when they went out to the parking lot and discovered the Mercedes was missing, but Butler couldn't fill in that information.

"Wow," I said. "Well, that was some crazy shit, when you just drove off in that Mercedes."

Butler twinkled at the comment, delighted that I recognized how he had pushed the envelope.

"Well, that's the kind of thing I would rather not have happen with a journalist from a reputable magazine watching," Butler told me. "But, between you and me, that wasn't nearly as crazy as some of the shit that goes on during some of my cases."

"Wow," I said again. "So that's it with Sharon, I guess. Case closed?"

"Case closed," said Butler.

If only.

5
PI Moms *Starts Shooting*

THE MAN IN CHARGE with bringing the PI Moms to reality TV stardom was Lucas Platt. Platt was a seasoned showrunner who had worked on many hit shows, including *Dog the Bounty Hunter* and *Steven Seagal: Lawman* before being hired as showrunner for *PI Moms*.

I interviewed Platt at length in 2013 to discuss the experiences he had working on *PI Moms*. He recalled meeting me briefly at the UFC Gym after I worked out with the Moms. Platt, like all cast and crew who worked on the *PI Moms* TV show, had signed a two-year nondisclosure agreement with the production company and cable network to protect the content of the show from leaking to the media. When we were finally able to chat on the record, we started at the point where we met, in the UFC Gym, a few weeks before the show's production commenced.

"I went there to meet [Butler and the PI Moms]. It was just to get a feeling for who they were in person," said Platt. "We were just getting started with the show and I wanted to see them in person, see how they interacted."

Platt said he knew going in that filming a show about private investigators in Northern California was going to be very challenging.

"It was a difficult legal landscape doing this kind of show in California. California is a two-party consent state, and they are very strict about it," Platt told me.

This meant if the show wanted to film an infidelity case like the one I witnessed, the production company would have to get permission from Sharon the Client and her fiancé before airing the episode. How many dudes who were caught cheating at the Holiday Inn Express would then consent to letting their image be used on a national network?

Platt devised an approach that could work in California, despite the two-party consent law.

"I thought we should focus on positive cases, where the moms could help someone—like finding missing persons," Platt explained. "We followed a case about two brothers who had been separated when they were very, very young. Linda found one of the brothers, and there was a tearful reunion."

Platt also liked an approach that showed the PI Moms investigating cases that involved criminal activity rather than a deluge of cheating husbands.

"I felt we could focus on cases that had real legal consequences," Platt explained. "For example, Denise was on this California board of PIs. To be a PI in California you have to be licensed, but a lot of people are not—they do investigations anyway and advertise themselves on Craigslist as an investigator. With Denise on board, we can reel in a case where we could find someone who was advertising himself as a PI, but didn't have a license, which is not legal in California." (As seen on *Dr. Phil.*)

"The other thing I wanted to do is get into the Moms' personal private lives. There was interesting material to explore there," Platt said, addressing one of the key components of reality TV. While the PI Moms' personal lives needed to be an important part of the show, Platt was concerned about the cross-section of onscreen talent at Butler & Associates.

"Normally, the kind of show that we were making would be put together in a different way," Platt explained. "You would do a wide casting search. You would hire a casting director and find women from at least the Bay Area or even all of California, because you could find women who would be a little more dynamic. But that is not what the network bought. The project that the network bought was this particular detective agency. They had already been on *Dr. Phil* and had been in *People* magazine."

The next trick was to figure out how many Moms to focus on, and which ones.

"We had multiple conversations with the network about the casting," Platt recalled. "The network wanted, like, seven characters, and I only wanted five. I did not think that there were seven Moms [in Butler's office] who were worthy of being part of the TV show. So, I thought that four or five was a good number of characters and we should pick one more as a backup."

Of the investigators working at Butler & Associates, Platt thought Charmagne Peters was one of the most promising characters for the reality show. She was attractive and articulate, equally involved in the PI business and her family. Denise Antoon, the other mother from my ride-along, was similarly strong, with her legal background and three children.

Michelle Allen, a single mom from Berkeley with two kids, also made the cut. Her background in acting made her a good fit for reality TV. Michelle, along with Charmagne and Denise, had appeared on *Dr. Phil*, the *Today* show, and in *People* magazine.

Ami Wiltz was another strong candidate. A single mom with a law enforcement background, Ami had a sad but compelling backstory—Wiltz had been a teenage mom whose son had passed away from a tragic illness. Now in her thirties, Wiltz was focused on obtaining her own private investigator's license while working for Butler part-time and raising three kids.

The final two spots in the cast went to Sharon Taylor, the blonde decoy from *Dr. Phil*, and a voluptuous Vietnamese woman named Linda Welch. Linda's history with Butler was colorful, and because she was the victim of a complex scam that could benefit *PI Moms*, she scored a role on the TV show.

The cast may not have been ideal, but by mid-October 2010, it was pretty much in place. Chris Butler would be the wise, experienced PI who owned the business; Sharon and Linda were cast to showcase the sexy decoy side of investigative work; and Charmagne, Denise, Michelle, and Ami would be the titular *PI Moms*.

As for cases, Chris Butler had assured Platt that his PI business was so busy that there would be no shortage of interesting investigations that would translate well to television.

"When we first started out, Chris would constantly brag about how he would deliver all these cases on our doorstep," Platt told me. "Butler said, 'I have so many cases, there's a line out the door.'"

After my UFC workout, I started writing my story for *Diablo*. I had not expected to witness so much action on the ride-along. I told my editor ahead of time that there was a good chance I would end up hanging out in the minivan, interviewing the PI Moms on a dull surveillance detail. That was my impression of what PI work was really like. Instead, I had witnessed the Case of the Napa Valley Swingers.

The action-packed ride-along exceeded my expectations, but the reason I was writing the story wasn't to showcase infidelity investigations. The point of the article was to offer a sneak peek at a national reality show filmed in *Diablo*'s backyard. And because the show would not air until the following March at the earliest, I wasn't in a hurry to finish writing. I still needed to do some research about the production of the show.

In early November, while I was working on the article, I received an interesting note from Chris Butler:

> Just a quick note regarding the PI Moms article you are working on . . .
>
> Charmagne Peters resigned last week, as she was given an ultimatum by her husband regarding the TV show and child custody. It was a very difficult decision for Char, but in her words, "her children come first." I have hired three interns who will be competing for Char's position. One is from San Jose, one from Concord, and one came all the way out from South Carolina.
>
> Our TV show commences production on November 8th. Let me know if you want to swing by at any time to get an inside look.
>
> Best regards,
> Christopher B. Butler, PI#21673

Rather than reply to Butler, I gave Charmagne a call. She and I had become Facebook friends since the ride-along and had exchanged a few texts. I left her a voice mail saying I had heard she left Butler & Associates, and I was curious as to why.

Charmagne called me back with some unexpected news: She was getting a divorce from her husband. This was a surprise, because during the ride-along, I was given the impression that both Charmagne and Denise were happily married and their partners were cool with the whole PI Moms thing.

"We've been headed for divorce for a while," Charmagne told me, sounding sad and a bit embarrassed. "We're just going to tell our kids about [it] this weekend."

Charmagne did not mention her soon-to-be ex-husband giving her an ultimatum about the show. She made it sound like not participating in Lifetime's *PI Moms* was her own difficult decision. Charmagne told me that the show's producers were interested in showing her—and her young children—dealing with the divorce on camera.

"There's just no way I could do that, put my kids through that," she said. "Everyone in America would have hated me."

Charmagne, who had appeared to be very excited about the show during the ride-along, was clearly bummed about the way things had turned out. I had pictured her and Denise and the other Moms getting together for pizza parties on Tuesday evenings to watch the show together. Now the show would go on, but with Charmagne on the sidelines.

But the conversation quickly turned glass-half-full, when Charmagne told me that she had secured a new job in the corporate sector. Her new gig came with health care benefits, something that Chris Butler did not offer his employees.

I wished Charmagne the best of luck, and told her I would keep in touch.

A few days later, *PI Moms* started shooting without her.

On November 8, production crews rolled into Butler's offices in Concord to begin filming *PI Moms*. Lucas Platt had recruited a small team of trusted TV pros to run the production, and a crew of freelance camera operators and editors were hired from the Bay Area talent pool.

"I picked supertalented producers to help put this together," said Platt. "Allison Howard, who has a really strong background in law enforcement television, and Lucy Lesser, with really strong personal TV experience. Between the three of us, we were going to make it work."

Platt explained his approach to the first weeks of production.

"Right from the start, we needed to get two or three cases up and running," Platt told me. "I wanted to have a bunch of cases running simultaneously. Cases get solved in waves, and I knew there would be downtime between the cases, so it was important to start getting footage. We could not wait around and do one case at a time."

So, what kind of cases would make for good reality television?

Psychic scam artists are always a good start.

One of the first cases filmed for *PI Moms* was a deliciously bizarre ordeal involving cast member Linda Welch, who was suspicious that a psychic had scammed her.

According to an interview I had with Butler, the weirdness began in May 2010, when Linda had been shopping in a Louis Vuitton store. A woman approached Linda and told Linda that she was equipped with strong psychic abilities and that she could see an evil presence hovering around her.

Cue "Tubular Bells" from *The Exorcist*.

Linda didn't take the news well and freaked out a bit. Then, to the psychic's delight, Linda asked for more information. After a brief conversation, Linda volunteered that she had been having marital problems, which the psychic blamed on the evil spirit.

Because the Louis Vuitton store lobby wasn't an appropriate locale for in-depth otherworldly exploration, the psychic told Linda that she needed to come to her house for a spiritual cleansing. Linda went along, and things got even stranger. The psychic told Linda that the reason her marriage had been so stressed was that her husband also was contaminated with an evil spirit, which Linda had passed to him during sex.

A supernatural STD.

Linda, now terrified, was told how she could exorcise her just-realized evil. The psychic said Linda needed to go to a grocery store and purchase a fresh tomato, then put the tomato in a shoebox with a picture of her husband and Linda together. The shoebox needed to be kept under the couple's bed as they slept. Linda complied and brought the tomato back to the psychic's house the next morning.

The psychic instructed Linda to strip nude, so the tomato could be rubbed all over her body. The psychic did this, while chanting and singing, then wrapped the tomato in a white t-shirt and smashed the fruit into pulp.

Linda watched as the psychic unrolled the t-shirt and pulled a black seed out of the tomato. The psychic said that the bad seed needed to be placed inside a vase, which would harness the evil and let Linda and her husband return to their happy marriage.

One hitch: The vase that the psychic would need to purchase to shelter the bad seed would cost at least $6,000. Linda, saddled with the existential dread of possible demonic possession, shivered with terror as she told the psychic she simply didn't have the cash.

The psychic told Linda there might be another solution: Put the demon seed into the snazzy purse she had purchased the day their paths crossed in Louis Vuitton, which the psychic would keep in a very safe place in a church.

The psychic added that Linda would need two pricey purses to act as seed vaults, because her demon-riddled husband would need to have his evil aura cleansed in a similar ritual. The psychic assured Linda that the purses would be returned after the evil spirits wormholed into an alternative universe of chaos and darkness.

So, Linda provided the psychic with another Louis Vuitton handbag, plus $300—which the psychic explained was an offering to the church. Call it a satanic materials handling fee.

Weeks later, Linda could not get in touch with the psychic and began to wonder if she would be getting her purses back. Concerned that she had been hoodwinked into believing that otherworldly evil had been excavated from her body in the form of a tomato seed, and that this ruse was simply a way to swindle her out of her favorite handbags, Linda decided that she might need some professional assistance in retrieving her goods.

Which is the single most interesting reason I've heard for someone to require the services of Chris Butler.

The gypsy psychic case was something *PI Moms* showrunner Lucas Platt described as a "tent-pole story," meaning it was a case that could sustain interest over a couple of episodes.

"To make the show work, we needed a couple of large cases that had have multiple beats and keep people watching from week to week," Platt told me.

On one episode, Butler and the PI Moms would get the full download on all the goofy details of the psychic's alleged scam. The next week, the PI Moms would set their plan into motion to build evidence against the psychic. Then, using undercover decoys and hidden cameras and other tricks from Butler's repertoire, they would catch the psychic red-handed, disappearing with a fancy handbag or taking cash for an unnecessary demon decanter.

But even if the PI Moms did bust the psychic, it was just one case—not nearly enough content to sustain an hour of reality drama from week to week.

So, what were the other tent-pole stories?

One was the case of a missing fifteen-year-old girl who I will call the Teen. She vanished in late November 2010. Her disappearance caused a ripple of concern in the East Bay area—fliers and Facebook notices were quickly circulated, and the Teen was listed on the Polly Klaas Foundation website.

According to several sources, the girl's family and friends suspected her disappearance had something to do with her boyfriend, a sixteen-year-old classmate. The teenage couple had been known to ditch school together, so one theory was that the Teen's vanishing was an elaborate game of hooky.

But as days went by with no sign of the Teen, her parents became understandably panicked. Investigators from the Contra Costa Sheriff's Office were producing no leads, so the Teen's parents decided to go to a private investigator, who charged a lot for services that produced no results.

A second PI also turned up nothing and took another wallop out of the savings account. Then the parents went to Chris Butler.

Butler assigned Carl Marino to investigate the speculation that the Teen's boyfriend had something to do with her whereabouts.

As Marino started snooping, Butler told the Teen's parents about the Lifetime reality show and convinced them that the cable network would cover his certain-to-be-weighty investigative fees—if the parents agreed to let their case be filmed for TV.

"The way that it was presented to me was that the family had engaged Chris previously to try to find the Teen," Lucas Platt told me. "[Butler] had done a lot of work for them and had even done a lot of stuff for free, but just could not keep going on the case for free, but was sympathetic to their plight and their missing daughter.

"The [family] had run out of money before the show got involved," Platt continued. "We thought, 'Wouldn't it be awesome if the network thought it was a case worth pursuing, and we would pay for the expenses, so that we were kind of helping each other out?' We were getting a potentially great case out of it for the show. We met the [family] and it seemed legit. So, we decided to go for it."

The Case of the Missing Teen was weird from the start.

The Teen's boyfriend denied having any knowledge of his girlfriend's whereabouts. The boyfriend's mother, who I'll call Anna, made similar denials.

Not only did Anna deny knowing anything about the missing girl, she also created a Facebook page dedicated to finding the Teen—and held a public prayer vigil for her.

As the Contra Costa Sheriff's Office, the website for Polly Klaas, Carl Marino, and an online contingent of amateur sleuths all searched for the Teen, the PI Moms jumped on the case, hoping to solve it in front of the cameras.

A perusal of the Teen's cell phone records showed that she had been chatting with a young man in Ontario, California. A team of PI Moms—and a crew of producers and camera operators—was sent to the Southern California city to stake out the man.

That investigation turned out to be a wild goose chase, although not without some excitement. At one point, law enforcement was called when one of the PI Moms saw a teenage girl in a pink wig, walking the streets of Ontario, and thought she might be the Teen in disguise.

But the pink-haired teen was just an Ontario kid out for a walk, which made the police helicopter called in to follow her an unnecessary use of resources.

Weeks more went by, with no sign of the Teen. Anna held another public prayer vigil. The situation equated to a logistical bummer for the reality show, and an unending nightmare of stress and worry for the missing girl's parents.

During the first weeks of filming, *PI Moms* started to gather footage of the previously mentioned cases, as well as some smaller investigations. For example, the Moms checked out a possible scam at an East Bay farmers market, where the owner of an organic ice-cream company felt that she may have been ripped off by a permitting and licensing scam.

Not exactly a tent pole.

The show made more progress building footage about the PI Moms' personal lives. Denise Antoon was shown going to marriage counseling with her husband. Michelle Allen, a single mom, was filmed having a first date with a guy she met through a single's website.

Ami Wiltz, whose son had died at a young age, had the most heart-warming personal story. The most tender moments filmed for the show involved Wiltz discussing her son's death, and finally getting a proper headstone installed on her son's grave.

As if Lucas Platt did not have enough trouble running the *PI Moms* show with California's two-party consent laws, a less-than-ideal cast, and possibly unsolvable tent-pole cases, there were other noticeable problems from the start of the show.

According to numerous sources who worked on the show, one major problem was the behavior of Chris Butler's right-hand man, Carl Marino.

Marino, who had moved to the Bay Area from New York after sixteen years and nine months of employment as a deputy sheriff with the Monroe County Sheriff's Office, made a pitch to be featured on the reality show just after production started.

"About the end of the second week of filming, we were at the gym filming the PI Moms training and Carl asked to talk to me," said Platt. "We went and sat in the front lobby of the UFC gym, and he confronted me directly. He felt very strongly that I was making a terrible mistake by not including him in the show."

According to Platt, Marino claimed, "I can really help make the show great. I have a big following from all my work on the *Trauma* show, and a big fan base."

"The *Trauma* show" was a short-lived NBC action series, *Trauma*, which filmed in San Francisco in 2009. After starting out as an extra, Marino had earned a speaking role on the show, a gig that led to his membership in the Screen Actors Guild.

Marino had also appeared on more than a dozen episodes of an Investigation Discovery true-crime show, *I (Almost) Got Away With It*, and a low-budget indie feature, *Sedona's Rule*.

Platt, whose career started with a job on the Oscar-winning classic *The Silence of the Lambs* before he went on to be showrunner on several network shows, was flabbergasted by Marino's requests to be featured on *PI Moms*. When Platt arrived in the East Bay to start production, he was under the impression that all the employees at Butler & Associates had been informed that the show was going to focus on the Moms.

"I felt kind of ambushed by Carl," said Platt. "So I just said, 'I hear what you are saying, but the show has been cast and the network has given approval, and the show is called *PI Moms*.'"

Unfortunately for Platt, his straightforward approach did not appear to satisfy Marino.

"[Marino] was clearly very upset. I did not want him to become more upset and cause problems, because I already had so much going on," said Platt. "I did tell him that the best thing he could do was support Chris, and help make the show a success in an off-camera capacity. If we're really successful in the show's first season, it's a rising tide, and maybe more opportunities would come. I made it very clear that it [being an on-camera character] was definitely not going to happen the first season."

Platt said that Marino continued to argue with him, becoming more irritated by the realization that he would not be a featured cast member on *PI Moms*.

"His reaction to my answer was to tell me, 'I'm really popular with women and I would be good for ratings.' He would not back off. He said to me, 'You should talk to the higher-ups, and I will go to them if you are not going to do it,'" Platt said. "I told him again that the show was cast and he was not in the cast. I did not want this asshole going to the network and saying, 'Well, Lucas said I should talk to you . . .' I wanted to be able to say in full honesty to the network that I always told Carl there would be no role for him."

As for Marino's side of that situation, he has given a range of responses about his desire to be featured on *PI Moms*. Over the next year, Marino told me on several occasions that he "never wanted to be on that show," but, in a March 11, 2012, article, he told the *San Francisco Chronicle*, "Of course I wanted to be featured on the show."

Probably most relevant was a statement Marino eventually gave to agents from California's Department of Justice.

"I was told [by Chris Butler] that there would be a role for me on the show," Marino told DOJ special agent Dean Johnston. "Then it turned out there wasn't a role on the show. I accepted that."

While Marino was causing headaches for Platt and the show's producers, the biggest problem the show had was Chris Butler. Before the show started shooting, Butler had promised Lifetime an overflow of cases to film and then failed to deliver.

"Chris Butler would constantly brag about how he would deliver all these cases to our doorstep," Platt said. "But Chris' cases just would not check out. This is speculation, but I think he just figured there were a bunch of producers from L.A. and he could just deliver a bunch of fake cases, and the producers would never know the difference.

"Both [producer Allison Howard] and I have done so much crime-oriented TV. We were not buying his bullshit. When we started checking up on the cases there were always problems. There was something else—the way that he characterized his police record [at Antioch,

California, PD] was that he was just too good; he was just going to make all these arrests, but the administration could not keep up with him. That was suspicious."

As the first weeks of shooting wrapped in early December, Platt had some good footage, but was not nearly as far along as he had hoped to be. For the Lifetime show to launch in March or April 2011, it would need a series of hour-long episodes, with some semblance of a television season—and Platt knew he was far short of that, contentwise.

So Platt brought on a freelance producer from the Bay Area, Chris Flitter, to help drum up some legitimate cases for the PI Moms to solve.

"When we found out that Chris Butler did not really have any cases, anything substantial, we brought on Chris Flitter because she's kind of an investigative reporter," said Platt. "We were going to have to go out and find cases that the PI Moms could work."

Production of the reality show took a break in mid-December to let the cast and crew enjoy the holidays, with plans to resume filming on January 10, 2011.

I was supposed to stop by Butler's office during the first weeks of filming, but my requests to set up a set visit were unsuccessful. This did not raise any red flags on my part; I understood that *PI Moms* was a complicated program, and the last thing the production needed was to slow down its work to walk a reporter around the show.

I gave Chris Butler a call on December 27, 2010, while production of *PI Moms* was on pause. It was a quiet Monday at his office, with no one else around, so it turned out to be a good time to chat. Butler was more than happy to discuss his childhood, his career, and his recent adventures as a reality TV star.

Butler boasted about the product-placement agreements the show had with Glock firearms, Oakley sunglasses, and UFC Gym. Butler also told me about the cases being filmed for the show—the gypsy psychic and the missing teen. He did say there had been some challenges with the production; it wasn't easy filming clandestine operations with multiple cameras and boom mikes.

Butler made no effort to tell me how serious the problems had really been during the reality show's early weeks of production. Instead, Mr. Cool made it seem like the uptight producers had been busting his balls a bit—just like his old cop bosses in Antioch, those fuckers—but the *PI Moms* reality show was still going to kick some ass.

PART TWO
A SECRET SOURCE

6
An Unexpected Email

LOOKING BACK on my September 11 ride-along, I should have known it was a fake.

There weren't just red flags but blazing road flares that indicated the case I had witnessed was 100 percent bullshit. But I was too naive, lazy, or maybe just plain dumb to figure that out on my own.

It never crossed my mind during that ten-hour ride-along that the whole thing was an elaborate hoax. That nine adults would conspire to lie to me, just so I would write a story about Butler and the PI Moms in a regional lifestyle magazine.

Little did I know.

My story changed forever on the first Monday in January 2011, when someone sent an email saying as much to the *Diablo* magazine general comments in-box. Every editor, and the publisher of the magazine, received the email, sent from someone calling him- or herself "Ronald Rutherford."

The email, received on January 3 at 11:21 AM, read:

> I am writing this as a courtesy to you. It would be a mistake to publish the article on the PI Moms and Chris Butler that you came and did a story on a few months ago. Chris totally played you. The case that you sat in on was totally scripted. All of the

participants were employees or paid actors. Sharon, the "client" actually works for the agency and was a former client. The "boyfriend" was a friend of Chris' named Al and his "mistress" is a hired "decoy" named Ryan. The entire Napa "trip" was planned out and the investigators knew exactly the course of events. The only reason Butler wants to be in your magazine is for advertising purposes. He has been trying to get into your magazine for a long time to get his business out to your subscribers through free advertising. The whole "PI Mom" thing has even been crafted just to get on a TV show.

You have a great and classy magazine, and I would hate to see it cheapened by someone of low character such as Mr. Butler. I just don't think it is right that he manipulated you just to try to get some publicity. He mentions the pending article now to all clients that come in for interviews. I am, obviously, an insider and do not wish to give out my name. I am not sure what your intentions are with the article, but I hope that publishing it is not in your plans. A lot of people know that this case was scripted as are most for the TV show. I hope that this information is helpful.

Thanks.

A concerned citizen

I read the email and immediately replied:

Hi, Ronald Rutherford. Can you give me a call to discuss?

I sat at my desk and read Ronald Rutherford's email again. Rutherford said he (or she) was "obviously an insider," and the name sounded as if it was made up for the purpose of contacting me anonymously. So did Ronald Rutherford's email handle: Therealtruthnow2010.

Several editors gathered around my desk with wide eyes, similar to the Monday morning following my ride-along a few months before when I had recounted, to the delight of the editorial team, all the crazy events and lurid details of the September 11 ride-along. No one had asked me if I thought it might be a fake.

Even though this email alleged that the ride-along was a hoax, the editorial team's consensus was that Ronald Rutherford was the prankster, not Chris Butler. One editor pointed out that Butler would be foolish to set up such a ruse for some exposure in a regional publication, and risk his reality show deal with Lifetime.

Diablo's managing editor questioned the size of the alleged conspiracy. "How many people were involved in the ride-along?" she asked. "That would have to have been such an elaborate plan, to get all those people to lie to *Diablo*."

It was a good point. There were nine people involved in the September 11 surveillance: Chris Butler; Charmagne Peters; Denise Antoon; Carl and Ilona Marino; Sharon the Client and her beefcake fiancé, Al; the tattooed Mystery Date; and the intern, Tracy, who drove Butler's Chrysler from the Holiday Inn Express back to Concord.

But as the cast of characters ran through my mind, it started to make more sense that everyone was in on the hoax. That would explain why Butler knew Al wouldn't stay in the gated community of Blackhawk. Or why the PI Moms weren't worried about sitting at the same patio table as Al and Mystery Date at the Rutherford Grill.

Or why Charmagne had stayed right behind the Mercedes all day long without being noticed. I had asked the PI Moms about that during the ride-along. "They have no idea—they're in their own little world up there," they told me.

As my head spun, my desk phone rang. I picked up, hoping it would be the mysterious Ronald Rutherford, explaining why he (or she) had made allegations about Butler staging my ride-along.

Instead, the caller was Chris Flitter, *PI Moms*' recently contracted freelance producer.

"Pete, I'm working on a reality show that's filming in the area," Flitter began, carefully talking around the name of the show. "You won't have heard of the show, because it's being kept a secret for now. But it's for a major network..."

I cut her off.

"Is it *PI Moms*?" I asked.

"How... how did you know that?" Flitter asked.

"Because I went on a ride-along on a case with the PI Moms a few months ago, and I'm supposed to write a story about the show," I explained.

"Oh, OK," said Flitter, still startled that I had even heard of the show.

It was difficult to assess who was more confused at that moment.

"Well, yes, that's the show I'm calling about," Flitter continued, "and, I'm calling because I wanted to know if you knew of anyone, from any other stories you might be working on, who might need the services of some private investigators."

"You want me to give you sources for the show?" I asked, gobsmacked.

"I've been hired to help the show find cases for the PI Moms to work," Flitter clarified. "And since *Diablo* magazine covers stories in this area, I thought you might be a good source for case leads."

I would later discover that Flitter had been working diligently to find real cases for the PI Moms to work, including one in a retirement community in which a somewhat sadistic neighbor harassed an elderly woman. There was also a corrupt landscape architect who might have swindled a suburban family out of half a million dollars. And the whopper involved the Alameda County District Attorney's Office, in which the PI Moms could have assisted on a major investigation involving a sex slavery ring, in which young Asian women were being smuggled into the United States to work in illicit massage parlors and brothels.

All of these cases—particularly the ugly business about sex slaves—would have allowed the PI Moms to provide a real community service by exposing the wrongdoers. And, of course, they could have made for some dynamic television.

However, the email I had just received from Ronald Rutherford made me wonder if the cases for the reality show were staged, similar to the alleged hoax I had witnessed.

"Let me ask you something—how do we know these cases that are being filmed are authentic?" I replied, thinking about the email I had received less than an hour before. "How do we know they aren't kind of staging stuff with actors to make good TV?"

"Why would you ask that? Was there something suspicious about the case that you went on?" she inquired.

"Oh, I'm not sure," I replied, realizing I should tread lightly before accusing Butler of defrauding me with a fake case. "It's just something that recently crossed my mind. Like, how do we know that what we'll be watching is really reality? I think everyone wonders that about reality shows, you know?"

At this point, Flitter clearly realized that her cold call was not going well. When she dialed my number, she was hoping I would offer, "You should talk to this local restaurant owner whose staff keeps stealing from the till." Or, "Have you heard about the unlicensed ADHD therapist who is bilking frightened parents for thousands of dollars?"

Instead, I was asking, "Is the show you are calling me about based on bullshit?"

Flitter wrapped up the call and wished me luck on my story. I hung up and went back to wondering just who the hell Ronald Rutherford was.

In my decade-plus tenure at *Diablo*, I've contributed more stories than any writer or editor in the magazine's thirty-four-year history. I've taken photos at countless society events, concerts, and fundraisers, and I've interviewed rock, sports, and movie stars.

However, one thing I have not done well is turn in my stories on time. I'm a perennial procrastinator who can always find ways to stretch out the definition of deadline, a trait that wreaks havoc on those whose work priorities are keeping the magazine to a strict shipping schedule.

When Ronald Rutherford's email turned my story upside down, I had a first draft about the PI Moms nearly finished, but key details about the reality show were still unreported. The most important missing fact was the month that the show would premiere on Lifetime, as the story needed to be pegged to that month's issue.

Thus, the story was still not ready, which caused great concern for *Diablo*'s editor-in-chief.

We were starting production on the March issue that week, but I was doubtful that the show had a chance of airing in March, which meant we would push the story back to meet the airdate. This meant that *Diablo* needed another feature story to fill those pages in the March issue, a situation my editor did not want to repeat month after month as production of *PI Moms* plodded along.

Now we had a new headache to deal with—the allegation that *Diablo* had been lied to by the people we had intended to publish a puff piece about. I was given an ultimatum to determine the veracity of the Ronald Rutherford email.

"Just call those Moms and Chris Butler and ask them if the case was real," my editor suggested. "If everyone confirms that it was, then finish your story and turn it in."

It seemed a reasonable approach: Ronald Rutherford's email had aggressively alleged that everyone in Butler's office had lied to me. I could just put them on the spot, and if their stories synced, we'd move forward.

But if they didn't, what then?

I started with Charmagne Peters, because she was no longer employed by Butler and was not a part of the show. If the ride-along had been a staged case, I felt she might have less motivation to perpetuate the hoax. I sent her a text asking her to call me. My phone rang a few minutes later.

I opened the call with some Happy New Year small talk. Charmagne was in better spirits than she had been the last time we had talked, when she told me that she had to bail on the reality show because she couldn't let her divorce become cable TV fodder. She had enjoyed the holidays, she loved her new job, and things were going well.

"So, I got the weirdest email today," I told Charmagne, addressing the elephant in my in-box. "It said that case I went on with you and Denise was a fake—that we were following actors hired by Butler."

"Wha . . . what?" Charmagne asked. "Who sent that?"

"I don't know," I replied. "But that doesn't matter. I just needed to ask you if it was a real case before I go forward with printing the article."

"Look, Pete, to be totally honest, I'm actually happy to no longer be working for Chris Butler," said Charmagne. "But that case you went on was definitely real."

"That's good to hear," I said. "But here's something I was thinking when I read this email. Let's say Chris just wanted me to see something exciting for my story, so he hired some actors to pretend to be out on a date. Is it possible that he did not tell you and Denise, because it was your job just to follow them and observe everything that happened? And that's why we saw all that crazy stuff in Napa, instead of just sitting in your van in the Twenty-Four Hour Fitness parking lot while the Fiancé worked out for a couple of hours?"

Charmagne shot that theory down.

"Pete, I know a lot of things happened that day that probably seemed strange to you, because you had never been on an investigation before,"

Charmagne told me. "But we saw that kind of stuff all the time. That was just another day on the job for us."

I thanked Charmagne for calling me back and clearing that up, acting as if I was convinced by her explanation, which I was not.

Next I called Denise Antoon and left her a message to call me back. Monday afternoon slid by, and I did not hear from her or the mysterious Ronald Rutherford. Toward the end of the day, *Diablo*'s editor-in-chief asked me what I had heard from the PI Moms.

"Charmagne says it was a real case. Denise hasn't called back," I said.

"What did Butler say?" asked the editor.

I dialed him next. Butler picked up immediately.

"Hey, Pete, what's up?" he asked in his monotone. I played it the same way I had with Charmagne, starting with innocuous chitchat about the New Year's weekend. Then I dropped the bomb.

"So, I got this email that said the ride-along I went on with the PI Moms was a fake case," I told Butler.

"What?!" Butler's cool-guy voice was replaced by a furnace blast of anger and confusion. "That is *bull crap*!"

"Yeah, it was weird," I said. "The email said that Sharon was one of your clients, but the guy we followed all day was one of your buddies. And that the whole thing was staged for you to get some free press in *Diablo*."

"First of all, I don't have 'buddies,'" Butler claimed, sounding like he might be close to an aneurysm. "And the guy you followed was absolutely my client's fiancé."

"Well, since I got this email, I thought I should run it by you," I said, playing nice, acting as if I believed Butler.

Pondering the limited information I had given him about the Rutherford email, Butler contemplated the short list of suspects who may have sent it.

"The only person who could have sent it is Charmagne," Butler said, more to himself than to me. "But why would she do that? She left on good terms."

It was interesting to hear Butler immediately throw Charmagne under the bus, not knowing that his former employee had already vouched for the ride-along's authenticity.

"Yeah, I don't know," I told Butler. "But I want to make sure that the case was authentic before we go to press with the story."

This snapped Butler to attention.

"I totally understand your position, and the position of your magazine," he said, the exact same reply he gave me when I told him I wasn't comfortable writing about the setup of an unsuspecting dude with a hot decoy.

"What do you need from me?" Butler asked. "I will do whatever it takes to show you that this was a legitimate case."

"I want to speak with everyone who was part of your investigation," I told him. "That's Charmagne and Denise, and Carl and his wife."

"No problem," Butler told me. "I will tell them to call you."

"But first, I want to chat with your client, Sharon," I told Butler. "The email I received suggested Sharon doesn't know that guy we followed around Napa all day. So, if I can talk to Sharon, and she can show me a photo of her and Al together from New Year's Eve a year ago, that would be a good start. Or, anything like that."

"That will not be a problem," Butler assured me. "I will get in touch with my client right away, and call you first thing in the morning."

Butler hung up and did not call his client. Instead, he sent a text to Carl Marino, who had been promoted to director of operations of Butler & Associates a few weeks after my ride-along, despite his unpleasant interactions with the producers of *PI Moms*.

The text read, "Call me ASAP."

I drove home with a grinding migraine. My wife could tell something was wrong when I walked in the door.

I told her about the email from Ronald Rutherford, and how aggressive and certain this anonymous emailer had been that Chris Butler had duped me for promotional purposes.

Because my wife had already heard every lurid detail about the ride-along, and had also seen Butler and the PI Moms on *Dr. Phil*, she disagreed with the theory my *Diablo* colleagues had offered—that the Ronald Rutherford email was the hoax, not the ride-along.

"Remember how my dad thought that case on *Dr. Phil* was weird too?" she asked.

My headache grew worse by bedtime, and I tossed and turned through the night. My back and neck were still badly injured from a nasty car accident weeks before, which, combined with the stress and confusion I was feeling about Ronald Rutherford's email, resulted in the first of many sleepless nights.

I spent the small hours of the morning replaying the ride-along in my mind. With each mental screening, the scenario seemed more preposterous.

Of course it was fake, I thought. *And* everyone *was in on it. They weren't stinging the Subject. They were stinging me. Soylent Green is people!*

The realization that I may have been lied to by Butler, by Charmagne and Denise, and by Sharon the Client made me livid. Adding insult to injury, the ride-along had taken place on a Saturday instead of a weekday, meaning I may have been suckered on my day off.

By dawn, I was a mess. But I was determined to find out what really happened on September 11 and write about the results.

Butler invited me to write a story about him, I thought. *And I am going to do just that.*

On Tuesday, January 4, I rolled into work, bleary-eyed and disheveled. I sat down at my desk expecting to see the red message light on my phone, as Butler had promised to have a message for me about Sharon the Client first thing in the morning.

There was no message.

I called Butler's office and one of his interns answered. I asked to speak with Chris Butler.

"He's teaching a first-aid class right now, so he can't take your call," said the intern, who sounded young and friendly. "Can I take a message?"

"Please go tell Chris Butler that Pete Crooks from *Diablo* magazine is on the phone and I need to speak with him right now," I snapped. "He'll know what it is about."

The intern didn't argue. Within a few seconds, Chris Butler picked up the phone.

"Hey, Pete, what's up?" Butler said. His cool-guy monotone was back to its factory settings.

This fucking guy is a liar, I thought. *He knows exactly why I'm calling.*

"What's up is that you were supposed to call me first thing this morning about when I can speak with your client," I told Butler. "So, I was surprised to get to work and not have a message from you."

Butler went into damage control mode.

"I have called my client but have not heard back from her yet," Butler said. "I did find out who sent you that email, though."

This piqued my interest. "Who sent the email?" I asked.

"I had an intern working here last year who washed out of the program," Butler said. "She didn't make the cut, and I had to let her go, and she was very upset."

Go on.

"What I did not realize was that this intern had begun having an affair with one of the PI Moms behind my back," Butler told me. "The relationship continued after the intern stopped working here. And my employee had been telling her about our cases, including the case that you observed."

"Wait a minute," I interrupted, trying to wrap my sleep-deprived brain around Butler's explanation. "This was a female intern having an affair with a PI Mom? These are two women hooking up?"

"That's correct," said Butler. "The relationship continued until the Christmas holidays and then it ended. And it ended badly. And now, the intern is trying to scorch the earth around everything having to do with me and my business, including this story you're writing for *Diablo*."

Butler then made a preemptive strike on my next question, by keeping these secret lesbians' identities a secret.

"Unfortunately, I can't tell you who this intern and PI mom are," he said, "because they could sue me for breaching their workplace confidentiality agreement."

I let Butler's explanation sink in for a second. Then I told him that the story did nothing to demonstrate that my ride-along had been real, despite its salacious imagery of two women kissing. If anything, Butler's story suggested he needed to do a better job of locking down his confidential case files. Surely, his paying clients would not appreciate their private information being whispered about.

"I still need to talk to your client," I told Butler. "And that needs to happen as soon as possible."

"I understand your position, and the position of your magazine," Butler told me again, sounding less confident than the first two times.

I told my editor about Butler's angry lesbian/scorched earth explanation, which provoked the raised eyebrow and pursed lip response the story deserved.

My *PI Moms* story was not getting any closer to being ready to print in *Diablo*, which was bad news for a writer who gets a "Needs Improvement" every annual review under the topic "Meeting Deadlines."

I knew the story was in serious danger of being killed. But I was not about to give up. I needed to know exactly what had happened on that ride-along, and if I had been played for a fool.

I called Charmagne again. She picked up right away.

"Chris told me who sent that email yesterday," I told Charmagne, who was eager to hear the explanation. I started to recount the tale of two lesbians. "Chris said that one of the PI Moms was having an affair with a disgruntled intern, who . . ."

Charmagne cut me off, with profane bluster. "He is *such a fucking liar*!" she screamed.

Wow.

Clearly, Butler's spurned saboteur excuse struck a chord.

"I will tell you exactly who sent you that email," Charmagne declared.

"Who?" I couldn't wait.

"It was Carl Marino. Carl is a jealous wannabe actor who has been stirring up all kinds of shit on the set of the reality show because he wants a part on it, but Lifetime doesn't want him."

This is an interesting theory, I thought. A jealous actor spilling the beans after being snubbed seemed much more plausible than Butler's story of an angry lesbian with an ax to grind.

"Carl sent you the email, I guarantee it," Charmagne said. "And Chris Butler is a fucking asshole who is fucking full of shit."

I would later learn, from several sources, why Charmagne took such offense to Butler's angry lesbian story. Months before my ride-along, Charmagne and an intern had asked to leave Butler's office early to go to a Lady Gaga concert together. As soon as they left the office, Butler went into gossip queen mode, telling his staff that the two women were certain to end their big night out with a white-hot hookup.

I told Charmagne I would be in touch again soon, then googled "Carl Marino," to explore the jealous actor theory. I found Marino's website promoting acting and modeling work in the Bay Area. Marino's résumé claimed roles in some big-budget films, including Clint Eastwood's *Hereafter* and Judd Apatow's *Funny People*, although a cross-check on the Internet Movie Database showed that Marino's roles in those movies were "uncredited," meaning he had been a background extra. Or his part wound up on the cutting room floor.

Marino's website also featured some of the cheesiest modeling shots I had ever seen. One featured Marino posed like Superman, "flying" faster than a speeding bullet, thanks to some remedial Photoshop.

Several shots showed Marino wearing the uniform of the Monroe County Sheriff's Office in western New York. The uniform jersey was unbuttoned and opened to expose Marino's bare, shaved chest.

There were some low-budget video clips as well, including one for a web commercial hawking online coupons. Marino, sitting in front of a desktop computer, pretended to be slapped across the face by a special-effect hand, which sprang from his screen. "I just saved fifty bucks!" exclaimed Marino.

I showed CarlMarino.net to my editor-in-chief, and then to *Diablo*'s publisher, Barney Fonzi, who had also received the original Ronald Rutherford email. I explained Charmagne's theory about who had sent the bombshell email and why.

"This guy is Ronald Rutherford," I told Fonzi, pointing to the Marino-as-Superman picture.

Later that afternoon, I received a callback from Denise Antoon. Instead of starting with small talk, I jumped straight to the allegation that the ride-along had been a fake.

"No, that was a real case," Denise told me, sounding extremely uncomfortable. I asked Denise about Sharon the Client, who cried in Butler's office when we all met on September 9, and seemed so comforted by Denise's hug.

"When did you first meet Sharon?" I asked, taking notes by hand.

"I met her that day," Denise said. "The same day you did."

That's funny, I thought. *Butler emailed me saying the PI Moms had been working with Sharon for weeks before I met her at the office.*

The stories didn't match up.

I inquired about the possibility that Butler had paid actors to pretend to be on a date, but that Charmagne and Denise had been none the wiser, just like me. Was it possible that the PI Moms were just doing their job, oblivious to the fact that they were following actors?

"No," said Denise, nervously. "Because Chris has so many cases, why would he go to the trouble to fake one? Besides, he wouldn't be that stupid, to do it in front of a reporter. Why would he risk doing that when he has a national TV show?"

"That's the thing, Denise," I said. "If Butler faked a case to get publicity when he has a national TV show, then this isn't just a *Diablo* story. This is a *Vanity Fair* story." (My apologies to the editors of *Vanity Fair* for the obnoxious presumption.)

I'm certain I could hear Denise gulp on the other end of the phone. The call ended awkwardly.

I checked my email and noticed that I had a new message from Chris Butler. I opened it, hoping that he had arranged for me to talk to Sharon the Client, as he had promised.

Instead, I got a long-winded runaround, with references to the angry lesbian who Butler claimed sent the email to *Diablo* and excuses about why Sharon the Client hadn't called me yet.

Butler wrote:

> I am disturbed to an extent over the email your publication received, but since I know who wrote it and why, I am not really concerned all that much. Disgruntled

former employees and vindictive parties are a fact of this business and will only become more frequent with the advent of our TV show.

What I am concerned about is how my former client may react when I advise her that you want to delve further into her case to prove that her case was real. I have left her two messages and am awaiting her call back; I cannot force her to call me back. When she does call me back, I will do my best to address her concerns and assure her that you have a legitimate need for further information.

Butler also wanted me to speak with Carl Marino and was clearly not aware that Charmagne had suggested it was Marino who had sent the email to *Diablo*:

Carl, my Director of Operations, was not available today, as his 101-year-old grandmother just passed away. Providing you with his cell phone number would not be a prudent thing to do without his consent, let alone given his loss. I have provided him with your cell phone number and he will be contacting you directly.

Butler ended the email by backtracking his promise to do whatever was required to prove the authenticity of my ride-along:

Please remember that while I want to help you with your story fact checking, I must provide my clients with [a] level of confidentiality and safety.

Best,

Christopher B. Butler, PI#21673

I stared at my computer screen, trying to figure out my next move, when it came in the form of a new email from Ronald Rutherford.

Thirty-six hours after I received Ronald Rutherford's original you-got-played message, my secret source sent me the following email, denying my request to talk on the phone.

Ronald Rutherford wrote:

> I would rather not call. I can answer any of your questions on here if it is possible. I was not joking and obviously need to be as anonymous as possible. I am trusting you not to divulge too much. I know you have called several people about this already including Mr. Butler. I am sure he is trying to do damage control now. I can give you any other information that you would like about this matter. I can tell you that the "girlfriend" from the stings', real name is "Ryan Romano" and she lives in Danville.

I put the name Ryan Romano into Google. A Facebook profile popped up, with a picture of the tattoo-sleeved woman I had watched scarf down two artichoke appetizers while being clumsily seduced by Smooth-Talking Al.

Hello, Mystery Date.

I replied to Ronald Rutherford, addressing the concern that I had reached out to Butler and the PI Moms about the original email. I regretted that now, because I was letting them prepare a defense to the allegation that they had lied to me.

Regardless, Rutherford seemed eager to provide more information that I had been duped, and I wanted to gather as much evidence as possible. I wrote back:

> I did reach out to both investigators and Chris after receiving your email. Obviously, these are serious allegations. It is certainly interesting to see how much information you have about this ride-along case.
>
> What other proof can you offer?

Rutherford quickly replied:

> The guy is Al Stewart [*sic*] who is a pilot somewhere in the bay area, the "fiancé" is Sharon Hooks [*sic*], and the "mistress" is Ryan Romano who has worked as a decoy many times for Mr. Butler. She started working for them because she is friends with [a woman I will refer to as Madame DD] who has been a decoy also for a long time. I believe that Mr. Butler has already been reaching out to the three of them to get them to have their stories straight. I am hesitant to share other things due to the fact that I am concerned with keeping my annonimity [*sic*]. Please be careful how much you divulge to Mr. Butler about what I tell you.

Before I could reply, Rutherford sent another message:

> I would also want to let you know that he did the same thing with the German TV network [RTL]. He scripted a case and used actors that were friends with one of the employees at the agency. I have all of this information also. They were lead [*sic*] to believe that the case was real and aired it on German TV already. Please don't share this information with Mr. Butler and I can give you more about this one with names and dates if you wish.

I replied that Ronald Rutherford should absolutely send any information about Butler staging cases for *Diablo* magazine or German television. I was intrigued by the allegation that another media outlet had been hoodwinked.

As I waited for a reply, I decided to have another look at CarlMarino.net.

I was on board with the theory that Ronald Rutherford was Carl Marino, just as Charmagne had explained. Marino's website made it clear that he was a small-time player in the Bay Area entertainment industry.

It made sense that Marino had gone along with lying to *Diablo*, thinking it would promote *PI Moms*—only to find out later he would not have a role on the reality show, at which point he felt it was time to expose the hoax and screw his boss and coworkers.

It was a bold backstab, a move someone would make on *Survivor* just before getting voted off the island. But in Marino's case, the cameras were not pointed in his direction.

I did not want to get involved in a pissing contest over who gets to be on a reality show, but I was determined to prove that Butler & Associates had tried to trick the media with fake cases.

The allegation that Butler had staged a case for a German show made me wonder about the authenticity of all of Butler's media appearances, including *People* magazine, *Today*, and *Dr. Phil*.

Maybe, Butler didn't just lie to me, I thought. *Maybe he's been lying to everyone, and hoodwinked his way into a reality show.*

That would be quite a story.

I had not slept in forty hours.

It was Wednesday, January 5, after midnight, and thanks to Ronald Rutherford's second email, I was studying the Facebook friends list of Ryan Romano, aka Mystery Date.

In a small-world surprise, I knew two of her Facebook friends: the woman who cuts what's left of my hair, and an East Bay nightclub promoter, Enrique Montero, whom I had written about in *Diablo*.

I also found the Facebook page of Madame DD, the woman who Rutherford claimed had a connection to Mystery Date. Sure enough, Madame DD's friends list included Romano, as well as Enrique Montero, Denise Antoon, and Charmagne Peters.

Finally, I found Sharon the Client. Ronald Rutherford had told me that her last name was Hooks, which was incorrect. A Google search for "Sharon" and the street that we had started the ride-along on brought me to a real estate website, which had a listing for a Sharon with another last name.

I dropped that name into Facebook, and voilà, there was Sharon the Client.

I made screen captures of all my Facebook discoveries so I could show my colleagues at *Diablo* the next morning. I was just about to try to pass out when Rutherford sent me one more email that proved the ride-along was a hoax without any doubt.

The email contained a forwarded message that had been composed by Butler and Charmagne Peters on September 10, 2010—the night before the ride-along.

In the email, Butler gave very specific instructions for the Fiancé and Mystery Date to park at the Holiday Inn Express, walk through the lobby of the hotel, and get into a Honda parked on the other side to make a getaway. There was even a Google Maps attachment, annotated with instructions about where everybody should park to make the sting work.

Charmagne's portion of the email listed all the addresses we had visited during the ride-along: the 24 Hour Fitness gym, the Napa Premium Outlets mall, the Rutherford Grill, and the Peju winery.

I had been played. Now I knew it for sure.

Which gave me something to think about as I stared at the ceiling until dawn for the second straight night.

Ronald Rutherford's email included this Google Earth attachment, showing how Al and Mystery Date could drive away from the Holiday Inn Express without being seen from the PI Mom van.

Wednesday morning, January 5, I dragged myself into *Diablo*'s office, looking like an extra on *The Walking Dead.*

As soon as I reached my desk, my editor asked where my *PI Moms* story stood for the March issue.

"I have some updates," I told her, and asked if all the editors could meet, so I could show them my work product from my all-nighter. Four editors and I gathered in a conference room and I laid out the printouts of screen captures.

I sounded half-crazed as I showed the connections from Mystery Date to Madame DD to the PI Moms.

"Check this out," I said, pulling out the "smoking gun" itinerary email I had received at 2:20 AM that morning. "This lists every place we went on the ride-along. And it was sent the day before the ride-along!"

Three of the four editors sat with wide eyes at my presentation, which was far more sensational than our editorial meetings for planning guides to summer fun or fall fashion.

As exciting as this unfolding mystery was, my editor-in-chief was clearly frustrated. The *PI Moms* story was supposed to be a fun piece about a reality show to run in the March issue. Now, it was morphing into something dark and weird, a story that required considerably more reporting. And, if the reporting demonstrated that Butler and the PI Moms were liars, the story would require an expensive lawyer to carefully review every word before publication.

None of these new wrinkles were going to get our next issue shipped to the printer on time, and the editor thought it might be time to kill the story.

"If Chris Butler lied to *Diablo* to get some free advertising for his business, then he doesn't deserve our attention," she said.

Even in my sleep-deprived stupor, I could see her point. And I realized that I was taking the allegedly fake ride-along much more personally than the rest of the edit team. Because I was the one who had spent ten hours on a Saturday being lied to.

But I couldn't let the story die.

"If Butler had lied to us about a case, just so we would publish a story about his PI business, then maybe he would not deserve our attention," I said. "But he has a reality show on a national network. Everyone wonders how real those reality shows are, and readers will be interested to see that Butler and the PI Moms faked this ride-along case for *Diablo*."

That argument bought me a little time.

"Besides, when this Lifetime show comes on the air and we don't do a story about it, our readers will wonder why," I said. "We could have had this amazing story about Butler taking me on a wild goose chase through wine country."

That bought me a little more.

I told the team about the connections I was working, people who knew Mystery Date and Madame DD. I wanted to go knock on those doors to see if I could get someone to admit the ride-along was staged.

I also planned to go after Sharon the Client, because there was no way she could prove that the Subject was her real fiancé.

Someone was sure to crack; then I could go back to Butler and the two PI Moms from my ride-along and make them admit they had lied.

"Keep us posted," my editor instructed, still skeptical.

When I came out of the editorial meeting, I had two voice mail messages on my desk line.

I hoped one would be from Chris Butler, saying I could speak with his client, but Butler remained aloof.

The first voice mail message was from Lucas Platt, showrunner for *PI Moms*, who was still in New York, preparing to come to California to resume filming. Chris Flitter had contacted him about the bizarre phone conversation we had shared just after I received the initial Ronald Rutherford email about the ride-along.

Platt seemed concerned that my article could damage the show's reputation, and invited me to come see that he was trying to film actual reality.

"Chris Flitter says you have some concerns about the authenticity of the case that you went on with Butler and the PI Moms," Platt's message said. "I don't know what happened on that case, but I wanted to point out that the show had nothing to do with it, that was all Chris [Butler]'s doing. We are working very hard on this show, and are making sure the cases we are filming are authentic. So, you're going to write what you're going to write in your article, but I would appreciate it if you would not suggest that the case you followed was part of the show, because it wasn't. What I can offer, is for you to come see what we are doing on the show, and we will be completely transparent about what we are filming and how we are filming it. Then, you can write whatever you are going to write."

It was a fascinating message, and I replayed it to make sure I heard it clearly. Platt, who had spent weeks trying to film a national TV show about Butler and the PI Moms, made no effort to cover for Butler and suggest that I had witnessed a real case. He only vouched for the authenticity of the cases being filmed for the show.

I sent Platt an email saying I would love to come visit the set of *PI Moms*.

Then I played the second message, which came from nightclub promoter Enrique Montero, who was Facebook friends with Mystery Date. Enrique picked up when I called him back, happy to hear from *Diablo* again. We had run a short story about his nightclub parties a few years before, after which he would occasionally give me updates about DJs I had never heard of coming in from Las Vegas for off-the-hook events in Walnut Creek.

"Yo, Pete, what's up, what can I do for ya?" Enrique always sounded as if he had just shotgunned a Red Bull.

"I'm working on a tricky story," I told him. "You know how you can be friends with someone on Facebook and then you realize they're friends with another person you know?"

Enrique said that he had experienced that social media phenomenon, but then quickly detoured into a diatribe about having his Facebook page shut down.

"I had like eight thousand friends and Facebook contacted me and said, 'You gotta make a fan page for that shit.'" Enrique said. "I was like, 'Fuck that,' then next thing I knew they shut my page down."

I waited for Enrique to vent his frustration about Facebook awhile longer, then steered the conversation back to the ride-along.

"I've been working on this story about a new reality show about these soccer mom private investigators, and I spent all day on a case with them," I told Enrique. "We spent all day following this guy and his mistress in Napa."

"Nice," said Enrique.

"It was pretty interesting," I said. "Anyway, like I said, I was looking through your new Facebook friends list, and I noticed that the mistress we were following is one of your friends."

"Really?" Enrique was intrigued. "Who is she?"

"Do you know a woman named Ryan?" I asked.

"*Ryan Romano?*" Enrique was surprised. "She's one of my best friends. I paid for her tits!"

I was also surprised. "You did what?"

"She used to come into this club I ran in San Francisco, and we had this go-go dance contest and the grand prize was a $5,000 boob job,"

Enrique said. "Ryan won the contest. Go look at my Facebook pictures, there's a pic of her with a giant check for $5,000 from the plastic surgeon."

I told Enrique I would definitely look for the picture, then asked him to tell me about his friend Ryan. Enrique explained that she was a full-time nanny for a wealthy family in Blackhawk, the gated community of mansions the PI Moms and I had out skirted on the ride-along. When Ryan wasn't being a nanny, she was at a nightclub, or traveling to Miami or Cabo or Hawaii or Las Vegas.

I asked Enrique if he knew if Ryan had been dating a big bulky guy with a crew cut.

"Naw, I never seen her with that guy," Enrique said.

I asked Enrique if he would give me Romano's phone number, which made Enrique pause. "If you want, I'll just call her and ask her what's up, and have her call you," he said.

"OK, that would be good," I said. "Just tell her she will want to talk to me before this story goes to print, now that I know who she is."

"No problem, bro," Enrique said. "If I talk to her, she will call you. She's one of my best friends."

Awhile later, Enrique called again.

"She's not gonna call you, bro," Enrique said. "I did what I could, but she told me there's no way she's calling you."

"Did you let her know that means she might be getting her name printed in the magazine?" I asked.

"Yeah, and she still said no. I also asked her if she knew about this reality show and she said, 'I can't talk about that,'" Enrique said.

Interesting. I thought. *The mistress would have had no way of knowing the PI Moms had a reality show.*

"Then I asked her if she was fucking some married guy," Enrique added. "And she just started to laugh and said, 'Enrique, it's for a reality show. We all know how real those things are.'"

Aha.

7

Do as Columbo Does

LATE THAT AFTERNOON, I got a call from Carl Marino. I had only exchanged a few unmemorable words with Marino in Butler's office and during the ride-along, but had received nine emails from Ronald Rutherford, who I believed was really Marino.

When I picked up Marino's call, I hoped that he would tell me that he had been emailing me under a pseudonym. But the call was strange, and Marino did not confess to moonlighting as Ronald Rutherford. Instead, Marino vouched for the ride-along's authenticity—although not as emphatically as Butler and the PI Moms had.

"I always assumed that was a real case," Marino told me, when I asked him if the September 11 ride-along had been legitimate. "We take cases like that all the time, so I would have had no reason to believe there was anything unusual about it."

I asked Marino why he had even been a part of the surveillance case, as it seemed like a second team of investigators wasn't a necessity. Marino said that his boss had instructed him and his wife to drive from their apartment in San Francisco out to the Concord office of Butler & Associates, where they were to pick up Butler's black Mustang. In the trunk of the Mustang, there had been a change of clothes for

Charmagne and Denise, should they have needed to change their outfit during the investigation.

It became clear that if Marino actually was the mysterious Ronald Rutherford, he wasn't just going to come out and admit it. To keep the conversation going, I asked him some questions about his background.

Marino told me that he was a retired cop from Rochester, New York. He said that he moved from western New York to San Jose at the end of 2008 to be closer to his family on the West Coast.

Later, background checks would show that Marino had two ex-wives and some court-ordered lien issues back in New York.

Shortly after arriving in California, Marino answered one of Butler's decoy recruitment ads on Craigslist, and then worked on and off for the PI throughout the next two years, during which time he also worked as an actor and model.

Marino met his third wife, Ilona, on the set of an independent film that I had never heard of, and seemed particularly proud of his role on the NBC paramedic show *Trauma*, a show I had never seen.

The phone call lasted for more than an hour, and Marino never let on that he was the one who was sending me information. If Marino was Rutherford, he wanted to keep that a secret awhile longer.

Later that night, Ronald Rutherford sent me three more emails, none of which mentioned me speaking with Carl Marino.

All three emails concerned Sharon the Client, and explained that she had been an actual former client of Butler's. Sharon had hired Butler and the PI Moms to set up her actual fiancé by flirting with him online, then sending Charmagne Peters to meet him for a date.

The sting sounded almost identical to the one Butler had offered me to follow in the first phone conversation I had with him. The one I had turned down, because it felt like entrapment.

I let Rutherford know that he or she had given me the wrong last name for Sharon the Client, but I had found her on Facebook. Rutherford apologized for the error, and confirmed that I did have the correct name.

I asked what would happen if I just went to Sharon's house and told her I knew about her real relationship.

"[She] will stick to the story, if she will even talk to you at all," Rutherford replied.

I continued to press Rutherford for as much inside scoop about Butler as I could get, and inquired about each of the players alleged to have been involved as decoys and actors: Ryan Romano aka Mystery Date, Madame DD, Al the fake cheater, and Charmagne and Denise. Rutherford recommended I cross-check everyone's Facebook friends lists, which I had already spent many hours doing.

The next day, Rutherford sent me three more emails. These messages included more details about Sharon the Client's original case, including the name, address, and phone number of her actual ex-fiancé. Because the new information was emailed in the late morning, it occurred to me that Rutherford was likely gathering it from Butler's case files in the Concord warehouse office—putting Carl Marino higher on my secret source suspect list, as Marino would have had access during the workday.

I would not hear from Rutherford again until the following Monday, January 10. The day the Lifetime camera crews returned to start shooting *PI Moms* again.

Every morning during that first week of January, my editor asked me where I was with the story. With each day, the pressure increased to get Butler or the PI Moms to fess up to the fake ride-along, or kill the story. The situation required a conference call with *Diablo*'s publisher, Barney Fonzi, and the company's president, Steve Rivera.

Rivera listened to me as I caught him up to speed on the ride-along and explained the even stranger events of the past few days. I argued passionately that this was not a story we should kill just because the principal characters might be shadier than the people *Diablo* tends to celebrate in its editorial pages.

"Everyone wants to know if reality shows are staged and scripted," I said. "Here's a guy who may have lied and faked his way into getting a show on national TV."

Rivera was intrigued by the premise and thought if Butler had lied to the magazine, he should be exposed. He came up with an idea to put Butler on the spot.

"Remember that old detective show, *Columbo*?" Rivera asked.

Of course I did. So did Butler. I had seen Peter Falk's eight-by-ten glossy on his office wall.

"Columbo would always be very nice to the villain, and string him along. Then he would say, 'There's just one more thing,' before dropping some bombshell of evidence," Rivera said. "You could go into Butler's office with a fact-checker, and go over the facts of the story—you went on this ride-along and these things happened. He'll say, 'Yes, they did.'

"Then you say, 'Just one more thing. We need you to sign this disclaimer that says 'this case was an authentic investigation, it was not staged or re-created, and there were no actors used.' Give him a document, and ask him to sign it in front of you, and see what he does."

I geeked out over the idea of pulling a *Columbo* on Chris Butler, and went back to my desk to send the man behind *PI Moms* an email, asking to set up a meeting with a fact-checker.

Unfortunately, Butler was getting more squirrelly with every contact, and said he would not be available to meet for my *Columbo* treatment.

"That won't work, as we will be back in full production at that time (16-hour days)," Butler wrote, adding, "If you did not get enough time on the phone with Carl, I will have him call you back. Just let me know!"

I assumed that meant Marino had checked in with Butler and said I had been convinced the ride-along had been a real case. Marino remained a mystery; it was odd that Charmagne had been so certain that Marino had sent *Diablo* the Ronald Rutherford email out of spite, but Butler still seemed to trust him.

As I noodled on that, Butler sent me another email, suggesting that he now wondered who contacted me about the ride-along.

Butler asked, "I almost forgot...could you please forward me the email you received from the unknown party? I have a government source that can trace the email source and IP. Thanks!!!"

This was interesting, because Butler was admitting that he did not know who sent the email, contradicting his claim from a few days before that it came from an angry lesbian with an ax to grind.

It was also disturbing; Butler had a guy who could trace the digital path between Rutherford and me.

I wondered if some government geek was using a provision of the Patriot Act to drill into my email. Lack of sleep and being lied to will make you paranoid like that.

"I can't send you that email for Journalism 101 reasons," I responded to Butler, and again tried to get him to meet a fact-checker so I could *Columbo* his ass.

This only made Butler more skittish.

He replied: "Since production on the show is resuming on [January 10], I won't be able to schedule any in-person meetings with any degree of certainty until production wraps up on [February 8]."

Meaning: "I won't be talking to you in person for more than a month, if then, so good luck fact-checking your story. Buh-bye, adios, nice knowing you, Pete."

What would Columbo do now?

8
A Dirty DUI

ON SUNDAY, January 9, 2011, Chris Butler had an actual case to work. Not a phony case to stage for the media or a reality show case to film for *PI Moms*, but a genuine case.

The case began in early November 2010, but had been slow getting started because of Butler's priorities with his TV show. The case involved a woman from the East Bay suburbs who had seen Butler and the PI Moms on *Today* and had come into the office to talk about her ex-husband. This prospective client had been engaged in an extended custody dispute with her ex-husband, who she claimed had a nerve-racking habit of drinking and driving while transporting their young son.

Butler offered a plan about how to deal with the situation: A specialized version of the undercover sting known as the Dirty DUI.

The sting worked like this: An unsuspecting fellow gets lured into a bar under a false premise, usually by a pair of hottie decoys. The girls flirt with the fella, do some shots at the bar, and then suggest that everyone drive to a nearby location to work off their overwhelming horniness in a hot tub.

Intoxicated by cheap liquor and the thought of a threesome, the mark would be likely to get in his car and follow the decoys—at which point

Butler would tip off a police officer about a drunk driver on the road, detailing the make of car, license plate number, and other identifying details.

These methods had proven effective in the past—before this January 9 case, Butler had successfully stung at least three unsuspecting men into being arrested for drunk driving, which led to custody trouble, changes in child visitation allotments, and other such headaches for the guys who fell for the hot tub invites.

But in the January 9 case, the client let Butler know that young drunk girls would not do the trick with her ex-husband. She said that her ex, a heavyset Turkish immigrant who worked in cell phone technology, wouldn't blink at bimbo bait.

A new plan was devised, in which a magazine reporter would interview the ex-husband about his success as a businessman and entrepreneur.

For Butler to lay the trap, he needed a few actors to trick the ex-husband into believing the sting was a legitimate meeting.

So Butler cast Carl Marino to play the role of the reporter. Marino called the ex-husband, pretending to be a journalist, and claimed to be writing a story about the East Bay's most successful immigrants for... wait for it... *Diablo* magazine.

The sting worked, and the ex-husband showed up for his "interview," which was conveniently held at a posh wine bar in the upscale town of Danville. Marino met with the man and pretended to care about his business over several flights of wine, while Butler waited outside in his Hummer.

During the interview, Marino kept Butler updated with texts, such as: "Going well... he likes to talk. Trying to get him to drink more."

Butler texted back: "OK. I imagine he will need 5 flights." The mark was a pretty big guy.

Marino chatted with the man from 6 PM until after 9, a late night of drinking in sleepy Danville. At 9:01 PM, Butler texted Marino: "What's your estimate of his level?"

Marino texted back: "I hope high. Mine is."

Twenty minutes later, Marino and the mark (who must have thought he was going to get quite a lengthy write-up in *Diablo*) were still sipping reds, and Butler grew restless.

"I am freezing my ass off out here," Butler texted. "How much longer???"

Carl Marino (left) modeling photo for a BACtrack personal breathalyzer device, a product that could have come in handy for the Dirty DUI setup victim of January 9, 2011. *Photo courtesy of BACtrack.*

Butler had kept his buddy, Danville Sheriff's Deputy Steve Tanabe, updated throughout the evening. By the nine o'clock hour, Tanabe parked his patrol vehicle in a position where he could watch for the ex-husband to leave the bar and drive away. Sometime before 10 PM, that happened.

The ex-husband was pulled over a few blocks from the wine bar for speeding. Deputy Tanabe's report said that, at 9:42 PM, the ex-husband was clocked driving forty miles per hour in a twenty-five zone for several blocks, and when he was pulled over, the smell of alcohol was immediately apparent. The driver admitted to having a few glasses of wine, consented to taking a Breathalyzer test, and blew a .118, well above California's .08 limit.

Busted. Handcuffs, drunk tank, the whole nine yards.

Marino left the wine bar and met his wife, Ilona, who had spent the sting having dinner across the street with Butler's wife, Rose. Rose was a former client who had hired Butler to investigate a previous ex. Ilona was there to play designated driver for the evening, and Marino made sure to thank his boss for the free wine and good times by texting him on the drive home.

"Ilona loved hanging out with Rose...they bonded," Marino texted, at 10:02 pm. Twenty minutes later, Marino asked about the outcome of the Dirty DUI.

"Did he have enough drinks?" Marino texted.

"He was arrested," Butler replied.

"Nice," Marino replied. "Because I would be too."

"He blew a .13," Butler texted, inflating the stat a little bit.

"Nice," Marino replied, signing off with a smiley face.

Another job well done for Butler & Associates.

What Does a Guy Have to Do to Get a Role on a Reality Show?

AS I ATTEMPTED to unravel the lies embedded in my ride-along story, there was more trouble between the *PI Moms* production team and a certain employee of Butler & Associates.

On January 7, 2011, just before the production crew returned to start filming the second round of *PI Moms* footage, showrunner Lucas Platt received a fourteen-hundred-word email from Carl Marino. Marino's diatribe addressed the issues he and Platt had discussed at the UFC Gym during the first weeks of *PI Moms* filming; chiefly, that Marino was not being featured as a principal cast member on the reality show.

Marino wrote to Platt:

> When you and I spoke, your advice was for me to just hang around and do what I was doing and maybe it would be seen that I should be used . . . I have been in this business a bit and have also been around the block a few times. I know when I am being "Okey-Doked." You and I both know that this isn't how it works. The longer it goes the harder it is to introduce me into a show that I should already have been part of. You can't all of a sudden go "Oh yeah, here is the director of

> operations that has been here the whole time, runs the office, assigns the cases, is the owner's right hand man, but you never saw. Now he is doing his job." That is very insulting.
>
> You also said that you would understand if I didn't want to work on things for the show. Do you realize how much I have already done for it and have just sat back while I am disrespected and insulted. This becomes very frustrating especially when I know what I can bring to the show.

Marino asserted that he was about to be interviewed by an Ohio-based radio show and a New York television show. According to Marino, both programs saw news value in a piece about a guy from western New York with a career in law enforcement moving to California and landing background parts on TV shows, such as NBC's defunct *Trauma* series. The email contained barely veiled threats that Marino might use this media campaign to question the integrity of the *PI Moms* reality show:

> Lately, I have become very confused as to what I am to say when asked questions about how the show and filming is going. I am unsure how I should answer the questions that will be asked of me on the upcoming media appearances [next week]. I have been asked many times in the past few weeks by family, friends, and coworkers who I have told about the project in the past. People have become very confused lately when I have answered that basically I have been told that I am not really allowed to be seen because the show was pitched a different way and things are not real at all.
>
> This has become very frustrating to me. I was working another show recently with a DP [director of photography] that has been the DP or main camera on many major projects. When I explained how I was not being utilized, he was amazed. His exact statement/question was, "They are shooting this show about your agency . . . and it is a show that will be seen on Lifetime, of all stations . . . and they aren't using your face in it?! Who the hell is in charge of that project?!"

Marino complained that his "fan base" would not get to see him on the Lifetime network, and that this would surely be a tragic missed opportunity for all parties:

> I can bring the show 10s of thousands of extra viewers with just a few posts and favors called on. This is significant for a show on Lifetime. I have a large network across the country. I also am the type of person that appeals to the demographic you are shooting for . . . the type of character you don't yet have represented on your show. Oh, trust me . . . I appeal to housewives.

Marino wrapped up the email by asking Platt to address all of his complaints with the powers that be at Lifetime—and, if Platt was unwilling to do so, Marino wanted to contact them himself.

Understandably, Lucas Platt thought that the threatening email was completely cuckoo. However, because the show was now more than two months into filming, and not as far along as it needed to be contentwise, Marino's threats needed to be taken seriously as a potential production nightmare.

"[The email] was this slightly insane screed, and he couched it as kind of 'I don't know what to do, because everything on the show is fake,'" Platt told me. "It felt like a very thinly veiled threat to ruin us in the court of public opinion. I felt like a teacher in an elementary school and Carl was going to tell everyone I was molesting kids, when of course I wasn't. But just making such a hideous allegation could be damaging.

"It was at that point where I felt that Carl was unhinged. That was the most generous interpretation of his behavior," Platt said. "I forwarded the email [that I got from Carl] to the network and we had an immediate discussion about what a problem Carl had become."

Platt and the network higher-ups decided that Marino needed to be contacted about the nondisclosure agreement he had signed for the production company before the reality show started filming at Butler's office in November 2010. Whether or not Marino had signed the document thinking he would be featured on the show wasn't relevant: The agreement had very specific language about giving any information to outside media about the show, so as not to spoil any surprises. It was the kind of boilerplate that keeps the outcomes of *Survivor* or *The Bachelor* from being revealed before the network broadcasts that valuable information to its viewers, between ads for beer and pharmaceuticals.

Platt said the network's attorneys sent a cease and desist order to the disgruntled director of operations, reminding Marino of the shut-the-fuck-up clause that he had signed and the legal implications that came with it.

"The letter that was sent to Carl let him know that he was not going to be contacting the media about the show for any reason, because he had signed a nondisclosure agreement, as had everyone who worked at the office," Platt told me. "I felt that if Carl gave a whit for the potential for season two of the show, or gave a whit about Butler his boss and friend, and if he did not want to be dragged through the courts by a network with a lot of legal firepower, he would back off."

Platt hoped the letter would make Marino stop interfering with the show, but wasn't convinced that it would. The intensity of the email diatribe that Marino had sent made Platt extremely uncomfortable.

"I got the feeling that [Marino] had spent the [holiday] break building a bigger and bigger head of steam about these people who were ruining his life, which all culminated in his sending this email that struck me as sad and confused about how the world works," Platt said. "It made me feel bad for the guy, but also worried about the safety for the cast and crew with this loose cannon around us."

Over the weekend of January 8–9, I didn't hear from Ronald Rutherford at all. Our last interaction had been four days earlier. But on Monday, January 10, Rutherford reached out to me again, inviting me to inform Lifetime that Chris Butler was a fraud and a liar:

> I was wondering if you have any updates or questions. The network is back filming this week. I believe they should know about the deception.

The message came one week to the day of Rutherford's initial contact, saying I should not publish an article about my ride-along because it had been a fake. This new message raised another issue: I should tell Lifetime that I had been duped by Butler and the PI Moms.

This was something I wasn't going to do, for several reasons.

First, Lucas Platt seemed to be well aware of the possibility that Butler had set me up with a fake case.

More important, I didn't want to tell Lifetime because I had no intention of damaging the show's chances of making it to the air. My exposé of Butler's reality show fame quest—with my firsthand account of my ridiculous ride-along—would be much more interesting if it was published in *Diablo* the month *PI Moms* premiered on Lifetime.

If the show never aired, would anyone care about the story? Anyone, that is, besides Rutherford, who seemed determined for me to let Lifetime know what a liar it was building its show around.

Would you be so offended by Butler's dishonesty if you had a spot on the show, Rutherford? I wondered.

Then Rutherford sent me a follow-up email, offering more evidence against Butler:

> Also, I am not sure you are interested, but I have the email chain from Mr. Butler showing how he engineered the article to be published in *People* magazine and the original script from both "sizzle" reels that they used to try to get the shows. The Lifetime people might be interested in seeing how he orchestrated that whole thing also. The whole thing is a sham.

These allegations were intriguing, as I had been wondering if any of the other media cases had been staged.

When I re-read the *People* magazine profile on Butler and the PI Moms, I had noticed that they were tailing a cheating husband driving a Mustang. A June 13, 2010, story in the *Contra Costa Times* reported that the moms were tailing a cheating husband in a black Mustang as well. Since Butler's black Mustang had made an appearance in my ride-along, I wondered if the same car had been used in all three stories.

I replied to Rutherford with an invitation to continue sending evidence of Butler's media frauds and thanked him for providing the information.

I told Rutherford that I wanted to address every possible angle on my case before contacting Lifetime, and mentioned that I had not slept much in the past week, due to my obsession with these new twists in the story.

That night, Rutherford replied:

> Lifetime knows nothing about the cases or about the way everything has been manipulated, they are just looking for cases because they have nothing else. They have been sold a product based on lies and bad information . . . [Butler] is very scared right now, because he knows this entire thing is based on lies and on the manipulation and misery of others.
>
> I understand how you would feel bad about this. This is how he deals with everyone. He doesn't care who he runs over or takes advantage of if things are to his advantage.

Misery of others, I thought. *Misery of who? A jealous actor who wants to be on a reality show?*

I had a lingering feeling that there was something more sinister than fame-whoring afoot.

There was.

10
A Cry for Help

DURING THE NEXT FEW DAYS, Rutherford continued to send me emails about how Sharon the Client got involved with Chris Butler. According to Rutherford, Sharon had hired Butler to investigate her actual fiancé, who she suspected of chatting with other women on online dating sites. Butler emailed Charmagne Peters' photo to the guy, with flirty notes, and the guy immediately agreed to meet for a drink.

Rutherford sent me the man's address and phone number and encouraged me to go check him out for myself. When I checked my email the morning of January 13, I found that Rutherford had emailed me three times the night before. He had been busy.

The first email informed me that Butler had still not told the Lifetime producers that he had staged a case for me to write about, even though the producers were asking about it.

The second email was a forwarded chain of messages between Butler and a writer from *People* magazine. The writer had done a similar ride-along with the PI Moms and filed a story—which eventually ran in the magazine in March 2010. However, the story took awhile to be published, and Butler wanted to expedite the process by having a PR flak suggest to the *People* reporter that Oprah Winfrey was interested in featuring the PI Moms on her daytime talk show.

"[The *People* reporter] will panic, as he knows that if Oprah puts the PI Moms on the show, *People* magazine loses the 'exclusive.' The article should be published the very next issue," Butler wrote to his team.

Then I read Rutherford's third email, which hit me like a gut-punch. Rutherford wrote:

> One more thing to tell you tonight and I am hesitant to tell you this.
>
> Mr. Butler is involved in some serious criminal activity right now. I can prove it and even have him "stung" if police or the DA is involved. If he is caught doing what he is doing, he would go away for a long time.
>
> I am not sure who to go to with it because he is very well connected in the police community and with the Narcotics Task Force. There are others involved that would be implicated that would probably make the news.
>
> I am not sure who to contact about this and I assure you it is serious. My window of opportunity is closing quickly to act on this if I decide to. I am not sure how to go about it and who I could trust in Contra Costa County.
>
> If you have any advice . . . please let me know. He is a very dirty person and believes that he can do whatever he wants without having to answer for it. Thanks again for listening and I look forward to your response.

Well, now, I thought. *This might be a bit more serious than phony ride-alongs and reality shows after all.*

I considered the allegations in Rutherford's email very carefully.

It had been nine days since I received the first message about Butler setting me up, and I had spent most of that time thinking Carl Marino was the one feeding me the information, believing Charmagne Peters' allegation that Marino's motive to tip me off was bitter, petty jealousy over face time on the reality show.

Until now, that was the most logical reason I could attribute to why Rutherford was so generous with inside information about Butler's business. Now I had to reevaluate my theories about both Butler and Rutherford.

I went back to the drawing board and studied Rutherford's newest bombshell very carefully.

"Mr. Butler is involved in some serious criminal activity."

What kind of criminal activity?

"He is very well connected...with the narcotics task force."

Narcotics. Butler is selling drugs? Or is he setting people up with drugs?

"I am not sure how to go about it and who I could trust in Contra Costa County."

Are there corrupt cops involved? How many? Who?

There was also the question of *Why Me?*

I'm an entertainment reporter. This is way out of my league.

I replied to the bombshell cautiously:

> I need to know more information about what type of criminal activity—these are much more serious charges than he faked a PR stunt to get a TV show or a magazine [article].
>
> I do know people in various local district attorney's offices, sheriff's departments, and police departments, including Concord PD. However, I don't know who you are implying [Butler] is involved with.
>
> Can you give me some indication of the type of criminal activity he is involved in, and who might be an associate in local government/law enforcement?
>
> I will keep a tight lid on this.

I hit SEND and waited anxiously for a reply.

It didn't come.

My editor asked what was going on with the story. I told her I was working on it, without mentioning the newest twist.

All day long, I checked my email in-box for a new message from Rutherford but heard nothing. By nighttime, I wondered if my source had gotten cold feet after revealing too much and was now ducking out on me.

I stared at the ceiling all night.

Then, on Friday, I received a reply, twenty-seven hours after I had asked for more details. Rutherford's response described allegations of Butler's criminal activities—and those of a key conspirator:

> [Butler] is selling large amounts of marijuana along with other drugs (prescription Xanax and Steroids) that has been confiscated by the Contra Costa County Task Force. You see, the commander of the task force is taking the drugs from raids and

giving them to Chris to move, he then gives them to . . . well me . . . to sell to someone else. The commander is a good friend of Chris' and they have worked together on things for years. So you can see why I am scared. I have not sold any and don't want to. I am not a drug dealer and do not want anything to do with this.

Stolen drugs.

Dirty cops.

I'm way, way, way out of my league here.

That fact seemed to be lost on Rutherford, who sounded desperate as he begged for me to help get him out of the very deep shit he was in.

Rutherford wrote:

I am willing to work with law enforcement or the DA to set up a buy, but as you can see [I] am very scared of both Chris and Norm (the task force leader). The window of opportunity is going to close soon on the stuff he has at his office because they are pressuring me to get rid of it quick and I feel they will move it somewhere else soon.

I have been conflicted about this for a while, but I think it needs to be done. Advise me soon what you think I could or should do. You can, of course, get the exclusive story if you wanted. I just want this taken care of. He is trying to come across on this TV show that he is such a compassionate and caring man, when in fact, he is a straight up criminal. He is a master of deception and thinks that he is untouchable.

Thank you for helping me. I need assurances that I will be safe and free from any prosecution if I help with this. I would be willing to meet with you and officials if interested. I am placing a lot of trust in you. Please don't leak anything that could comprimise [*sic*] me. I will await your reply.

Rutherford has been conflicted about this for a while. And his big move was to ask an entertainment reporter to do something.

My head throbbed from the realization that the ball was entirely in my court on a possible corruption scandal that would blow the lid off a sleepy bedroom community, all because I was supposed to write a puff piece on some local soccer moms getting a reality show.

Now, Rutherford—who wouldn't even tell me his actual name—wanted me to do something about the commander of the CNET task force selling drugs with his con man boss.

On top of that, Rutherford wanted me to make sure that he would be safe and free from prosecution. Because, of course, the entertainment writer at *Diablo* has that kind of pull with the DA's office.

Let me get right on that.

I Googled "Norm," "Task Force Leader," and "Contra Costa Narcotics Task Force," which led me to the name Norm Wielsch, the commander of the Central Contra Costa County Narcotics Enforcement Team, aka CNET.

Norm Wielsch was one of Butler's best friends in high places, as far as law enforcement went. Wielsch and Butler worked together at Antioch PD, before the squares behind the desk gave Butler the choice of quit or be fired from law enforcement.

As Butler's cop career fizzled in the mid-1990s, Norm Wielsch's soared. Wielsch went from Antioch PD to a job working for California's Department of Justice Bureau of Narcotic Enforcement, the longest-running narcotic enforcement agency in the United States. Wielsch worked his way up at the DOJ to become the commander of the CNET task force, a rotating crew of carefully selected police officers from the same East Bay region that *Diablo* magazine covered.

CNET's mission was to investigate high-level drug traffickers in the area; the task force had been operating since the 1980s and was held in high esteem in the law enforcement community.

Butler loved having a close contact at CNET and frequently took Wielsch out to lunch for cop talk. Butler would boast of his relationship with CNET to prospective clients; he kept a stack of Wielsch's business cards in his office to hand out, telling anyone who would listen that his PI firm frequently helped the task force with its official undercover bad-guy-busting business.

Butler had even bragged about CNET to me, the day of my ride-along, while showing me that his motorcycle's mirror had been damaged in a deep-cover operation.

Wielsch was similarly impressed by Butler, who drove slick Mustangs and Hummers and Mercedes sedans, was always surrounded by sexy female investigators, and claimed to earn a six-figure income with his PI business. As Butler's deal with Lifetime was heating up, Wielsch's own career was slowing down—Wielsch had been in law enforcement for twenty-five years, had some serious health issues to consider, and was thinking about retiring.

Butler told Wielsch not to worry, because when he retired, there would be a spot at Butler & Associates waiting for him. And by that time, the TV show would be a smash and there would be PI Moms franchises opening from Seattle to Miami.

Until then, Butler and Wielsch had plenty to do together. Wielsch used Butler as a confidential informant on a few CNET vice stings on sensual-massage parlors, and Butler asked Wielsch to help with some of his cases as well—which I will get to soon enough.

I found dozens of articles quoting Wielsch about various drug busts around the East Bay—CNET found $30 million worth of marijuana in Brentwood, a couple pounds of crystal meth in Concord. Wielsch was also often used in media stories as an expert source to talk about narcotics abuse, such as the rampant rise in Oxycontin abuse by teenagers. I even found a quote from him in a 2005 *Diablo* article about the rise in prescription painkiller abuse by suburban moms.

Ronald Rutherford's allegation that the top drug cop in the area was putting people in jail for selling drugs and then putting those drugs back out on the street (and keeping the money) made me sick to my stomach.

But as abhorrent as the allegation against Wielsch was, I had serious doubts about Rutherford's motivation. It was still possible that my inside source was really a jealous reality show wannabe, hiding behind an alias, which made me wary that he might be willing to slander a law enforcement officer out of spite.

Still, all the information Rutherford had given me about my ride-along had checked out. And if I have learned anything from a lifetime of watching cop shows and noir movies, the number one thing a guy has to worry about after snitching on drug-dealing corrupt cops is getting whacked.

Rutherford was begging for my help, and I had reason to believe his life was in danger.

At the very least, I thought the allegation that Norm Wielsch was selling drugs out of the CNET evidence locker had to be checked out by the appropriate authorities.

I sent an email to Rutherford, offering this plan:

> I can meet with a person in the Alameda County DA office and let her know, in very ambiguous terms, that I have come across a confidential source who might want to reveal important information about serious criminal activity.
>
> I can pass this information along this weekend, off the clock, and not as part of the official research of the story, since I still can't prove the confidential source isn't just an angry employee with an ax to grind over more trivial matters who is throwing wild smears.
>
> I'm interested in offering an outlet for an appropriate stream of information to the appropriate authorities, to do the right thing. I don't know how a sting or buy would be set up . . . but I think I can put you in touch with the right people to help you do what's right.

Rutherford wrote back, explaining how he got sucked into a criminal conspiracy with Butler and Wielsch:

> They are pressuring me a little, but I have been stalling . . . It was presented to me asking if I know people who smoke weed and would be interested in large amounts. I said I know some people like that. That's when I was told about everything and felt a little pressured to help out with it. I actually have 2 of the packages that I really don't want to be in possession of. I have told him that I have a buyer, when I really don't and they are waiting for me to set up the sale. I did this to stall them. That is why this is time sensitive. I think I have a week or a little more before they put more pressure on me.
>
> I am not a drug dealer and I hate the position that I have been put in. I want to get past this terrible part of my life and am not sure who to trust. I really do appreciate you helping me with this. I owe you a lot just for listening and believing.

Rutherford then added allegations about a stash of contraband, located in Butler's office, which was much more dangerous than marijuana:

> He has about 7 more pounds [of marijuana] in the office, along with thousands of Xanax, and even a couple of pounds of C-4 plastic explosive. .

Oh, shit.

The military-grade explosive C-4 is more powerful than dynamite. I knew I had to help Rutherford, because I would not be able to live with myself if those explosives were somehow detonated in my hometown.

Then I reached out to the one law enforcement source I knew I could trust.

11
The Cavalry Is Named Cindy Hall

I'VE KNOWN CINDY HALL for more than twenty years. I met her long before I became a journalist.

In the 1990s, I spent a good part of my twenties as a somewhat shiftless vagabond, taking hourly wage jobs in Guam, Australia, and the Grand Canyon National Park. Between these trips, I would come back to my hometown of Walnut Creek and save some money while working as a teacher for an elementary school's after-school center. Cindy Hall was one of the parents, and her son, Kyle, and daughter, Courtney, were sweet young students in the program.

Cindy was one of my favorite parents at the school. She was friendly and cool, and very engaged with her children. She also had a fascinating job, working for the Alameda County District Attorney as an investigator. She would come in to pick up Kyle and Courtney, give them a hug, and then tell me fascinating stories about law enforcement—undercover narcotic investigations, murder scenes, dangerous arrests.

I have several specific memories of the first few years I knew Cindy Hall, back in the early 1990s. One came at a soccer field on a Saturday morning, when I ran into her at a city park where her son, Kyle, was playing in a soccer game. Cindy was cheering for Kyle with as much enthusiasm as every other parent. But when she talked to me, she smiled and said that she was exhausted because she had been on duty the night before, investigating a horrific scene at 3 AM. A woman in East Oakland had been smoking crack in her apartment, passed out, and started a fire with a lit cigarette. The apartment went up like a tiki torch, barbecuing the crackhead beyond recognition.

As Cindy told me about it, I could sense three layers of exhaustion: from not having slept, from experiencing the unpleasantness of such a graphic crime scene, and from differentiating this fresh experience from the many nightmarish crime scenes she had seen in her career.

But she still showed up for her son's soccer game, cheering enthusiastically for Kyle, immediately after pulling an all-nighter sifting through corpse ash.

I thought of the chat at the soccer field, as well as another incident in which Cindy faced a parent's worst nightmare. I thought about her daughter, Courtney, who died from complications of meningitis.

I was teaching at Courtney's school at the time, having returned to my hometown between stints in Guam and the Grand Canyon. I adored Courtney and so did everyone who knew her. She was a happy, beautiful little girl, an absolute joy of a child who befriended every kid in her class.

When Courtney would see me each day at school, her face would immediately beam and she would run over to me and give me a happy hug. Nearly twenty years after her passing, whenever I think of Courtney, I can still feel her slam into my legs with one of her bear hugs, and I can hear her giggle.

But one Sunday morning, Courtney never woke up. She was rushed to the hospital, slipped into a coma, and had to endure several aggressive surgeries. And then, she was gone. Her shocking death broke the heart of every child in her class, as well as every teacher and parent at the school.

I went to Courtney's funeral in an old Catholic church in Walnut Creek. I can still picture Cindy in the funeral procession, touching Courtney's tiny coffin all the way out of the sanctuary.

All of these memories came rushing back when Ronald Rutherford asked me if I knew a law enforcement contact who could be trusted. I knew I could trust Cindy Hall. And that she would be the best bet to advise me about Rutherford's next move.

As frightened as I was by the situation Rutherford had pulled me into, I felt a weird sense of comfort in my decision to contact Cindy Hall. It was as if I could feel little Courtney encouraging me to call her mom. I knew that the sweet little girl who has been gone for so long would have been happy—and proud—that her mom could help me.

I sent Cindy Hall an email on Friday, January 14, asking if she could meet for coffee to talk about an important story for *Diablo*. She wrote back right away that she could meet the following Sunday afternoon and was looking forward to catching up. It had been several years since we had seen each other; our last run-in had been at a fundraiser for an animal rescue nonprofit that Cindy volunteered for.

I emailed Rutherford and said that my contact would meet me on Sunday. Rutherford thanked me again.

"I really do appreciate you helping me with this. I owe you a lot for just listening and believing," Rutherford wrote.

As I waited for the Sunday meeting with Cindy Hall, I had time to rethink my theories about Ronald Rutherford and the possible motivations for telling me about the phony case for my ride-along.

The idea that Rutherford was really a jealous and petty small-time actor named Carl Marino no longer seemed as significant. In my mind, the threat of C-4 going off in a local shopping mall or high school and the implication that the area's highest ranking narcotics officer was selling drugs out of the evidence locker trumped the theory that my source was provoking a pissing contest over face time on some silly reality show.

Meanwhile, my sleeping disorder of the past two weeks now had a new component: nightmares. When I would finally drift off to sleep, I was constantly disturbed by horrific dreamscapes—vivid hallucinations of the aftermath of a bomb attack in my hometown.

The surreal images were random, psychotic, and terrifying; they made *Jacob's Ladder* seem like *The Little Mermaid*. I saw faces melting into walls of fire, dismembered limbs scattered amongst ashes, long hallways covered with dripping blood, small children screaming in confusion and pain.

In each dream, I was paralyzed and mute; I would watch the horror unfold, without being able to talk or move or help. Without fail, I would awake from each dream sobbing and soaked in sweat.

My wife could tell that the stress I was under was kicking my ass. Over the past two weeks I had become twitchy, nervous, and exhausted, and now, extremely paranoid. I had reason to believe that Chris Butler was not only a liar and a fraud, but a dangerous man—and the public safety threat of loose C-4 brought a sense of urgency.

Whatever Cindy Hall was going to advise me to do could change my life, as well as Rutherford's. And if the allegations were true, Butler's and Norm Wielsch's reputations and lives would see some dramatic changes as well.

My anxiety was extended another twenty-four hours when Cindy called me on Sunday morning and asked if we could postpone our meeting another day. She mentioned that she was dealing with a neck injury and had had a particularly unpleasant night and was still feeling very groggy.

"I'm not sure what you want to talk to me about," Cindy said, "but I want to be clearheaded when we meet."

I wanted the same thing.

Cindy and I finally met for coffee in Lafayette on the Martin Luther King holiday, Monday, January 17, 2011. She gave me a warm hug in front of the chain café and we walked inside and ordered cappuccinos. We had a lot of catching up to do—it had been years since our last conversation—and I felt bad that I hadn't scheduled a coffee with my friend in so long.

Whether it was my machine-gun foot-tapping or my shaking hands, Cindy could tell I was not in my perpetually laid-back state that she remembered from when she knew me as an after-school teacher and world traveler, twenty years before. She tuned right in to my anxiety.

"So Pete," she said, sipping her coffee. "What did you want to talk about?"

I started at the beginning and described how I was introduced to Chris Butler and the PI Moms. I told her all about the ride-along, with its bizarre twists and turns, and its sordid resolution.

"Wow, you saw a lot," she said, skeptically. "Sounds too good to be true."

"Exactly!" I said, moving on to the Ronald Rutherford emails, which exposed the ride-along as a fraud. I told Cindy that I suspected my source was a jealous actor who got cut out of the reality show and that I intended to expose Chris Butler and his associates as liars.

Cindy nodded and sipped her coffee. Her expression asked, "So why the urgent calls to meet for coffee?"

I explained, carefully. "It was bothering me that this guy would go to so much trouble to snitch on his boss for faking these stories in the media," I said. "But I kept emailing Rutherford, and he kept sending me more information... and then he sent me this."

I had printed out the emails that Rutherford had sent me alleging Butler and Wielsch's criminal behavior. I read them to Cindy. She nodded. No wonder I was freaking out.

She didn't seem terribly surprised by the allegation that Norm Wielsch was selling drugs. Not that she had ever heard of Wielsch, she hadn't. But the temptation is always there for narcs to go bad, and the allegation that a couple of pounds of weed fell off the evidence truck was not necessarily going to instigate a deep-cover investigation.

It was the C-4 allegation that made Cindy's eyebrows go up.

"That's what they're going to want to go after," she said softly. I hoped "they" were people Cindy could introduce Rutherford to.

I explained that Ronald Rutherford had offered to flip and start buying drugs for law enforcement, and that I didn't have a clue about how such a plan might be arranged.

"OK, first things first," Cindy said, with the mater-of-fact authority of someone who had spent three decades as a professional investigator. "Your source is dirty. I'm sure there's more going on than he's telling you. I have no idea what that might be, but there's no way he's just some good citizen who wants to do the right thing."

I had imagined that Rutherford must have some dirt on his hands, if Butler and Wielsch were willing to ask him to sell drugs in the first place. But whatever trouble Rutherford was into, his emails did state that he drew a line at selling drugs with Butler and a dirty cop.

"I believe that this guy is frightened for his life," I told Cindy. "He has no idea who to talk to—and he certainly can't go to the head of the Central Contra Costa Narcotics Enforcement Team."

Cindy nodded and said, "If these guys are brazen enough to sell drugs, that means they are greedy and they'll keep trying to do it until they think they might get caught. The trick is not to tip them off. You really don't want to go to anyone in local law enforcement—because even if they're not dirty, they could compromise the situation. If the CNET commander thinks someone is watching him, this case will go away."

Cindy calmed my nerves considerably when she volunteered to call her boss at the Alameda County District Attorney's Office in the morning to give him the full download of my unexpected adventure. Her boss, another veteran of the DA's office, knew all the important people in neighboring Contra Costa County where Wielsch worked, and would know how to proceed without tipping anyone off about the investigation.

"Meanwhile, I want you to get a phone number for your contact," she told me. "You'll need to pass it along to my supervisor, if he decides to look into this."

Although she was clearly the right person to go to, Cindy was in a bind about being able to help. The car accident that had caused her neck injury was an on-the-job incident. Consequently, she was on injured leave and had strict orders to stay home and rest, meaning that she wasn't even supposed to pick up a phone to do anything work-related. If she was found to be working on any cases, it could affect her employment. As Cindy was quickly approaching her thirtieth year working for Alameda County, she wanted to be able to retire with a full pension, a prospect that was already in question because of her injury. I did not realize this until many months after our meeting.

But Cindy Hall, having more integrity than just about any other person in this story, was not going to shrug off my urgent request for help because of some bureaucratic red tape. She told me not to worry and that I could let Rutherford know that he would likely receive a call from a safe law enforcement source soon.

"There's one more thing you should know," Cindy told me. "Once he goes undercover, you might not ever hear from your contact for months, or years, or ever again. Once he becomes a confidential informant for law enforcement, you probably won't hear anything until the news that there has been an arrest."

That night, I sent Rutherford a detailed message about the meeting, explaining that I had met with a contact from the Alameda County DA's office who would call her supervisor in the morning.

I was careful not to offer Cindy's name or position, as I still did not trust Rutherford. And I certainly did not mention Cindy's outright claim that Rutherford would prove to be more deeply involved in criminal activity when the facts of the investigation shook out.

Due to my paranoia that Chris Butler could read my emails, I used thinly veiled code language for the email, suggesting that the drug allegations were a television script pitch, that the law enforcement officials I knew were producers who might be interested in reading the script.

I let Rutherford know that it could take a couple of days for a "producer" to contact him, as the information was new and coming out of left field. I ended the email by letting Rutherford know that if he did become a confidential informant, we would no longer be able to communicate about the case. Due to the protocol required of undercover narcotics investigations, Rutherford needed to know that confidential informants shouldn't correspond about the details of drug sales and criminal activity with journalists during the investigation.

I wrote:

> This is important: Once you make contact with this producer, if you arrange a script deal, I will lose contact with you, and won't have any way of knowing what the proposed/planned storyline is. I will simply continue to research my *PI Moms* story and have to play catch-up, if any plot twists arise in the criminal storyline not immediately connected to my [ride-along] story.
>
> Please let me know that you received this and let me know that you understand the approach. I don't need any more information about what details you know, how much of what is in whose possession, etc., I have passed enough info along about that and it is best that I don't know any more. That way the investigation can proceed as cleanly as possible.
>
> Hopefully I will be able to contact you in the next 48 hours with a contact. If I have not heard anything in 48 hours, I will contact you with that information as well. OK?

I felt a little sick after sending the email, for a couple of reasons. First, the idea of losing contact with such an inside source nagged at my inner journalist, but I had decided that the allegations of fire sales on stolen narcotics and weapons-grade explosives outweighed my magazine story about Chris Butler lying to *Diablo* magazine.

Second, I was worried that Rutherford would be tossed into a pit of snakes and not be able to get out. It was my contact that would advance the investigation, and I wished that Rutherford could have figured out how to contact law enforcement on his own. But, he didn't. Rutherford came to me, and it was up to me to do the best I could do to expose Butler and Wielsch safely and expediently.

Rutherford responded to my email:

> I appreciate this and understand completely. I await your information and would love to meet with a trusted person. Thank you again.

12
Reality Sabotage

THE DAY AFTER I MET with Cindy Hall was one of the strangest days on the set of *PI Moms*.

Showrunner Lucas Platt and his team were on their second day back following the holidays, and they had an important case to film. It was a sting on an unlicensed PI who was advertising investigative services on Craigslist.

Setting up unlicensed PIs was a Chris Butler specialty. Butler had successfully run this sting already on *Dr. Phil*, as well as with San Francisco's ABC7 news. In March 2010, Channel 7 ran a story that followed Butler and the PI Moms on a series of fake PI setups.

One poor bastard who was stung by Butler claimed to have no idea it was illegal to advertise himself as a PI on Craigslist. He had gotten the idea of moonlighting as a PI from HBO's *Bored to Death*.

I had to laugh when I heard the earnest ABC7's news reporters warning viewers to make sure that the PI they hire has a license, like Chris Butler of Butler & Associates. The most compelling factor of the ABC7 piece is that, as far as I can tell, the entire piece involved no media fakery whatsoever, a unique distinction on Chris Butler's television résumé.

The case that was scheduled to be filmed on January 18, 2011, for Lifetime's *PI Moms* show, was another real case in that there really was a guy in the East Bay hamlet of Piedmont who was advertising investigative services without a license. The show filmed the Moms making an appointment with the unlicensed PI, and the next big step was to film him accepting payment for his services.

Platt sent producers and a camera crew to Piedmont, early on the morning of the 18th, but things did not go as planned. The unlicensed PI never came.

"The PI Moms were scheduled to meet him at nine AM, so they made sure to get there at seven AM to set up," Platt told me. "Nine AM came and went, then ten and eleven AM. I started getting calls from [my field producer] saying, 'No one is showing up.'"

Platt instructed one of the PI Moms to call the unlicensed investigator and ask why he had missed the appointment. "[They asked,] 'Why didn't you show up?'" says Platt. "And the PI said, 'Because I got a call that it was all part of a TV show and if I had shown up, I would have been busted on TV.'"

Someone had tipped off the unlicensed PI.

Given that this sabotage had occurred just about a week after Carl Marino had threatened to go to the media to say that the show was filming false cases, Platt and his production team had a principal suspect in mind.

Platt told Chris Butler to call the unlicensed PI to see if they could smoke out the mole.

Butler was able to convince the unlicensed PI to drive out to his warehouse office in Concord. The unlicensed PI explained that he was getting ready when he received a phone call from a man who claimed that the appointment was a setup for a reality TV show. The male caller warned the unlicensed PI not to show up, or he would be filmed being arrested.

Butler and the *PI Moms* crew wanted to see if they could catch the mole red-handed. They had PI Mom Linda call Carl Marino to talk about office work on speakerphone while the unlicensed PI sat and listened to the call.

"The PI identified Carl as the guy who had called him," said Platt. "Carl was caught red-handed."

The incident was more than a little disturbing to Platt, who was already very concerned about Marino's unhinged email from the week before. Platt contacted Lifetime about the incident, following the meeting with the unlicensed PI.

"The network lawyers wrote [Marino] a much more serious letter and told him they would suspend any work from Butler & Associates, and he had to stay away from anything that was being filmed for the show," Platt told me. "It was a very strict contract, and I confronted Chris and Carl with it, and [Marino] signed it, and we all countersigned it."

The same day that Carl Marino was sabotaging the TV show's unlicensed PI case, I had a phone call with Cindy Hall's supervisor in the Alameda County District Attorney's Office. Cindy had given him the information, and the supervisor wanted to hear it from me as well.

I went through the details again: I had been invited to write about a new reality show, covering the PI Moms who had been featured on *Dr. Phil* and in *People* magazine. I had gone on a crazy ride-along, then started receiving mysterious emails saying that I had witnessed a fraudulent investigation. During my email correspondence with an anonymous source, I was informed that Norm Wielsch, commander of the Contra Costa Narcotics Enforcement Team, was selling drugs out of the evidence locker, and that he and Butler were also looking to unload a couple pounds of C-4.

The supervisor gave the same analysis of my secret source that Cindy had given: Rutherford wants to snitch to get out of trouble.

The supervisor also pointed out that an allegation from an anonymous source was far from slam-dunk evidence; it was hearsay. The information wasn't nearly solid enough for the Alameda County DA's office to launch a corruption investigation about a high-ranking cop in a neighboring county.

"What I can do is talk to a trustworthy source in Contra Costa County," the supervisor told me. "That person is Paul Mulligan, and I can speak for his credibility and integrity without any reservation."

Mulligan served as the Chief of Inspectors in the Contra Costa District Attorney's Office, and several trusted sources would later vouch for his integrity as well. I told the supervisor that the plan sounded fine, and I would keep Rutherford abreast of the details and explain why the investigation needed to begin within Contra Costa County. I also passed along the phone number that Rutherford had given as a safe-contact number.

"OK, I want you to make up a code name right now, a name that only you and I know," the supervisor told me. "Then give that name to your source, and tell that person to expect a call from someone asking for that name."

Immediately, I knew what name to give the confidential informant: Angel. My favorite television show, and also the greatest detective show of all time, is *The Rockford Files*. Fans of the show remember the character Angel Martin, a shady con man and ex-convict, played by the wonderful character actor Stuart Margolin. Margolin won two Emmy awards playing Angel, a conniving and duplicitous snitch who was always getting Jim Rockford into trouble.

In an amazing case of art-life serendipity, Margolin also played a private detective for two seasons on a Canadian series called... wait for it... *Mom PI*. In the show, Margolin's character, a grizzled veteran PI, took on a single mom as a crime-solving sidekick.

"The name is Angel," I told the supervisor.

"OK, Angel it is," the supervisor repeated.

When I first checked in with Rutherford following my meeting with Cindy Hall, he seemed to understand that the process might take a couple of days, and that my contacts in Alameda County needed to talk to someone in Contra Costa County.

"Received and appreciated... thanks again," Rutherford wrote back, at 9:52 AM on Tuesday, January 18.

But just a few hours later, he started getting squirrelly. He wrote to me at 12:40 PM. There was a definite sense of panic in his tone:

> UH OH... something is happening... Norm has asked Chris for all of the packages back due to "he thinks that someone might know they are missing" he is being adament [*sic*] enough that Chris is going to drive into San Francisco to pick up the one that I have in my possession. I am not sure if or who you spoke to, but it seems like possibly that Norm was tipped off. Remember, he is the task force commander. I

have a feeling that if anything was to be done it has to be done now to this evening or all will be lost. I know exactly where he has the packages hidden in the warehouse. I am getting scared that he suspects something and may try to set me up. I know what he is capable of. I know he won't move the stuff out right now because they are filming at the office now... Please advise... This needs to happen now... I am willing to talk to anyone as long as this happens today... I know he could try to set me up somehow... Please and Thank you... The clock is definitely ticking.

The email freaked me out—how could Rutherford have been compromised already?

I had no idea that Butler had plenty of incentive to collect whatever illegal drugs that could be tied to him, as he knew he had a mole in his organization and that the mole was aggressively sabotaging Butler's dream of becoming a reality show star.

I replied to Rutherford that I would contact my law enforcement sources with an urgent update, and reminded him that they were only learning about the allegations that day, and it might take awhile for him to get a call. It didn't feel great saying that, as I wasn't the one sitting on a couple pounds of stolen narcotics, worrying that I was about to be set up. But Rutherford needed to hang tight for this to work.

I heard back quickly from Cindy Hall that her supervisor still had not talked to anyone about the allegations, so there was no way Norm Wielsch had been tipped off. I sent this information to Rutherford immediately. Rutherford replied:

Okay, THANK YOU! I have been freaking out a little bit about this. The timing was strange, but Norm has been pressuring Chris to pressure me to sell it, and I have been stalling. He could just be fed up and have another outlet. I have a bad feeling once Norm gets it back tonight, it will be out of my hands. I have complete access to the office and can bring anyone in late if needed. Thanks again.

A few minutes later, Rutherford sent me another message:

Chris will have all 8 pounds of [the marijuana] in his truck after he comes to get the one that I have in SF. I considered calling SF PD and telling them about it... or running over to Concord PD right now and explaining it is there and they need to get it before it is gone...

I didn't like the sound of this. I was worried that Rutherford was wound too tight, and that he might make a mistake with the evidence and blow the case. I called Cindy again and said that Rutherford was talking about walking into a police station with a pound of weed and claiming it came from Wielsch.

"If he does that, the case goes away," Cindy said.

I emailed that message to Rutherford:

> My contact says DO NOT just go to any random law enforcement in CoCo county. Stay cool.

I tried suggesting Rutherford do some more evidence collecting while he waited for the call:

> Can you take cell phone photos of the stash in the warehouse before it gets taken away? If not, don't worry . . . don't do anything to draw attention. If they've tried this once, they will try it again down the road.

This seemed to calm my source down a bit. Rutherford replied:

> I can't do anything as far as pictures go right now. The funny thing is that all of the production people are sitting and have been sitting right next to it throughout the filming and have no idea. It is in a big locked heavy-duty black lock box. I know where the key is. I can take a picture of the two pounds that I have in my possession before Chris comes [to] get the one later tonight.

That evening, Rutherford sent me a picture of two pounds of shrink-wrapped marijuana, laid out next to a tape measure:

> I attached a picture of the 2 packages that I have in my possession (each one is a pound). Chris will be coming to pick up one of them tonight to take back to Norm with the rest of them. He doesn't realize I have the other one . . . I had to give my own money for it because he was pressuring me. I told him that I sold it to "my guy."
>
> I still haven't heard from anyone yet. Thanks.

During the afternoon of Tuesday, January 18, I received an email from Lucas Platt, who made good on his promise to invite me to come to the set and watch how *PI Moms* was being filmed for Lifetime. Platt wanted to make sure he gave me a chance to see that the cases being filmed for the TV show were authentic, and that I would differentiate between the show's cases and whatever Chris Butler had done to stage my ride-along with actors and a contrived investigation.

Platt sent me an itinerary of the shooting schedule for the next day, Wednesday, January 19. At 10:30 AM, they planned to interview Linda, the intern who had been sucked into the scam with the gypsy psychic. At 1 PM, they would interview Chris Butler. During the afternoon, they would be filming PI Mom Denise Antoon and her husband, Jeff, in a marriage therapy session, but I would not have access to the therapy session. Then, at 7:30 PM, they would do a one-on-one with Denise to discuss the day's events.

I told Platt I wanted to attend the interviews with Butler and Denise, as they had both played a role in my ride-along, and I wanted to see each of them face-to-face. I felt I might be able to get Denise to come clean about staging the ride-along, if I looked her in the eye.

Butler was another story, and I wasn't sure how to approach him on set. Just a week before, I wanted to *Columbo* him; drop a legal document in his lap and see if he would sign it. Now, I knew that law enforcement sources were whispering about Butler being involved in some truly heinous behavior.

Of course, Butler did not know that I was aware that he was moonlighting as a drug dealer and C-4 salesman, but he certainly did suspect I was planning on writing an article that could damage his dream of becoming a reality show star.

Rutherford had sent me a note saying that Butler had mentioned me in the office, saying that he had not heard from me in a while and was hoping that was a good thing. Butler had his fingers crossed that he had managed to get to all the players in my fake ride-along before I did, and that I might just kill the story.

I wondered what he would do when I showed up on the set of *PI Moms*.

On Wednesday, January 19, I drove to the address Platt gave me for the reality show taping, making sure to arrive a full hour before Butler was scheduled to show up. The "set" was actually a couple of conference and hotel rooms in a Hyatt Summerfield Suites in the East Bay city of Pleasant Hill. There was an elaborate production crew spread around several rooms; tired-looking tech geeks, sitting in front of screens and editing docks and cables and cords and power strips.

Lucas Platt showed me around and introduced me to his production crew, who were mostly Bay Area freelancers hired part-time to work on the show. As freelance work went, *PI Moms* was a nice gig for the Bay Area's TV production scene—Lifetime was pumping a good amount of money into the show to make sure it could stand next to *Project Runway* and similarly slick shows on the cable network.

I didn't get the sense that Platt had warned the crew about my presence. I did receive a number of compliments on my *Star Wars* t-shirt, but that seemed par for the course for A/V clubbers whose chosen career path involved spending sixteen-hour days in front of editing docks.

During the tour, I asked Platt if he had told Chris Butler that I would be attending the afternoon's filming session.

"I did not," Platt said. "Did you want me to?"

"No, that's fine," I said, wondering what Platt thought of Butler after spending more than two months filming *PI Moms* with him. "I'll just say hi when he gets here."

Butler arrived a few minutes later. His jaw hit the floor when he saw me.

"Hey Chris, how have you been?" I asked. I tried to sound nonchalant and friendly, but the voice I heard come out of my mouth sounded like a crazy person's. Butler looked down and avoided eye contact.

"I've had better days," he said.

"Oh yeah?" I said. "What's wrong?"

Butler didn't mention his recent hassle with a saboteur on his staff, at least not specifically. "It's just internal stuff," he told me, looking at the ground.

I followed Butler into a makeshift studio, a two-room suite with the windows blacked out by heavy curtains. Bright lights and a neutral-colored backdrop were set up in one room, and Butler took his spot on a stool in the spotlight. Camera and sound operators lurked in the darkness, and a field producer talked to Butler about the cases the show had been filming.

Butler's role for the day was to play the wise sage PI, giving feedback about how the PI Moms had performed on various cases: the farmers market–permit scam, the harassment case at the senior residential home, the gypsy psychic, and the missing teenage girl. The tape of Butler's commentary would be edited into the show and appear after the footage of the PI Moms working each case.

I sat a few feet in front of Butler, just out of the rim of the lighting. As the field producer started asking Butler questions, I started writing in my reporter's notebook, recording Butler's quotes and also taking notes about his demeanor with the camera rolling.

It was a surreal experience to watch Butler under hot lights, being peppered with questions. The scene was somewhat reminiscent of Sharon Stone's infamous interrogation sequence in *Basic Instinct*. Butler wanted to give the impression that he was in charge, the way Stone was when she flashed her crotch at Michael Douglas and Newman from *Seinfeld*.

What was truly fascinating was listening to Butler freestyle his tough-guy PI philosophy for the camera. When asked about why it was so easy for someone to scam purveyors at a farmers market, Butler said, "People are usually too lazy or too trusting. And that's exactly what a criminal is looking for."

Does lazy and trusting apply to journalists as well, Chris? I wondered.

The field producer spent the most time on the case of the missing teenager. Clearly, the show had invested more time in this case than any other. One recent incident involved the missing teen's phone record showing a phone number in Ontario, California. Butler and the Moms discovered the number belonged to a man in his twenties, and thought the Teen might be shacking up with him down in Southern California.

Butler seemed confident that the Teen was in several kinds of trouble, suggesting that there was statutory rape involved in the Ontario situation as well as sexual abuse in her family history. Butler was vague about how he gathered this information, saying, "We all know about the craze that is Facebook. Even if you don't know somebody, you're going to be able to find someone who knows somebody. There's always a link."

Useful tip, I thought, scribbling in my pad and thinking about how Rutherford's identification of Mystery Date as Ryan Romano led me to connect the dots between several of the PI Moms and Butler's decoys through Facebook.

The field producer pressed Butler about his team's investigation. Butler said he had one of the PI Moms working on her teenage friends, in case one knew of the missing girl's whereabouts. Butler thought his employee could charm the information out of another teen—even one sworn to secrecy—by playing the do-the-right-thing card. "There's snitching for the wrong reasons and snitching for the right reasons," Butler said. "I think here it is for the right reason."

Is Rutherford snitching for the right reason? I wondered.

The interview wrapped with the field producer asking Butler how he would feel if he found out his teenage daughter was shacking up with a twentysomething dude halfway across the state.

"I would not be a happy camper," Butler said to the camera.

The field producer asked for another take. "Can we get a stronger response, Chris? 'Not a happy camper' sounds like you just dropped a sandwich on the floor," said the producer. "I want to know how you would feel if you found out your teenage daughter was secretly dating an older man."

"I'd be out for blood," growled Chris Butler, Tough Guy PI.

"That's good," said the producer. "That's certainly stronger than 'happy camper.'"

The interview with Butler lasted two full hours, with me scribbling away in my notepad the entire time. My mind raced with questions, such as: Had Rutherford been contacted by Contra Costa investigators yet? How dangerous would Butler be if he knew law enforcement had been tipped off about his stash of drugs and explosives? What should I say to Butler if I got some one-on-one time with him after the interview?

Butler did not offer me a shot at the latter. When the interview wrapped, he was out the door in a flash. I bolted out the room after him, only to see him disappear out a hallway exit into a parking lot.

By the time I was outside, he was gone.

I told Lucas Platt I would be back to the set in a few hours to watch Denise Antoon's interview.

I went out to my car and checked the emails on my iPhone. Rutherford had pinged me, saying that there was still no contact from law enforcement asking for Angel. I wrote back for him to sit tight and that I would text my contact again to say how nervous the informant was about being set up. I also wrote:

> I just got done watching Chris being interviewed for two hours with the show people. I think he was very surprised to see me there.

Rutherford quickly replied:

> I bet he was surprised. He didn't mention it to me...and he would have if he had known. I would be interested in knowing the context of that interview, after what transpired today at the office right before it. I honestly can't wait to be over with this so I hope it is soon. Thanks again.

After a few hours, I went back to the Summerfield Suites and waited for Denise Antoon to arrive. Lucas Platt intercepted me and said that Denise was uncomfortable about letting me watch the interview, because she was going to be discussing some very personal details about her marriage; things that had come up in that afternoon's marriage counseling.

There was some hypocrisy to Denise's privacy request, of course, as she was being filmed for a national television show the whole time.

At the same time, I was sympathetic, because the experience I just had watching Butler being filmed was both intense and intimate. Assuming that Denise was going to be uncomfortable around me anyway, I was fine with not freaking her out during filming, just as long as I could talk to her when she was done.

As Denise went into the darkened studio, I sat in one of the editing rooms with Lucas Platt and had a long talk about the show. Platt strengthened my opinion that he was a straight shooter, as he told me about various problems the show had experienced during production, all of which seemed to hinge on Chris Butler not being reliable.

I told Platt that I appreciated him letting me visit the set that day, and I would make it clear in my story that anyone involved in the Lifetime production had nothing to do with the case I had witnessed—the one that seemed to have been fraudulent, according to Ronald Rutherford's first email.

"You realize that the person who emailed you was a disgruntled employee, right?" Platt asked.

We looked each other in the eye and both thought about the same person: Carl Marino.

I had no idea that Platt had spent most of the last twenty-four hours dealing with Marino's shenanigans as a reality TV saboteur. And Platt had no idea that Chris Butler might be selling drugs with a corrupt narcotics officer. So I decided to take Butler's own explanation of the email for a spin.

"Butler told me it was a disgruntled employee," I said. "He said it was a former intern who had been having a secret gay affair with one of the PI Moms. Butler told me this former intern is out to scorch the earth around him now."

Platt groaned and put his head in his hands. "Goddammit, Chris," he said.

Out of the corner of my eye, I saw Denise quickly walking through the editing suite, heading for the same exit door where Chris Butler had disappeared earlier in the day. I sprang up and followed her out to the parking lot.

"Denise!" I called out, running after her. Denise stopped and turned to face me. She looked exhausted.

"How did the interview go?" I asked, my fake-friendly tone sounding forced.

"It was fine," Denise replied.

"Did you want to talk anymore about the ride-along case, or the conversation we had last week?" I asked.

"Not really," she said, jingling her car keys. "I have to get home to my kids."

"OK, Denise, let me just say this before you go," I said, looking her in the eye. "I'll check in with you again before the story goes to print.

You don't want this story to go to print without having a chance to talk to me. OK?"

Denise looked sad under the dull fluorescent lights of the parking lot. She nodded, walked to her car, and drove away.

The next morning, Rutherford sent me an email at 9:37 AM to let me know that he had received a phone call from a lieutenant in the Contra Costa District Attorney's Office. I was thrilled to hear about the call, as Rutherford's increasingly panicked emails during the week had me feeling uneasy about his behavior, not to mention his safety.

Clearly, Rutherford felt the same way:

> I feel somewhat relieved already . . . they will be contacting me again in about an hour to decide what we are going to do about it. Thanks again! I will keep you updated.

So far, so good. I drove to the *Diablo* magazine office feeling better than I had in nearly a week, since Rutherford had told me about the drugs and C-4. Going to Cindy Hall had been the right move. I felt that I still couldn't tell my editor or publisher about the criminal allegations, so my plan was to carefully keep chipping away at sources about the fake ride-along while playing dumb about more serious matters.

I didn't want my reporting to jeopardize the investigation involving Chris Butler. If he was as dirty as Rutherford suggested, I wanted to see him get busted. Same went for CNET Commander Norm Wielsch—if he was putting people in jail for selling dope and then putting those drugs on the street anyway, he needed to go down.

When I got to the office, I had another email from Rutherford, but it wasn't an update about further contacts from the DA's office. Instead, it was more melodrama about the reality show.

> You obviously know who I am now, but I need to ask you to back off the identity if you could. I just got a frantic call from Chris saying you called [Lifetime] Production and told them you figured out who it was that was sending the emails and named my name. I, of course, denied everything.

I had done no such thing. When I spoke with Lucas Platt, I repeated Butler's claim that a vindictive lesbian was sending me messages. Rutherford asked me to provide cover:

> Is there any way you can tell them you don't know who sent the original email? I don't know what to do and I am worried that this will jeapordize [*sic*] the thing with the D.A.'s office. I adamantly denied it was me that sent any of this, of course and shifted blame.
>
> Please keep me as a confidential source . . . I beg you . . . there are other factors involved that could put me in danger . . . Thanks again for everything you have done so far.

Although I believed Rutherford was terrified, I wasn't about to start offering subterfuge services for his hassles with the Lifetime production crew. I fired off a response, letting Rutherford know that if Butler and the production crew were saying I had ID'd him, they were bluffing:

> I definitely DID NOT say that you were the source. I gave the angry lesbian story that [Butler] gave me and told the producer we got two anonymous emails. Obviously, I can't tell them that I received this tip from you. I'll shoot Lucas an email saying thanks again for the help last night.
>
> I DID NOT tell production your name. I DO NOT know who you are. I could make a good guess, but I DO NOT know. Stay cool, Angel!

This calmed Rutherford down. He replied:

> That's great news . . . he was testing me then . . . I did audiotape that conversation as well where he admits the whole thing was staged and he talks about how he silenced the actors involved . . . Thank you . . . Thank you . . . thank you.

To make sure Rutherford was on the same page, I wrote back to let him know exactly what I had told Lucas Platt about receiving emails, concerning the integrity of Chris Butler and the PI Moms:

> I told Lucas I received two anonymous emails, which Chris said came from an angry lesbian/disgruntled former employee . . . I let them know I was waiting to hear back from Chris to confirm that the Client was really in a relationship with [her

fiancé] for three years and the case was real. I wanted to believe him but Chris never even got back to me, so I had to start checking out Facebook, etc. and came across the mistress. There are FB connections with the mistress to someone who is FB friends with all the PI moms. If Lucas asks again I will say the same thing.

I don't want to be too gotcha about this, but I am annoyed that I went along for such an elaborately staged ride-along, which is why I have insisted [on] getting to the bottom of things instead of just killing the story we thought we had.

Rutherford replied with another Butler-is-a-dirtbag diatribe:

Your annoyance is very understandable. Many, many people would feel the same way if they realized how they were manipulated by Chris. It's not only the lies though... his business practice is pretty much based on criminality. Besides his narcotics sales (which hopefully we can end soon) I could write paragraphs of the illegal practices that he is involved in. It seems like there are very few of his practices that don't involve some sort of criminal activity on his or his investigators' part.

Then, Rutherford passed along some chilling info, claiming that Butler had designs on setting me up to even the score:

Chris has told me personally that they are working on you, to make you believe everything was true. They need you for marketing purposes for the show, to advertise it and his company. He is worried (as I would think he should be) that you could write the truth and hurt his credibility. He discussed trying to "sting" you somehow so he could have some leverage over you to just go away.

I called Cindy Hall as soon as I read Rutherford's message and let her know that Butler might try to sting me.

"If I get caught with a pound of heroin or a severed head in the trunk of my car, I told you something might happen," I blurted.

Cindy said she would pass along my message of paranoia to the powers that be. I drove home imagining that every headlight in my rearview mirror was Chris Butler, right behind me, planning his revenge.

13

A Dirty DUI, Part Deux

AS I HAD HOPED, Cindy Hall was the right person to call. Her contacts got in touch with exactly the right people to begin a crackerjack investigation of Butler and Wielsch—her Alameda County supervisor called Paul Mulligan in Contra Costa, who assigned a trusted lieutenant to inform Norm Wielsch's boss of the allegation that Wielsch was stealing and selling drugs. On the morning of Friday, January 21, Lieutenant Daryl Jackson of the Contra Costa District Attorney's Office called the California Department of Justice and asked to speak with the director of the Bureau of Narcotic Enforcement.

"Daryl Jackson called our director, Larry Wallace. Jackson needed to talk to someone in DOJ, so that was a good place to start," Kent Shaw, who is now the deputy director of the California Department of Justice's Division of Law Enforcement, told me during an interview at a coffee shop in Fairfield, California, in 2012. "The information was immediately passed to me."

"It's not unusual to have a lot of wild allegations against our folks, due to the nature of the work," Shaw said. "Fortunately, almost exclusively that information winds up being bogus or fabricated. However, we have an obligation to ferret these things out, and we always do."

Shaw assigned DOJ representative Gary Pitkin to go that evening to Contra Costa County to meet with Rutherford. Pitkin was to conduct a preliminary interview to see if this person besmirching Wielsch's conduct had any credibility.

Pitkin and Jackson scheduled an interview with Rutherford at the Contra Costa District Attorney's offices in Richmond. Pitkin wanted to meet with Rutherford as soon as possible, but the informant claimed to have a professional obligation that would last until at least 3 PM. So Pitkin and Jackson agreed to meet Rutherford at the end of the afternoon.

Exactly one week after telling me about Chris Butler's criminal activity and Norm Wielsch's corrupt behavior, Ronald Rutherford finally had a meeting scheduled with a safe law enforcement source.

Rutherford had two people to thank for that meeting: Cindy Hall and me.

Friday, January 21, was a busy day for Carl Marino. He had a juicy role booked in the East Bay city of Livermore, a suburban sprawl at the far southeast end of *Diablo* magazine's readership area.

The gig wasn't anything like the standard-issue day work that Marino had been getting since moving from New York to California, such as playing a SWAT team member for the low-budget true-crime show *I (Almost) Got Away With It*, or posing as a cheerful fiancé in a TV spot for a local jewelry store.

For this gig, Marino got to play a TV producer for a nonexistent reality show that was fabricated to trick another East Bay husband into getting arrested under Butler's Dirty DUI method.

This setup was a doozy, a Butler & Associates special production. A two-part episode, in fact.

Part one had taken place one week earlier, on the night of January 14, 2011. Carl Marino had set up a Livermore Valley winemaker by inviting him to meet for drinks in Danville to discuss a possible reality series about independent wineries for the A&E cable network.

Marino identified himself as John Brownell, a producer for a company called ArtistFilm. ArtistFilm is a real production company, the one that gave Marino his first acting job in an independent thriller called *Sedona's Rule*.

Marino told the winemaker he was creating a new reality show that would compare wineries in the lesser-known Livermore Valley to powerhouses in the Napa Valley, with hopes that the A&E network would pick up the winery show.

The con worked like clockwork.

The winemaker met Marino to talk about his business and be tempted with the prospect of fame and free publicity via reality television. Much wine was consumed as Marino spun a web of bullshit about a TV show that didn't exist. At the end of the night, Marino said he would follow up soon after contacting the bigwigs at A&E. As the meeting ended, the winemaker stayed at the bar's entrance to chat with some other people that he knew. Marino met up with his wife, Ilona, who again had been having dinner across the street with Butler's wife during the scam, along with two other decoys. The female foursome had even come into the wine bar to add some sugar to the sting—pretending to be a group of wine lovers on a girl's night out, they oohed and ahhed over the winemaker's bottles.

"Text me what he blows," Marino messaged Butler, who was positioned outside the bar in his Hummer. Ten minutes later, Butler messaged Marino that the winemaker was in cuffs.

"Oh no. LOL," Marino messaged back.

".15 BAL," Butler texted proudly, after getting an update from the arresting officer, Steve Tanabe, who had also arrested the businessman Butler and Marino had set up five days before.

"Oh yeah, I can handle that," Marino replied. "I'm just pissed he stood outside for 30 minutes or I would have had him at double the legal limit."

The winemaker setup was a tricky one, because there were complications after the arrest. Butler's client—the winemaker's wife—became concerned that her soon-to-be ex-husband knew he had been set up, and that she had been a part of it. So, she hired Butler and Marino to continue the lie a week later.

That's why Marino and two friends—Butler & Associates intern Jessica Carter and Bay Area actor James Galileo—drove out to a Livermore winery with a video camera one week after Marino set up the winemaker. Marino continued his role as John Brownell, make-believe television producer; Carter played the camera operator; and Galileo portrayed Marino's big financial backer. Marino later told authorities that Galileo was paid one hundred dollars for his role in the lie.

The trio of phony TV professionals took a tour of the winemaker's business, shooting video and saying how great the winery would look on television. The winemaker told his staff to be on their best behavior, in case this turned out to be a big break. He even had his mother come by the winery to meet the producers.

During the scam, Marino made sure to text the client that everything was going as planned. Marino also messaged his wife, Ilona, about another bit of business he needed to take care of that afternoon.

"Bring the package home," Marino texted, referring to the shrink-wrapped marijuana Ilona was hiding in her desk in an office located in San Francisco's Presidio district, where she worked as an executive assistant for a private equity firm.

Part two of the winemaker setup wrapped with Marino and two other liars saying thank you and good-bye to the winemaker and his gracious staff in the Livermore Valley.

Marino then drove the fifty-mile commute to his San Francisco neighborhood where he picked up Ilona and two pounds of marijuana, which had been stolen from CNET's evidence stash several months before. And then (finally) Marino drove thirty miles (in Friday afternoon Bay Area traffic, ouch!) to the Contra Costa District Attorney's Office in Richmond.

That's where Marino finally revealed himself to be Ronald Rutherford and turned over the dope to law enforcement, snitching on Chris Butler and Norm Wielsch.

PART THREE
THE INVESTIGATION

14

The DOJ Gets the Download

DURING THE FINAL DAYS of January 2011, I found myself overwhelmed by the stress of a story in which I had unintentionally become a key character.

Rutherford's daily emails kept me privy to a situation with far higher stakes than any story that I—or anyone—had ever reported for *Diablo* magazine. Rutherford's warning that Butler had plans to set me up had me looking over my shoulder constantly.

In the *Diablo* office, the PI Moms story had become something of a sore subject. I just kept telling my editor that I was still working on it, and that I was sure Butler had set up the ride-along, but I wanted to check out some more sources. I didn't mention the more sinister twists that I was aware of and just kept stalling, saying that Lifetime was delaying the airdate by a few months so we still should have time to fit the story in at a later date.

Fortunately, I had scheduled vacation time for the first week of February. As I do every year around that time, I used my vacation days to attend as many screenings as possible at the Noir City Film Festival, a hugely popular ten-night retrospective of film noir at the historic Castro Theatre in San Francisco. The festival always screens a few noir standards, such as *Sunset Boulevard* or *The Postman Always Rings Twice*, but specializes in resurrecting—and sometimes saving—prints of long-forgotten B-pictures the studios cranked out in the 1940s and '50s.

It so happened that the theme of Noir City 2011 was "Who's Crazy Now?" Each of the twenty-four films featured some character with mental illness or amnesia or shellshock or some other horrible psychological ailment, which led the character to fall into that rabbit hole into which noir characters descend. Artistic serendipity for the Strange Case of Ronald Rutherford.

Night after night, as Ronald Rutherford was working undercover for the Department of Justice, I sat in the dark at the Castro Theatre, taking in stories about desperate souls in downward spirals while trying to wrap my head around the very noirish reality I had been living since Rutherford had tipped me off about the fake ride-along.

Fortunately, Rutherford was in very good hands with the team of DOJ agents that were brought in to work the case.

Of all the characters I interviewed for this book, California DOJ's Division of Law Enforcement Deputy Director Kent Shaw is one of my favorites.

Shaw reminds me of a G-man out of an old Warner Bros. crime film, a straight-arrow lawman who has dedicated his life to fighting crime. Shaw speaks clearly, always wears a suit, and works tirelessly to fight California's tidal wave of illegal drugs. Shaw spends his days overseeing investigations of drug cartels, prison gangs, meth manufacturers, and other shady characters.

When he's not sweating over those highly dangerous operations, Shaw campaigns against pharmaceutical companies that produce the chemicals that create crystal methamphetamine, and assists in the crackdown on prescription narcotics abuse by pillheads and doctor shoppers.

Most of Shaw's cases involve much higher stakes than what Carl Marino suggested Butler and Wielsch were involved in. Two pounds of weed ("garbage" weed at that, according to a couple of pot enthusiasts who Butler let sample the product) was not explosive evidence, but the corruption it was connected to represented something far more insidious: that a DOJ agent was selling the dope he was supposed to be taking off the streets.

On January 21, Carl Marino met with Department of Justice representative Gary Pitkin and Contra Costa DA investigator Daryl Jackson for several hours at the Western Operations of the Contra Costa District Attorney's Office in Richmond. Marino handed over the two bags of shrink-wrapped weed that he had been hiding in his closet for the past several weeks, and told Pitkin and Jackson that the dope came from Chris Butler via Norm Wielsch.

Pitkin knew Chris Butler and Norm Wielsch from their days at Antioch PD, long before Wielsch became the commander of the Contra Costa Narcotics Enforcement Team. Wielsch, to that point, had a clean record as a DOJ agent. But Marino's detailed descriptions of Butler's interactions with Wielsch warranted further investigation.

"Pitkin called me back and said this was something that needed to be looked into," Kent Shaw explained to me. Shaw said that Marino's statements did nothing to prove that Wielsch was involved in criminal activity, because the only criminal behavior Marino had witnessed was by Chris Butler.

"Nothing that Carl had at that time included Norm being involved in criminal activity," said Shaw. "[Marino's] big concern was that he was in possession of marijuana that he was supposed to sell. And he brought the marijuana with him. So, based on that, Pitkin thought [Marino's allegations] were plausible."

Shaw explained that Pitkin, who had been a task force commander like Wielsch before moving up to a management position in the Department of Justice, carefully considered the information that Marino presented: Marino received the drugs from Butler, who claimed they came from Wielsch.

"Just that what [Marino] was saying was possible, was enough for us to do our due diligence to look further," Shaw said. "We at least knew that we had to investigate Butler, because of Carl's firsthand knowledge working for him. If Wielsch was connected in any way, then we had to investigate that as well."

Shaw spent the weekend of January 22–23 assembling a team of DOJ agents to come to the East Bay and begin a top-secret investigation. Shaw said that the case was a tricky one, due to Wielsch's law enforcement connections in the area, as well as Butler's background as a cop.

"We were dealing with current law enforcement and someone with a lot of previous law enforcement," Shaw said. "Additionally, [Butler] was very savvy about surveillance and countersurveillance. So, you go into the operation assuming the worst is possible."

Shaw told me that he decided to assign the case to a team from outside of the Bay Area, so he called Dean Johnston, an all-star DOJ special agent supervisor with a stellar reputation in the field. Johnston is the recipient of the 2010 Alfred E. Stewart Award for California's Narcotics Officer of the Year, among many other accolades for his work with the Department of Justice.

"We have a lot of agents that could have done that assignment, but I knew I was going to assemble the best of the best," Shaw told me. "That team, and what they had been doing in major investigations at the time—and Dean in particular—gave me a greater sense of confidence that it was going be done right."

Dean Johnston had never heard of Norm Wielsch or Chris Butler or the PI Moms before getting the call from Shaw. I asked Johnston to explain his reaction to hearing the allegation that a fellow DOJ agent was selling dope stolen from evidence seizures.

"These were serious allegations," Johnston told me. "Even in this profession, it is still shocking when you hear [allegations against a DOJ agent]. It is a surprising thing, but it motivates you to get your A-game on."

Johnston said he really did not know what to expect from the assignment. It certainly wasn't his job to jump to any conclusions.

"When I came over here, I did not know if it was just going to be a two-day fact-finding mission," Johnston said. "[The first priority was to] find out what is true, what is factual, and what could be investigated. If you really apply yourself, the facts will fall out. It might take a while—it might take years—but the facts will come out."

Just before driving to San Francisco to interview Carl Marino for the first time, Johnston did a Google search on Chris Butler. Johnston watched Butler's appearance on *Dr. Phil*, to get an impression of the private investigator and the PI Moms. There wasn't much online about Marino, other than his acting and modeling website.

"I wanted to interview Marino, the guy who brought these allegations," Johnston told me. "So I brought a couple of guys who are fantastic at interviews. And I always bring someone I call my devil's advocate, who sees the holes in the story. As an actor, [Marino had] a propensity to be better than us at acting and lying. So we went over there to find the lies in the story."

Before he met Marino, Johnston had the same instinct that Cindy Hall had expressed to me when I gave her the initial confidential informant's allegations. Both Johnston and Hall have seen enough snitches to know that they tend not to be squeaky clean.

"Most [informants] come with baggage," Johnston told me. "They have been arrested, or [are informing] because they were slighted by an individual. Rarely do you give up your best friend because it is the right thing to do. They are there because they want to get out of [trouble], or because they have been slighted or burned."

On Tuesday, January 25, Dean Johnston and two other DOJ agents met Carl Marino at his one-bedroom apartment in the Marina District of San Francisco. I have reviewed the recording of the interview, a fascinating document of Marino's account of the events that led to his come-forward moment. After giving his first and last name and date of birth, Marino told Johnston that I was the one who aided his safe passage to the meeting with the DOJ.

"I had been in contact with an editor," Marino said, responding to Johnston's 'why are we here today' question. "A guy who did a story—we actually fabricated [a case] for him—and he was going to print a story based on that."

"And who is that?" asked Johnston.

"Peter Crooks, senior editor for *Diablo* magazine," Marino responded.

Johnston had already heard a bit about me, and *Diablo*, from the chain of information that Kent Shaw had given him.

"I noticed [*Diablo*] covers stories on restaurants," Johnston commented, trying to comprehend how a lifestyle magazine editor figured in to the allegations that a top narcotics agent was selling stolen drugs.

Marino explained that *Diablo* covers everything about the East Bay area, the region where Butler and the PI Moms are based.

"So he was doing a story based on this fabricated case, and he was going to print this article, not knowing the truth," said Marino.

"You felt it was necessary to tell him about that?" asked Johnston. It was a good question, because Marino had played a role in organizing and acting out the ride-along sting without any apparent ethical dilemma.

"Honestly, I thought it was a pretty nasty thing to do; it was going to jeopardize his career possibly," Marino said. "Chris Butler did it for his own PR purposes, to get business."

Marino continued to dish on Butler's aggressive media whoring.

"[Butler] has done this quite frequently," Marino said to the DOJ agents. "He did it to the *Dr. Phil* show, and he did it to *People* magazine. He creates these elaborate cases for writers to go on these ride-alongs."

After Marino described Butler's fraudulent media stories, Johnston steered the interview back to its main purpose: to investigate the allegation that Norm Wielsch was selling drugs. Johnston asked Marino how he had come into the possession of the two pounds of marijuana that had been handed over to Gary Pitkin and Daryl Jackson the previous Friday.

Marino claimed that he had been holding on to the two pounds of marijuana for quite a while. The first pound came into his possession on November 19, 2010, a few weeks after *PI Moms* started filming. That Friday evening, Marino explained, all the other staff had gone home for the day and Butler brought Marino into the warehouse part of the office for a chat. Butler opened up a footlocker that contained nine shrink-wrapped packages of marijuana, each containing approximately one pound.

After showing off the stash, Marino claimed that Butler had asked, "You know people that smoke weed?" to which Marino replied, "Sure."

Marino said that Butler then gave him instructions to sell weed. "Here's what I want you to do. I'm going to give you a packet of marijuana, and why don't you try to sell it?"

After Marino made this claim, there was a quiet pause in the interview—the DOJ didn't ask a question. It is my opinion that Marino could feel the DOJ agents' eyes on him, asking the obvious, "Why didn't you just tell Butler you weren't interested in selling drugs?"

Without being asked, Marino had an explanation. "[Butler] is very manipulative, I guess at the time I should have said, 'No, I don't want to have anything to do with it.' But he's that kind of a guy who can guilt you into doing something, and say, 'Well, now that you know this . . .' He can be a scary person. I know how he sets people up. Chris' main goal is to get information on everyone else so they can't say anything."

"And, at that point, he told you this stuff comes from Norm?" Johnston asked.

"At that point, I pretty much knew the stuff came from Norm," Marino responded. "I know their relationship, it just all made sense. But then he mentioned Norm's name. He said, 'If you can possibly get rid of this—all of this—here's the deal: Whatever money you make on it, half of it goes to Norm, the other half we split.'"

So, Marino took a pound of the marijuana, drove it thirty miles from Concord to San Francisco, and hid the package in his apartment. Marino said he held on to the weed for the next month and that Butler was constantly pestering him about selling it. Eventually, Marino said, he and his wife took more than $1,200 out of their bank accounts to pay for the pound and get Butler off his back.

Marino paid for the pot on December 16 in a surprising place.

"It was at the Tracy Police Department gun range," Marino said.

Johnston asked why Marino and Butler would be hanging out at a police department gun range (let alone conducting illegal drug transactions there).

"As part of the [*PI Moms*] show also, we go there and shoot," Marino said. "[Tracy PD] gives us full access."

"OK," said Johnston. "So you give him the money, and did he give you [another] package then, or later?"

Marino said that a day or so after he paid Butler for the first pound, his boss gave him another shrink-wrapped package to sell. Realizing he would quickly empty his bank account by buying pounds of weed, Marino never offered to pay Butler for pound number two.

"He's been asking me about it, if not every day, at least every other day," Marino complained, adding that he did not have a clue what to do with the evidence. "I did not know who to go to in Contra Costa County, because I was almost 100 percent certain those packages came from the task force. I know Norm, I've been around Norm quite a few times. I know he and Chris are best friends."

Johnston knew that Marino's claims of Butler and Wielsch's close friendship did nothing to prove that Wielsch was the one actually providing the drugs. Johnston shifted gears and inquired about the culture at Butler's office. The DOJ agent asked how often Marino went into Butler's office. Every day, said Marino, but during the past week he had not been anywhere near the office—because he had been suspended from work. Marino eased into the story about the unlicensed PI.

"It was an incident where I was trying to have [Butler] fire me, but he still [wouldn't]," Marino explained.

The interview continued, and Marino, sounding considerably more irritated about the reality show situation than he did about being asked to sell stolen drugs, complained that the reality show was spoiling the daily business at Butler & Associates.

"Chris has been telling us that we would run the business as usual, and then the production company comes in and they push us all around," Marino said. "They take our cases away from us because they want to use them for the show, and they basically treat us like shit."

Marino described his motivation for sabotaging the show by tipping off the unlicensed private investigator.

"I took an opportunity, where I knew Chris was going to realize it was me, because there was only one person it could be," said Marino. "I called the kid and told him not to show up. I knew it was going to disrupt the show a little bit, and I could make a statement: 'Look, you screw with my job, I can screw with yours a little bit, too.'"

"What did Chris say about that?" Johnston asked, wondering why Marino would make such an aggressive move against Butler's show, especially if Marino was in possession of stolen drugs at the time of the sabotage, and concerned for his own safety.

"He was more hurt that I did that to him," Marino said. "I told him, 'Chris, you're a big boy.' He knew I didn't like Lucas Platt, the showrunner, because he and I have butted heads the entire time [the show has been filming], because of all the stuff he has done without caring about the business."

Johnston asked about Marino's relationship with Butler, inquiring if Marino owed his boss any debts. Marino said the only outstanding loan was the second pound of marijuana.

"So the only debt you owe him is for the pound?" Johnston asked.

"Or, to bring the weed back," Marino replied.

Another DOJ agent piped in, surprised, and asked, "Has he said that, 'Bring the weed back?'"

Marino replied, "Well, he did at one point, when this whole thing [with the unlicensed PI] went down. He pulled me outside the office and said, 'Norm's getting real worried, he thinks they might realize it's missing, you need to bring it back and I need to get it today.'"

Marino said that Butler's behavior made him worried that his boss was going to set a trap to get Marino arrested, to stop him from sabotaging the reality show again. Marino said that the night of the unlicensed PI tip-off, Butler called to say he would drive in to San Francisco and pick up the marijuana Marino had not sold yet.

That evening, Marino said he saw an unmarked police car in the alley behind his apartment, and was certain the car was there as part of a plan to catch him in possession of the drugs.

"I think he was trying to set me up that night," Marino told Johnston. "In fact, there's no doubt in my mind he was trying to set me up, and get me arrested."

Marino—as Ronald Rutherford—had emailed me about the unmarked police car as well, and the incident spiked my paranoia that corrupt CNET officers were everywhere, following both Rutherford and me. I believed at the time that there was an unidentified dirty cop in Butler's employ, who was staked out to slap the cuffs on Marino for possession with intent to sell. However, there is no evidence that the unmarked cruiser had anything to do with this case. The car was very likely in the alley for reasons totally unrelated to Carl Marino, Chris Butler, or Norm Wielsch's stolen marijuana.

Marino and I weren't the only ones to experience some paranoid fantasies during the investigation. During his initial conversation with Marino, Johnston wondered if it was possible that the whole crazy story was an elaborate setup to sting the Department of Justice and use the footage on a reality show.

"As Carl was talking to me, I looked across the room and saw this clock on the wall," Johnston said. "And, I wondered if there was a hidden camera in the clock, filming me, trying to punk me for some TV show."

Johnston's interview with Marino lasted just over an hour, during which time Marino made many scandalous allegations. In addition to the drug dealing and media stings, Marino said Butler had steroids for sale, which may not have come from Wielsch but from the victim of one of Butler's many stings. Marino also talked about the time Butler mentioned having a few pounds of C-4 in his possession—Marino said he had not seen the explosives, but believed Butler when the PI said he was concerned about driving around with plastic explosives in the trunk of his Hummer.

There was certainly enough from the interview for Johnston to request a search warrant for Butler's office, but nothing substantial against Wielsch.

Johnston then defined Marino's informant status.

"At this point you are a citizen informant," Johnston told Marino. "That's different from a criminal informant, or what people would say would be a snitch. A snitch is trying to get out of trouble for something."

Johnston explained that because Marino came forward with the allegations—rather than talking after he had been caught selling or transporting drugs, or being involved in other criminal activities—Marino's informant status would carry more credibility than other types of informants. Nonetheless, Marino's status was far from Eagle Scout.

"One of the first allegations will be that you're a disgruntled employee," Johnston said to Marino. "We have to prepare for that."

Marino said he understood why Butler would claim he was disgruntled, but debated the semantics a bit. He brought me back into the conversation in his defense.

"My contact [with Pete Crooks] happened way before [Butler] even suspended me," Marino claimed. "I have been trying, for a while, to see who to go to. And this guy [Pete Crooks, again] found someone in Alameda County who found someone we could trust [in] Contra Costa County."

Johnston asked Marino if he decided to reach out to law enforcement as soon as Butler gave him drugs to sell, in November of the previous year. Marino did not answer the question directly.

"That's basically when I decided I didn't want to work for Chris Butler anymore," Marino replied. "He's put me in a lot of situations that I wasn't comfortable in, and we've taken down a lot of good people on kind of bullshit things."

Marino began to describe the Dirty DUIs, placing all the blame on Butler for the setups, and alleging that other corrupt cops were involved.

"His number one thing is he gets people on DUIs," Marino said. "He lures people to places on false pretenses, they have drinks . . . and he has the Danville police in his pocket too, so as soon as the guy pulls out, he calls them on his cell phone. He did that twice in one week, a couple of weeks ago."

Marino did not immediately mention his own leading role in both of those setups. Johnston asked if the stings involved divorce or custody situations.

"Sometimes it's custody, but a lot of times, these women are just angry," Marino said.

Johnston continued to ask about how the Dirty DUI scam worked, asking how the mark would be lured into meeting for drinks.

"He put that on me; to create the stories," Marino admitted. "We'd go in with the false pretenses that we are doing an article for a magazine, or doing a TV show. Meet me at this bar in Danville, and I'll interview him.

"Chris will come up with these things—like the one [victim] was a Turkish guy. So we'll do [an article about] the twenty-five most influential immigrants in the East Bay," Marino explained, conveniently omitting the fact that he posed as a *Diablo* reporter in that setup. "This guy was all over it [and] drinks a lot of wine. As soon as he leaves, Butler makes a call on his cell phone and they pull him over."

"Gotcha," said Johnston. "Obviously, [Butler] doesn't have a problem with some moral stuff."

Johnston would later describe how repulsive he found the Dirty DUI sting to be, when Marino explained how the con worked. "That's just wrong on so many levels," Johnston told me. "It's wrong to set up a guy, it's wrong because you're setting up the situation where it's easy for him to drink, and it's wrong because you don't give him an out and tell him to take a cab."

Marino's admission of participation in the setups quickly dropped his informant status from citizen to criminal.

"Once he told me about these things, it created a situation that was like, 'Look, Carl—you're involved in criminal acts.'" Johnston said.

Marino's criminal informant status wasn't a total game changer, it just meant the DOJ team had to be that much more careful in dealing with him. In any case, it was time for Marino to step up and call Butler, with the DOJ listening in.

"We tested him right on the spot and said, 'Make a phone call, and [we'll] record it. Let's see you do it,'" Johnston told me.

After an hour of Q&A with Marino, Johnston was ready to put his new informant to the test.

"What we'd like to do today," Johnston told Marino, "is have you place a call to him and establish the credibility that you know him.

Marino dialed. Butler picked up after the third ring.

"What's happening?" asked the PI, sounding like Bill Lumbergh, the soulless boss in *Office Space*.

Butler immediately inquired about the Case of the Missing Teen, as the reality show was counting on the case as a tent-pole. Marino's role in the investigation—before being suspended—had been to fish for information from Anna, the mother of the missing teen's boyfriend. "Got any good news?"

"Yes, I do, actually," Marino answered, explaining that he had scheduled a lunch the next day with the mother. Butler laughed with delight at the thought of Marino sweet-talking the worried woman over lunch.

Butler shifted into alpha-male mode and instructed Marino how to play the mark. "OK, so take her to lunch—and this is what you want to get through to her: 'Look, I know that [your son] is still communicating with her; he has to, she's his girlfriend.' Then you start working on her. You say, 'You gotta do the right thing here; be the mom.'

"This is her opportunity to show that she is protecting this girl, and this girl has a story to tell, and [the mom] will be the heroine of this whole story," Marino said. "And if she doesn't, when we find her, she's gonna look like the villain."

"Yeah," said Butler. "We want her to look like the hero. That is what we want. We don't want [the Teen's father] to look like the hero, after he's already been on television crying."

Butler proceeded to make boo-hoo noises, mocking the emotions of a father whose daughter had been missing for two months.

"Exactly," said Marino.

Butler seemed pleased. Then, with a graceful gearshift, Marino changed the conversation to drug dealing.

"Oh, by the way, I sold the package that I had, finally," Marino told Butler, who sounded surprised.

"Woo-hoo!" Butler offered his best Homer Simpson impression.

"The guy wants three more packages," Marino said. "But he wants to know if we can do it for $4,000 for the three. He'll have the money tomorrow."

"Tell him yes," Butler responded, immediately, unaware that three narcotics agents were listening to him offer a fire sale on the stolen marijuana.

Marino discussed the logistics of picking up the three pounds of pot around his lunch with the mother.

"I might have my guy post up somewhere nearby, just so I don't have to drive the stuff over the bridge," Marino told Butler, setting off a minor alarm.

"I don't want him to see me!" Butler cried. Marino assured his boss that the fictional drug contact would be waiting a few miles away, so he needn't worry. Butler would get his money, Marino would drop off the dope, and maybe they'd even get lucky with information about the missing teenager.

"I'll let you know tomorrow when I get done with [Anna]," Marino said, wrapping up the call. "Hopefully I won't have to take her to a hotel afterwards."

Butler loved the zinger, laughing merrily. "That's a scary thought."

"The thought of that disgusts me," Marino added, his chuckle fading in the presence of law enforcement. "Honestly, I have to block that out."

The silence of the three DOJ agents listening to Butler and Marino joke like frat boys was deafening. Marino wrapped up the call and hung up.

"He obviously still has it," Marino said to the DOJ agents, referring to Butler's stash of stolen ganja.

As I said earlier, I was clued in that the person sending me the emails under the name Ronald Rutherford was Carl Marino, and I suspected that Marino's motive for tipping me off about the ride-along was spite. But the drugs and the C-4 had thrown my perspective for a loop.

When I had met with Cindy Hall about Rutherford becoming an informant, she said that once he made contact he would become the invisible man. I had made that very clear to Rutherford in my emails, telling him that I expected to lose contact with him, and that I would have to keep my knowledge of his involvement with the DOJ top secret.

However, Marino did not comply with the invisible man imperative, and continued to email me under the Rutherford alias once in contact with the DOJ. Following his interview with Dean Johnston, Rutherford emailed me a vague update about the meeting, with allegations that the conspiracy could be far-reaching.

> You might want to steer clear of Chris for a little bit, and, per the DOJ, don't mention a word about this to anyone. It may go even higher. I will keep you updated as I get things. They may need to talk to you also when this is over. You are obviously the only person I am telling this to and the only one I trust right now (besides my wife). I am very appreciative of the help you gave me getting this to the right people. Thank you again.

I can find nothing in the interview transcript that suggests the DOJ agents told Marino that Wielsch and Butler's criminal behavior possibly involved a conspiracy with law enforcement higher than CNET. I suspect that the narcotics agents simply issued a general zip-your-lip request regarding the investigation (which, of course, would extend to contacting me as well).

Rather than continue to remind Rutherford that I really should not know the details of the investigation, I decided I would let him keep me abreast of the goings-on, if he was willing to keep sharing that information.

I did feel that Rutherford and I had formed a bond in our three weeks of secret emails—he was the guy on the inside, collecting information and evidence; I was the stealth outsider, putting him in touch with the law and reporting on the crime and corruption, ready to blow the whistle and expose Butler and Wielsch when the time was right.

Clearly, Rutherford seemed greatly appreciative of my assistance, as his email thanking me for setting him up with Johnston was about the twentieth message of gratitude he had passed along since asking for my help.

I made sure to let him know I thought he was doing the right thing, and emailed back, offering words of encouragement:

> You have thanked me many times for helping you connect with the right people. I appreciate that recognition. But I also wanted to let you know that I admire what you are doing and am glad to be of assistance. You have to go face to face with some incredibly corrupt and powerful dudes—you seem to realize it's the right thing to do. We can chat more about this down the road I am sure, but for now, just know that I am very impressed by what you're doing. So thank you too.

Rutherford replied at 1:04 AM. His email started to reveal a deeper personality behind the anonymous pseudonym as Rutherford opened up about how it felt to snitch on his boss:

> I really appreciate that. I have struggled mightily with this, going over and over again if I am doing the right thing. I have never been in this type of position. I actually like Chris Butler for some of his traits and know that I could be giving up some great opportunities, but I do not want to be the person that he thinks that I am or the one that he is trying to create.
>
> I don't feel heroic at all, in fact, I feel more dirty, like I am a traitor being disloyal and ungrateful. These are the feelings that I have fought with for several months. Deep down I know I am doing the right thing and I will take it to the end now, because I have started something that I can't stop.
>
> I just hope the future fallout will be favorable to me and the people who judge me will see it the way you do. Tomorrow will be another crazy day full of turmoil, and I will let you know how it goes. And, as always, I am very appreciative of what you have done for me. It means more to me than you realize. Thanks again.

15

Stolen Drugs at Rock-Bottom Prices

ON JANUARY 26, Carl Marino drove from San Francisco to Walnut Creek, where he met special agent Dean Johnston and team members from the Department of Justice. Marino had already spoken with Butler about paying for the pound of weed that he had taken from Butler's office around December 17, 2010, with the premise of selling it to Marino's cousin in San Jose.

Johnston gave Marino several thousand dollars and helped hide a wire recorder in Marino's jacket, then coached his new informant about how to approach Butler about buying more of the stolen marijuana. The DOJ agents told Marino to relax and know that they had eyes on him at all times.

Marino and Butler had planned to meet at 12:45 PM in a supermarket parking lot near the Walnut Creek suburb of Rossmoor. The location was convenient for Marino, who had scheduled his meeting with Anna to talk about the missing teenager at a diner in the same parking lot.

The missing teen wasn't the only case for the Lifetime show that was on Marino's mind as he started his new role as a confidential informant. Just before driving to Rossmoor, Marino sent his wife a text, saying,

"You can call the psychic and tell her that stuff. Confirm it is the right one. I think Linda saw her yesterday."

Ilona Marino replied, "OK."

Since Carl had already received a cease and desist order from Lifetime's attorneys, followed by an official notice of suspension when he tipped off the unlicensed PI, it made sense that the gypsy psychic be tipped off by someone other than him. Preferably with a woman's voice.

As Marino drove from the DOJ meeting to the parking lot, he received a call from Butler, who had already arrived and parked in front of the supermarket. Marino pulled in a few minutes later, parked his Mazda, and got into Butler's Hummer.

"What's up?" Marino asked, then jumped right into the drug transaction. He pulled out the wad of cash that the DOJ had given him just a few minutes before.

"Here's what he gave me," Marino said, showing Butler the stack of bills. "He gave me thirty-four hundred dollars, which covers the first package and full price—the fifteen hundred dollars—for the second two packages, because he couldn't get enough together for the third package. But he still wants it."

Butler spoke in his low monotone—Mr. Cool, but with a twinge of paranoia. "Do you trust him?" Butler asked.

Marino didn't answer the question. His "guy" was a lie, there was no one to trust. So, Marino kept following the instructions that the DOJ had given him—to offer to take the third package and owe Butler the money.

"If you want, I can just take the other package and hang on to it," Marino offered.

"Might as well, it's not doing me any good," Butler mumbled.

"Then he'll owe another fifteen for that one," Marino encouraged.

Butler and Marino spent a few minutes trying to figure out the math on how to split up the money, with Marino getting a 25 percent cut. On the wire recording, neither Butler or Marino demonstrates expedient math skills, but eventually they were able to come to an agreement.

Then, Marino added a little bullshit about his source being very happy with the quality of the stolen weed.

Butler was distracted by other people in the parking lot. The PI was paranoid that he was being watched by undercover law enforcement.

"That guy is just sitting in his car with the headlights on," Butler said to Marino, who reassured the PI that the unidentified man looked like a businessman.

Marino would have no way of knowing if the man was an undercover agent, as the DOJ operatives made sure not to reveal all their players in front of him. ("Today's informant is tomorrow's criminal," Johnston told me.)

As Butler worried, Marino's cell phone buzzed and he picked up the call. He quickly told the caller he would call back in a little while.

"Get out of the car now, we're moving on you!" Butler joked, pretending the call had been from the cops.

"Don't even say that!" Marino replied, laughing.

Marino offered a little more bullshit about his fake buyer, saying that he wanted more down the road. "Is Norm able to get more stuff, because you said that's a possibility. This guy seems like someone who would want to keep buying it, once he starts moving it."

Butler groaned at the mention of Norm's name. "I don't know," he replied.

"OK, well, if he does, we definitely have an outlet," said Marino. "This guy, he assured me that he is able to move it now."

Butler shifted gears from drug dealer to reality show wannabe, changing the subject to the lunch meeting Marino was about to go into. He asked Marino how he planned to approach the meeting with the mom.

"I'm going to smooth-talk her and make her feel like she is the heroine and is protecting [the missing teenager]," Marino said. "I'll schmooze her. This is her chance to talk on national television. I'm sure she'll want to be on camera."

Butler told Marino to make sure he kept the receipts from the lunch meeting, then asked if Marino had all his cash from the drug deal. Marino said he did, took a shopping bag filled with three pounds of marijuana back to his car, and locked it in the trunk.

It was a job well done, confidential informant–wise.

Then Marino went back into PI mode and drove across the parking lot to meet with the mother of the boyfriend of the missing teenager to see what he could find out about her. He left the three pounds of weed locked in the trunk of his car and went into the Rossmoor Diner to have lunch with Anna.

The lunch conversation between Marino and Anna lasted about eighty minutes, during which time Anna admitted that she knew exactly where the missing teen had been hiding since disappearing about sixty days before. The Teen had been staying with her boyfriend at Anna's house.

During those two months, the missing girl's parents were worried sick, the PI Moms had gone on a wild goose chase searching for her in Ontario, California, law enforcement was combing the Bay Area, and the Polly Klaas Foundation website had posted the girl's picture.

After many months of ignoring my requests for comment, Anna finally told me that the Teen and her son had engaged in an elaborate game of hooky. According to Anna, she did not know the Teen had been staying with her son until after missing fliers were circulated and a prayer vigil was held in a local park. After realizing that the Teen was safe, Anna agreed to continue the ruse because she was afraid her son and the girl would run away for real. But as days passed by, Anna's anxiety grew exponentially, and she wanted to tell local law enforcement—or someone who could help—that the girl was staying in her house.

It was a wildly complicated situation—made even more complicated because the missing girl was the single most important case still being filmed for *PI Moms*. Finding the Teen, safe and sound, would have been a great get for the reality show.

When Anna met with Marino for lunch, she confided right away that the Teen was staying at her house. According to Anna, Marino instructed her not to talk to anyone else about the situation and demanded to meet the missing teen that day.

Then Marino texted Chris Butler—just three hours after making his first drug buy as a confidential informant—to let him know that the teenage girl had been located. And that the first thing Butler should do was to tell the *PI Moms*' showrunner the good news.

Marino wrote, "Tell Lucas Platt I found [the missing teenager]."

Butler texted back, "WHAT?????" and then, "Call me ASAP."

Butler had every reason to use all caps. It had only been a few days since he had officially suspended Marino from his business, at the order of the reality show producers, because of Marino's behavior. After Marino had sabotaged the unlicensed PI case, there was serious discussion of pulling the plug on the show for good.

Now Marino was the only one with the scoop on the show's most important case.

"Carl, please don't just go off and 'find' her, as we need it for the show," Butler texted to Marino, adding ten exclamation points to show how serious he was.

Instead of listening to his boss, Marino drove to Anna's house and met the missing teen, making sure to take a cell phone picture of himself with the girl.

That night, Ronald Rutherford emailed me with an update, telling me about the drug deal and finding the missing teen. The message began with another spooky warning about me staying away from Butler:

> Wow... what a day. The events of today alone would fill a feature film. I really think you need to stay clear of Chris now. The first deal went down today without a hitch... there is no turning back now and I believe that soon no amount of pumping or bailing will work on the sinking ship. Wow, those DOJ guys are very impressive. Immediately after the "deal" was done, I went to interview someone for a case I have been working on for Chris and the show... even though I am suspended... and guess what I did... I found [the missing teenager]... the teenager that all of the police in the area, the police in LA, the detectives, or other private detectives were unable to do for 2 months. I actually spoke to her face to face and made sure she took a quick picture with me to prove she is alive and well.

Rutherford complained that he was not going to get credit for finding the Teen, especially while the show was filming. Clearly, he was upset about missing out on the spotlight that could come from finding her:

> It is a case that I spent a lot of time and energy on that Chris took away from me to give to production. They got nowhere with it and the PI Moms were useless again

> so Chris had to put me back on it to solve it. Now I am in a dilemma. Chris and Lucas are so very happy with my success that they want me to hand it over with no cares for [the missing teen] or the woman who helped her to the PI Moms to solve on the show.
>
> Unbelievable, I break one of the biggest mysteries of the year (all by myself and while I am "suspended") and I am supposed to sit back and give the credit to people who have done nothing but treat me like crap.

Then, just as he had asked for my help getting him in touch with law enforcement, Rutherford asked for my advice about what he should do about the information regarding the missing teen:

> I'm also not sure what to do because I have an obligation to take this to the police because now that I am involved and don't tell anyone and something happens to her, I am responsible. What do you think that I should do about [the missing teen]. I feel like I need talk to someone about it that cares about these people and not just so a show succeeds.

I really did not know what to say about the missing teen—but I was concerned about Rutherford blowing his cover in the DOJ case by bitching about not getting credit for finding her. I replied to Rutherford, and said not to worry if the reality show "found" her, the most important thing was that the girl was safe and that Rutherford did nothing to jeopardize the narcotics investigation.

Rutherford wrote back, still bitter about the TV show and the PI Moms. He then offered me access to the girl as an "exclusive":

> She was local the whole time, and if they let me do my job originally I could have saved them a lot of money, because I knew that the whole time . . . I just proved it today . . . The PI Moms were useless, as usual. They haven't solved a case that I can remember without Chris or myself doing it for them. I think Chris was kind of embarrassed when I texted him a picture of me with [the missing teen]. I was informed that my suspension was over and purged from the record. Apparently they aren't afraid of me anymore when I have what they want. On the other hand, you can have the total exclusive if you want it. I interviewed [the missing teen] myself tonight at an undisclosed location for two hours. I can give you access to her if you want it.

This was the second time Rutherford had offered me an "exclusive." The first time had been when he asked for my help with law enforcement. I had not contacted Cindy Hall because of the offer, I helped because I thought there was a public safety threat from the C-4 and that the allegation that Wielsch and Butler were selling stolen drugs needed to be checked out.

Offering the missing teen as an exclusive was a much different scenario, and not an attractive one. I wasn't interested in exploiting a missing child's story so Rutherford could stick it to Butler, the PI Moms, and Lucas Platt.

More important was the matter of confidentiality—if I suddenly published a big story about Rutherford finding the missing teen, it would be obvious who had tipped me off about the fake ride-along, which also would not be a good thing for the top-secret investigation into Butler and Wielsch's wrongdoings.

Ultimately, Rutherford—Marino—did the right thing, and informed the DOJ about the missing teen situation.

"The PI Moms were working a case about a missing juvenile, and there was a fight about who gets to find the juvenile," Special Agent Dean Johnston told me. "No one seemed to care that the juvenile was missing. It was, 'Is the show going to find her first or is Carl going to find her first?'"

Johnston continued, "[When Marino] shared that information with us, I said 'Look, Carl, I'm a law enforcement officer. I have to deal with [the missing teen information] right now. You have to call the police department and tell them what you know.' His side of it was, 'Yeah, but if I do it this day, they are going to know I'm the one who found the juvenile, otherwise the other guys will get the credit.'"

Johnston had to explain to Marino why he needed to disregard the reality show spotlight and do the right thing, not just for the missing teenager's safety, but for the integrity of the DOJ's undercover narcotics investigation.

"I had to work with [Marino] on that," Johnston explained. "I told him, 'You just told me [about the missing girl] so I'm going to deal with it. It's either going to be me that goes out to the house, or the local department. It's better if it's a local department, because it's better if people don't know we're in town. If our guy [Wielsch] finds out, he's like, 'What's DOJ doing in town with a missing juvenile [that Butler was looking for]?'"

Johnston was able to convince Marino to contact the Contra Costa Sheriff's Office to tell them where the missing girl had been hiding.

"Carl ended up doing the right thing," Johnston told me. "But, clearly, because I told him, 'What happens if she's chained to a bed?' The point was, I couldn't give him the green light to wait for the producer to show up with a camera next Tuesday."

After Marino took a photo with the missing teenager, he informed the Contra Costa Sheriff's Office of the girl's whereabouts. Apparently, the detective in charge of the case was not overly impressed by Marino's investigative work. "The detective actually told me that if I had not come in when I did, he would have been feeding me bologna sandwiches in his jail," Marino later told me.

Meanwhile, Butler was desperate to save the sinking ship that was his reality show. On Friday, January 28, producers from the show set out to finish filming one of the show's tent-pole stories, the Case of the Gypsy Psychic. *PI Moms* cast member Linda Welch had been in touch with the psychic, and promised to bring another expensive handbag to a hotel room in Oakland in exchange for more psychic services.

However, the gypsy had been tipped off. She never showed.

Showrunner Lucas Platt spent the morning in a hotel room with a miserable Chris Butler, with nothing to do but watch the show fail.

"So there we are in the hotel, waiting for the gypsy to show up. And we are waiting around for hours," Platt told me. "After several hours, Chris shows me a text message from Carl that says, 'Lucas needs to include me in the series or I will scuttle this case.'"

Platt was furious that Butler waited for hours to show him the text message.

"I said to Chris, 'Why didn't you show me that text four hours ago?'" Platt said. "Chris said, 'I didn't think Carl was actually going to do it.'"

That was the end of another tent-pole story for *PI Moms*.

Which meant that there was just one tent-pole case left: the Case of the Missing Teen. Butler had originally told Platt that Marino had located the missing teen and wanted to be able to help the show out.

"Chris told me that Carl really wants to make [finding the Teen] part of the show, and I said, 'OK, great. We have to do it right away,'" Platt recalled. "Then, the gypsy hotel thing happened. As soon as the gypsy case fell apart, I had a conference call with my partners [the L.A.-based producers on the show] and I said, 'Either Chris or Carl scuttled this, and this was supposed to be a tent-pole case.' It was a huge blow."

By the time the gypsy case had fallen apart that Friday afternoon, Platt realized it would be the final straw for the powers that be at the network. But since that official decision probably would not be made until the following Monday, the *PI Moms*' showrunner sent his cast and crew to Anna's workplace to confront her about why she had been hiding the missing teen for two months and lying about it when interviewed by law enforcement.

The PI Moms and production crew arrived at Anna's office—located in the same parking lot where Marino had bought drugs from Butler just two days before—and staked up their cameras outside the front door. Knowing that she was going to be filmed, Anna panicked and called Marino.

Marino happened to be just a few miles away, picking up a rented tuxedo to wear to the Screen Actors Guild awards in Hollywood that weekend. Marino told Anna that he would come straight to the scene, and by the time he arrived, the shit had hit the fan.

First, Chris Butler had pulled a major no-no, flashing his Hummer's strobe lights like it was a police vehicle and then assaulting Anna by grabbing her as she tried to run to her car. Anna became hysterical and hid behind a Dumpster in the parking lot, sobbing.

In front of dozens of stunned witnesses, Marino tried to escort Anna away from the gaggle of PI Moms and camera operators. That's when the PI Moms freaked out, screaming accusations that Marino had helped Anna harbor the missing teen all along.

Marino responded by screaming, "Shut the fuck up," and waving the business card of the Contra Costa Sheriff's detective that Marino had contacted about the missing girl. The local police were called to break up the melee.

"It was a total nightmare," Lucas Platt told me.

Late that night, Marino emailed me (still using his Ronald Rutherford pseudonym) to describe the scene, claiming he had brokered a deal with law enforcement to make sure the missing teen was safe and sound, and then diffused the nightmarish melee with the PI Moms, the reality show crew, and the local police. Marino said that Butler had assaulted Anna during the incident. Anna was threatening to sue Butler, the PI Moms, and the reality show, but Marino claimed that he calmed her down and talked her out of it.

Meanwhile, Marino described how he watched as the missing teenager was finally reunited with her parents by telephone. My "secret" informant let Butler know what a beautiful and poignant moment that had been. He wrote:

> When I described the tearful reunion scene to Chris and what a fantastic, emotional moment it was for everyone involved, [he said,] 'Yeah, that would have been great TV.' That statement pretty much sums up Chris Butler.

Chris Butler saw Marino's behavior in the missing teen case as that of a vindictive actor who had not gotten a part on the reality show. He wasn't that far off the mark.

"It has become apparent that you intend to destroy this show. And you have," Butler texted to Marino after the parking lot melee. "I'm resigned to that. I just didn't deserve this."

Marino replied with vehement denials of having any intentions of sabotaging the show (with the exception of sabotaging the unlicensed PI case, for which he had been caught red-handed), and claimed that he had done more to help the show than any of the PI Moms had.

Meanwhile, Marino sent a message to the father of the missing teenager, requesting kudos in any comments the family might give to the media.

"If you could give me some credit in your statement today, I would appreciate it," Marino wrote. "If you want to direct any press or questions my way, feel free to give my number."

That weekend, Marino got to take a break from his first week as a criminal informant for the DOJ, so he and Ilona could drive to Los Angeles to attend the Screen Actors Guild Awards. According to a SAG representative, Marino was on the waiting list to buy tickets to the awards show dinner and had been selected at the last minute. That's why he had been picking up a rented tux in the vicinity of the missing-teen melee.

The SAG Awards was a top-shelf event for the aspiring actor and model to attend, and Marino made sure to upload all his celebrity photobombs (Steve Buscemi! Sofia Vergara! Betty White!) to Facebook.

Marino also made sure to text Butler during the star-studded party to let him know what life was like on the other side of the velvet rope.

"Had a drink with Kyra Sedgwick," Marino wrote to Butler. "And saw Morgan Freeman's penis in the bathroom."

The day after Marino bragged to Butler about sneaking a peek at an Oscar winner's genitals, a newspaper in his hometown area of Hornell, New York, ran a story about his big weekend.

"Sunday night was the night of the Screen Actors Guild Awards in Hollywood, and Hornell native Carl Marino was there, walking the world-famous red carpet," reported the *Canisteo Valley News*. "Marino, a former Monroe County Sheriff's Deputy, now works as both an actor on numerous projects such as the Discovery Channel's *I (Almost) Got Away With It*, and as an investigator for a detective agency in California.

"And if walking the red carpet weren't high honors enough, it should also be noted that Marino is excelling at his work as an investigator. He just solved a missing child case in California. You may have heard about the case in the national news."

When I had passed on the "missing girl exclusive," Marino gave his hometown newspaper the story. He gave the *Canisteo Valley News* a quote that would have made Chris Butler cringe. "I actually had the father on the telephone, he had called me while I was sitting there with his daughter," Marino told the paper. "I was able to say to him, 'I'd like you to be able to speak with your daughter,'... it was quite a moment."

The article ended by acknowledging that the missing girl's family had thanked Marino on their Facebook account for finding their daughter.

It was not the first time the *Canisteo Valley News* had reported on Marino's acting career. In 2009, the paper ran a short piece about the hometown actor securing a background role on the NBC series *Trauma*, and included a picture of a smiling Marino standing in front of a fire truck. That article identified Marino as a graduate of the West Point US Military Academy, with a degree in environmental engineering, and a seventeen-year veteran of the Monroe County Sheriff's Office.

"[*Trauma* is] a lot of fun. I'm going to take what I can get from this, and keep working with things as they pop up," Marino said in the 2009 article, which did not mention his work with Butler & Associates. "I think a lot of people are out here to be a big-name actor, but we'll just wait and see what happens."

As the Marinos played in Hollywood, Chris Butler and Norm Wielsch were up to no good in the East Bay. On the morning of Sunday, January 30, Wielsch told Butler to meet him at the Central Contra Costa County Narcotics Enforcement Team office in Pleasant Hill. The CNET offices weren't identified in any formal way and were part of a nondescript office complex in which most tenants had no idea that one of the neighbors was a crack force of narcs.

Butler brought the remaining few pounds of marijuana that he was holding on to from his original ten-pound stash, of which Marino had acquired five packages. Despite Marino's recent ability to sell the original stash, Butler told Wielsch that a good pothead authority informed him that the dope was "garbage."

During the same week that Marino was finally introduced to the DOJ and became a confidential informant, Wielsch's CNET team had seized fifty pounds of marijuana from a search warrant bust. This stuff wasn't garbage; it was primo bud with a heavy THC payload—the sort of stuff that sells for top dollar at the Bay Area's many medical marijuana dispensaries.

Since the large seizure had just taken place a few days before, this new stash of high-quality pot was still entirely in storage at CNET's office. When the team came back to the office on Monday, a ten-pound sample would be transferred to the drug locker at the Contra Costa Sheriff's Office as evidence for prosecutorial purposes.

The rest of the weed would be destroyed, which gave Butler and Wielsch a bright idea: Switch out their remaining dirtweed (the stuff that only Marino had been able to sell) for some nuclear-grade ganja, then sell the good shit for top dollar.

So that's what they did. Early that Sunday morning, Butler and Wielsch stole twelve pounds of killer buds, in one-pound bags marked "Purple Kush" and "Bubba," which Butler drove back to his warehouse office and hid in the trunk of his tricked-out surveillance Cadillac.

16
So Long, PI Moms

ON MONDAY, JANUARY 31, Marino drove back to the Bay Area where agent Johnston was waiting for him to do more informant work. Marino had told Johnston that Butler had a stash of steroids for sale, in addition to the marijuana, explaining that he thought the steroids might have come from a sting Butler had staged on a drug-dealing community college student. Johnston worried that they came from Wielsch—or worse, from another corrupted law enforcement officer that was in cahoots with Butler.

"[Early in the investigation] we were very focused on the drugs—we were concerned that [the narcotics were coming from] an open locker," Johnston explained to me later. "If our guy [Wielsch] was doing it, what's to say he doesn't know five other guys [who are also involved]."

Back at Butler's office, things were not looking good for the *PI Moms* reality show. The weekend had been grim—the incident with Marino and Anna the previous Friday all but assured that Lifetime would shut down production on the troubled program.

On top of that, Butler had to deal with an unexpected mutiny at his PI business. Michelle Allen, Denise Antoon, and Ami Wiltz—the principle PI Moms from the reality show—each marched into Butler's office and handed in their letters of resignation. The cameras crews showed up one last time to record each resignation on tape.

Ami Wiltz had another surprise in store for her boss: She had secretly been studying for the state's private investigator test, and planned to open her own investigation business and compete with Butler.

Butler realized that Wiltz's PI ambitions were bad for his business for a number of reasons, especially when it came to the reality show. Wiltz had gotten the most on-camera time during the first two months of filming, far more than Butler had. Her personal story was already compelling; Wiltz had lost a child as a teenage mom. Years later, she raised kids while working as a sheriff's deputy in Northern California.

Butler knew that if Wiltz went and opened her own PI business in the area, there was no reason that *PI Moms* couldn't just follow her story and leave him in the dust, with nothing but Dirty DUIs and drug dealing on his résumé.

"My whole world was crumbling down around me," Butler would later say.

That week, the DOJ had Marino place another recorded call to Butler to talk about paying for drugs and steroids. Butler picked up after the second ring.

The PI sounded down in the dumps, but perked up a little when Marino said he had some more "salad" [cash] to deliver.

"Why don't you come on back and we'll inventory what we have?" Butler asked, sounding like he could use the company. "Everyone else left, because apparently there is a wrap lunch [for the reality show], which I wasn't invited to."

Marino laughed. "Neither was I," he said. (I have interviewed a number of people who did attend the wrap party, which was held at a nice Italian restaurant in Concord. By all accounts, the party was a dismal affair, as dozens of freelance television professionals glumly snacked on appetizers and complained that Butler and Marino had teamed up to train-wreck what could have been a successful series.)

With the PI Moms and show producers at the wrap party, Butler invited Marino to disregard his suspension agreement and come meet him at the office to deal some more drugs.

By the time Marino reached the office, Butler was talking with his Beverly Hills publicist, who had no idea what a disaster *PI Moms* had become. Butler was acting like it was going to be the next big reality show to hit television.

Butler took Marino outside of the office and gave him a larger list of available steroids. Marino told his boss that the buyer was interested in moving "everything." Then Marino poked into the subject of where the steroids were coming from, asking if the steroid stash had been obtained during a case in which Butler set up a teenage drug dealer, then stole his stash.

"No, no, I didn't get steroids from the kid, I got Xanax," Butler said. "I got steroids from another source."

"If you have them right now, I was going to drive down to San Jose tonight," Marino said.

"He's interested in the Xanax?" Butler sounded excited, as he was sitting on a stash of somewhere around four thousand prescription pills.

"No, he's interested in the steroids. The Xanax, he hasn't really said anything about," Marino clarified, reemphasizing that his connection in San Jose was going to be able to move a lot of steroids.

Marino pulled out an envelope containing just over a thousand dollars. He gave the money to Butler and said it was for the third pound of marijuana that he had taken the week before in the Rossmoor parking lot.

"That stuff, he's moved it all," Marino said, suggesting his San Jose connection had baggied several pounds of dirtweed into eighths and quarters and sold the stash.

"Well, then, here's the cool stuff," Butler said and began to tell Marino about the new supply of killer weed he and Wielsch had stolen during the weekend.

Then Butler reached out and patted the front of Marino's jacket.

"Are you wearing a wire?" Butler asked. Marino laughed and said no. (I'm sure he was not laughing on the inside, though.)

Butler laughed as well. "With everything that has happened lately, I'm beginning to wonder why is my world coming to an end."

Marino laughed again.

Butler continued. "Let's just say the source, because I don't want to use names anymore. I took the remaining three packages that had not moved, because my source said [to] bring it back, and we'll get something that's ten times better. What happened was, there was fifty pounds—but we just can't walk off with fifty pounds—so we skimmed off twelve pounds, took the other three, and kind of fluffed them all up to replace it."

"OK," Marino said, letting Butler do all the talking.

"So, I have eleven-and-a-half pounds of really good stuff," Butler told Marino.

Butler talked about the grade-A ganja he and Wielsch had stolen from the CNET office, how the bags were labeled "Purple Kush" and "Northern Lights" and "Bubba." Butler said his source said each pound was selling for $4,000 on the street, so they needed to sell it for at least $3,000. Marino offered to take a pound to his San Jose source right away, so he could make some money for an upcoming trip to Las Vegas.

"Just remember that's three grand [you'd owe]," Butler said to Marino, who responded, "No problem."

Butler took Marino back inside his office and opened up a safe to show him more stolen stash. Butler pulled out a bottle of ephedrine tablets and explained that ephedrine was a key ingredient in the manufacturing of methamphetamine.

"This should sell for, I don't know, five grand," said Butler. "Ask him if he can move ephedrine pills."

Marino asked for a sample. Butler gladly complied and took Marino over to his Cadillac, which was loaded with hidden surveillance cameras. Butler remarked that he wanted to use the vehicle to sting the Walnut Creek cops who had intervened in the melee involving Anna and the reality show camera crew several days before, to get them back for fucking up his dramatic on-camera confrontation with the harborer of the missing teen. Then Butler pulled two half-pound bags packed with Purple Kush that he had stashed in the Cadillac's trunk and gave them to Marino to sell to his guy in San Jose.

"Is Norm going to be able to get more out of the same stockpile?" Marino asked, deftly dropping Wielsch's name again.

"Depends on how quickly we move it—if we move it fast enough, then yes," Butler responded. "Speed is the key."

Marino told Butler that his source in San Jose was going to be able to move as much weed as Butler and Wielsch could steal.

"This guy had a lot of money right now. I guarantee you I'll sell two tonight," Marino said. "And hopefully one more tomorrow before I go to Vegas."

Butler reminded Marino to push the Xanax stash on his buyer. "That's where we make the most amount of profit, if we sell each one for a dollar. If you and I split that, it's two grand."

Next, Marino and Butler reviewed an inventory of steroids that Butler had been holding.

Butler boasted that he was already selling testosterone to a steroid user at low, low prices. Marino said that his source was interested in testosterone and another steroid, which Butler said he would sell at forty-five dollars per unit.

"I have to give that to Norm," Butler said, implicating Wielsch further as Marino peeled off ninety dollars for two vials of the steroids. Butler then gave Marino a fatherly lecture about how to maximize profit from illegal drug sales.

Listening to the recording of Butler coaching Marino about selling drugs reminded me of reading C. S. Lewis' *Screwtape Letters*, in which Satan's demonic agent carefully outlines instructions to his demon nephew to show him how to convince a human to fall into sin by encouraging individual benefit and greed.

"If you can negotiate a price higher [than your cut], I don't fucking care," Butler told Marino. "If you turn around and sell it for a million, I don't fucking care."

The two went back to counting out testosterone vials and cash, and splitting the money three ways, with a cut for "Uncle," which was the nickname Butler semiregularly used when talking about Wielsch. Marino performed exceptionally well, informant-wise, by asking if Wielsch could provide more steroids than Butler currently possessed. Butler said that he would ask Wielsch to provide a detailed shopping list, and reminded Marino again that he could set his own prices with the buyer.

Marino asked if the boxes of steroids that Wielsch could get would be counted by someone else, drawing unnecessary attention to the criminal scheme at hand.

"No, [the steroids] are getting ready to be destroyed," Butler replied. "That's why we don't want to walk off with something that's going to trial, because there goes the evidence."

"Gotcha," said Marino.

Butler handed Marino a sheet of the entire remaining inventory, saying the stash could be sold for fire-sale prices. Then Marino boldly asked about the C-4 explosives and suggested that his weed-and-steroid-buying contact in San Jose might be interested in some military-grade fireworks as well.

"He knows some shady guys who might be interested in the C-4," Marino said. "Is it in two separate pounds?"

"One," Butler said, abruptly.

"One brick of C-4," Marino said. "Any idea on a [price]...I have no idea."

On the recording, Marino's conversational cool was remarkable. He might as well have been asking Butler about the cost of a twelve-pack of Coors Light.

"I have no idea either, so, whatever," Butler said. "Otherwise, I was going to turn it over to be destroyed. I was going to give it to my uncle and say, 'Say you found this on a search warrant,' and get rid of it."

"Well, let me run it by him and see if he knows someone who is interested," Marino said. Butler blanched a bit at the idea of selling the plastic explosives.

"Be very careful, because possession of that—you get pulled over and they find that in the car...," Butler warned.

Butler was stating the obvious: Get caught with a pound of Purple Kush and you're in a fair bit of trouble. Get caught with a pound of C-4 and you are fucked with a capital *F*.

But as usual, Butler couldn't help but talk into the wire, and he went on to describe the alleged explosives to Marino.

"I've never touched it. It's wrapped in two bags and says 'Centech,' or something on it," Butler explained. "The guy that got it for me said it's extremely safe, it's not just going to go off. But if you bury a cherry bomb in it, then you're going to have a world of hurt. Something like that will take out a couple of houses."

"Oh yeah, two pounds of it?" Marino replied, offering a colorful anecdote from his life before coming to California. "We used that in the army. We used to take railroad ties, and just pinch it right off."

"Well, if they want to buy that, great," Butler said, adding potential black market explosives dealer to his résumé. "[Your guy] seems to be flush with cash right now. Cash talks."

Marino wrapped up the steroid samples and inquired about the Northern Lights and Purple Kush, knowing the DOJ would want to have a peek at more of the new shit. Unfortunately, Butler had the rest of the good ganja stashed somewhere away from the office.

Oddly, Butler said he had a series of potential client appointments scheduled at the office, one after another. Not the fake *People* magazine kind or the reality show variety, but actual paying clients, inquiring about his investigative services. Which meant he couldn't go pick up the stolen marijuana to sell to Marino.

So Marino got into his car and drove away from the office. Within minutes, he got a call from a DOJ agent about where to go to debrief and drop off the new stash of evidence.

That night, Marino sent me the following update about the day's events. He caught me up to speed on the PI Moms turning in their resignations and said that he had purchased more dope for the DOJ:

> I went to the office, after meeting with DOJ and made more "deals." Chris is digging deeper and deeper. Apparently their [*sic*] is access to "a lot" more product and of a much better quality...I was also given several samples of vials of steroids to give to my "guy" with a list of what Chris has and what the prices are...He really believes he is untouchable. This story gets crazier and crazier every day.

Marino left for Las Vegas on Thursday, February 4, leaving the DOJ agents with a long weekend of work to do without their informant. Marino scheduled absences several times during the investigation—the SAG Awards weekend and the Super Bowl—causing the DOJ significant irritation.

"[Marino] had other jobs—he would go shoot a movie for two days, and we would go work on other things," Dean Johnston told me.

I wanted to know how closely the DOJ team informed Marino of their investigation strategy. Johnston assured me that Marino was on a very strict need-to-know basis.

"He would not know what we were doing," said Johnston. "He was not one of my teammates, he was just an informant."

Johnston said that he would make sure to schedule meetings with Marino in different places, and would make sure that he did not see the entire team of investigators, out of concern that the investigation could be compromised at any time.

"A lot of things we did with Carl were a little different because he was intelligent. I didn't want him to see all of our guys," said Johnston. "And I didn't want him to arrive thirty minutes before I [did] and set me up. I have a responsibility to my guys and myself, so I didn't want a film crew being there to shoot me and jeopardize us and our identity."

Johnston said that his careful handling of Marino was nothing personal, but standard procedure for dealing with criminal informants.

"Honestly, I don't trust him, because it's not my job to trust him," said Johnston. "I would be letting my guys down if I trusted him."

While Johnston knew not to trust Marino from past experiences with criminal informants, I grew not only to trust him but also consider him a friend.

I felt a bond with my secret source, who I only knew through private emails. I felt like we were a team—he was the guy on the inside, staying close to a criminal sociopath and gathering evidence to expose Butler and Wielsch's corruption. I was the guy on the outside—a victim of one of Butler's setups—who was helping Rutherford get out of trouble by guiding him to the right people.

It was all very exciting, like the vintage noir films I love to watch at the Castro Theatre.

I thought Marino was doing brave investigative work for the Department of Justice because he knew how dirty Butler and Wielsch were, and that someone needed to do something about it. He sent me dozens of appreciative emails about all the help I had given him.

For weeks, my secret source sent me emails that read like a cliff-hanger detective story, and I kept this thrilling information top secret. I kept Marino updated about my reporting, letting him know what angles I was working, in case something I did might tip Butler off that he was suspected as more than a hoaxer.

I was also keeping in touch with other sources and tracking down information about the cast of characters on my ride-along—Ryan Romano, the tattooed decoy who liked horseback riding and artichoke appetizers, and Sharon the Client, who cried so believably as she described how she felt her fiancé might be fooling around. Marino had emailed me the contact information for Sharon's real ex-boyfriend—the one Butler had stung by sending two PI Moms to meet him for drinks and flirtation in a bar.

I delayed contacting the ex-boyfriend, because doing so might have gotten back to Butler, which could expose Marino.

Meanwhile, sources besides Marino would check in with me. One was Charmagne Peters. Even though Charmagne was no longer working for Butler—and no longer a part of the show—she kept in contact with me by text and phone to see how my story was going.

On Super Bowl Sunday, Charmagne gave me a call to fill me in on all the drama that had gone down in the final days of the reality show. I listened to Charmagne for an hour and a half, taking copious notes throughout the call and never letting on what I knew about Butler's dirty business with Wielsch.

Most of what she told me I already knew, since Marino (still under wraps as Rutherford) had emailed his version of the events. But it was interesting to hear Charmagne's account of the *PI Moms* meltdown, which was different enough from Rutherford's to create a *Rashomon* reality effect.

Charmagne explained that all the PI Moms had given their resignations to Butler, with the camera crew recording the action. The show had been a disaster, she said, but the producers had enough good material with Denise, Michelle, and Ami to put together a two-hour movie from the footage filmed during the past few weeks. This meant there was still hope for *PI Moms*. If the pilot played well, then Lifetime could still build a series around Ami's new investigations business, and leave Butler out.

Next, Charmagne reemphasized her belief that the person who had emailed me about the ride-along was Carl Marino and that his motivations for contacting me were petty and spiteful. From Charmagne's point of view, Marino lived his life like Richard Hatch, the scheming, double-crossing, backstabbing winner of the first season of *Survivor.* She told me that Marino was insanely jealous of the reality show—that he was wrecking cases left and right, including the Case of the Missing Teen.

Charmagne said that Butler "worshipped Carl Marino and his wife, and said many times that they would be the 'Mr. and Mrs. Smith' of *PI Moms.*" When Lifetime didn't want the Marinos, Charmagne said that Carl Marino wigged out and started waging war on the production by sabotaging the cases.

Charmagne told me that there was something mysterious going on between Chris Butler and Carl Marino, and that the main reason the PI Moms quit is that Butler would not fire Marino after all he did to sabotage the show. She suggested that the only explanation that she and the other PI Moms could come up with about why Butler did not send Marino packing was that Marino might try to blackmail Butler about all the secrets in Butler's case files.

There was a lot of truth in what Charmagne was saying. But at the time I did not believe anything she told me, because I knew Charmagne had lied to me during the ride-along and lied again after I confronted her about the allegation that it was a setup.

And because I knew about these more sinister, deeper layers—the stolen drugs, the C-4, and the CNET connection—I didn't care if she thought Marino was a jealous and vindictive tool. I thought he was a good guy who was risking his neck to do the right thing.

Looking back, we were both right.

Several days after Marino returned from Las Vegas, Butler organized a road trip to Los Angeles to try and drum up some interest in a new reality show, which was based on a Los Angeles satellite office that did not yet exist.

Despite the train wreck of the *PI Moms* show, Butler took Carl Marino along for the trip to meet with a publicist in Beverly Hills, as well as with former Marine captain and FBI agent Charles "Chuck" Latting. After retiring from the FBI in the early 1990s, Latting had created an East Bay–based private investigation firm, with a clientele of high-profile corporate clients.

Latting also supervised private security operations for the Oakland Raiders football team, which led to his introduction to Chris Butler, who had seen Latting with former Raiders tight end Rickey Dudley at a shooting range. Butler, always impressed by celebrities, gravitated toward the Raiders' 1996 first-round pick, met Latting, and made the most important contact of his career after leaving the Antioch police force.

Butler went to work for Latting, who soon handed over the business after going back to work for the State of California's correctional system. Butler kept in touch with Latting from a distance, calling in favors when he needed to exploit the retired FBI agent's laurels—like when Latting appeared on the *Dr. Phil* show, giving the appearance that he had something to do with advising the PI Moms. Which he did not.

I met Latting for lunch in a south Pasadena coffee shop, long after the investigation concluded. He told me about the meeting he had with Butler and Marino in early February 2011, in which they discussed Marino opening a satellite investigations office in Los Angeles, which would become the first PI Moms training facility.

Latting, a former Marine captain who was awarded a Bronze Star for his efforts in Vietnam, told me that he was not impressed by Butler's choice for a director of operations.

"Chris kept telling me how he had to use Marino, that he was an exceptional employee," said Latting, who had no idea about the drugs, dirty DUIs, or any of Butler's corruption at the time. "When I met Marino, I couldn't believe that Chris spoke so highly of him. He wouldn't look me in the eye, and he spent the whole meeting sulking in the corner like a little weasel."

17
Tickling the Wire

IN CRIMINAL INVESTIGATIONS involving narcotics, undercover investigators have all kinds of tricks to build a caseload of evidence against drug dealers. Because they are monitoring phone calls and conversations, narcotics agents will introduce specific red flags for cash payments or other verifiable evidence, hoping to get their targets to mention the red flags on wire recordings.

"We call it tickling the wire," DOJ assistant chief Kent Shaw told me.

After Butler and Marino returned from their L.A. expedition, DOJ agents gave Marino a thick stack of marked singles, fives, and tens—more than $2,000—to buy drugs from Butler. Marino handed the wad of bills to Butler, who bit the bait like a jumbo-shrimp cocktail.

"All these fuckin' fives!" Butler said, laughing. He started counting the money. "He must have a lot of kiddies coming by for their weed."

It is clear from the recordings that Butler had faith that Marino's drug-slinging contact was a cash cow.

"Oh, well, [Norm] will like a nice big fat wad," Butler went on, dialing Wielsch's number. Wielsch had taken his elderly father to an Indian casino to play nickel slots all day, but he picked up when Butler called.

"I've got an envelope for you," Butler told him, gilding the lily a little before bringing up the topic of crystal meth. Butler had told Marino that Wielsch might be able to get his hands on some potent stuff. Of course the DOJ was interested, and asked Marino to say his San Jose contact was interested. Butler passed the information along to Wielsch, explaining that he had a guy waiting to buy the crystal meth at $10,000 a pound.

"I got this guy right now wanting to do it today. All I know is that he showed up today with the biggest fuckin' wad of cash I've ever seen in my life," Butler said, stealing Marino's line, before pausing to let Wielsch talk. "Hold on one second and I will get the answer to that question for you."

Butler turned to Marino. "How do we know that this guy is not a cop?"

"This guy is nasty dirty," Marino responded. "He's my buddy's guy; he's been dealing with him for years and years."

"This guy has been doing this for years and years," said Butler, again taking Marino's line. "It's not like some guy who just started. I feel really good about it, so don't worry."

On the other side of the phone call, Wielsch expressed concern about moving up the drug ladder from weed to meth.

"I know this is a whole different level, that's why I wouldn't worry about it on your end," Butler replied, playing the chill card. "I'm worried about it, because I'd be taking the hit. I'll see you later today when you come to get your envelope."

Butler hung up the phone and told Marino about the plan he had worked out with Wielsch to get the crystal meth.

"It's in evidence, and he has to write a destruction order," Butler said. "And he can't just walk out of there with it. So, he and I are going to go to the dump and have something buried in the hole. We can put some bags of flour; I need to take bags of flour to be destroyed," Butler said, laughing.

Butler reiterated that Wielsch had been very nervous on the phone about the whole situation. "When I told him this guy showed up with the biggest wad of cash, he started saying, 'That's what cops do! That's what cops do!'" Butler told Marino.

"Well, that's what scumbags do, too, the kind that sell drugs," Marino pointed out.

Butler was easily convinced, "Oh, I know, but [Norm] is nervous. He's never done anything like this before."

Butler began hypothesizing about how much dope he could sell to Marino's fictional drug connection.

"I wonder if he would buy those Xanax too," Butler said. "Maybe we should tack it on, make it a rider."

"You've got like four thousand of them, right?" Marino said, instinctively tickling the wire.

"Yeah," Butler confirmed. "You could say, 'OK, we'll sell you one pound for the ten [thousand],' but then it's like, 'Now you have to do me a favor. I've got one thousand Xanax, take 'em off me for a grand.' If he wants that meth, well, his profit margin goes down a little, but that way we can get rid of 'em. It's an extra five hundred bucks!"

Butler's voice started to sound dreamy as he told Marino about all the missed opportunities he had to sell drugs for Wielsch. He described a trip to the CNET office after Wielsch's task force had snatched a massive supply of Ecstasy.

"You should have seen the bag full of Ecstasy pills just sitting on his desk. There had to be 10,000, no, he told me it was 13,000 pills," Butler drooled. "Each one of those went for $10, so that's $130,000! And [Norm] went and destroyed them."

Butler asked Marino to drive him to an auto shop so he could pick up his Honda. Marino agreed but said he wanted to use the bathroom first. In the bathroom, Marino texted the DOJ with an update, then flushed the toilet. When he came out of the bathroom, Butler was back on the phone with Wielsch.

"Hey, I've got a quick question. What if we swapped out what was in there, with like flour, and just took that on destruction day?" Butler asked. Wielsch was irritated to keep having his day at the casino interrupted, but Butler was persistent. He reemphasized that the drug connection was in town with a wad of cash, and asked if Wielsch would be willing to swap out a pound of meth for flour that night, so they could make the sale.

Wielsch had to explain that the meth was not in the CNET office but in the Contra Costa Sheriff's evidence locker, and getting the drugs would require a more complicated process of fraud and robbery. Butler apologized for the confusion, then emphasized that they would also need to steal a lot of steroids when they did break into the evidence locker.

"He's telling me that he thinks there are three pounds, or slightly under three pounds," said Butler. "I thought it was in his office in the evidence room, but it's in the sheriff's evidence room. On Monday, he's going to get the destruction order [from a county judge]. And then Tuesday, I'll drive him in the Hummer and we'll dump flour in the hole."

On the drive to the auto shop, Butler fantasized about selling three pounds of meth and paying his tax debt with the money. Then he changed the subject back to the reality show, which had slipped further from his fingers.

"I got a text from Lucas that we've been approved for a two-hour pilot," Butler said. "But I know what's going to happen. They're going to give [the show] to Ami. *Ami, the Mom PI.* So, I've got to lock up the *PI Mom* trademark."

"When are they thinking of airing [the pilot]?" Marino asked Butler.

"I don't even fucking care anymore," Butler said. Mr. Glass-Half-Empty.

Butler tried to cheer himself up by talking about a possible decoy sting on four young women who had recently answered his Craigslist ad. The plan was to road trip with the girls to his brother's house in Southern California, which had a hot tub. Butler, Wielsch, and Marino had used the house in January 2010 for a similar sting, in which two of Marino's actor friends were hired to pose as drug dealers.

"Some of this money can fuel our decoy test down in L.A.," Butler told Marino. "The girl that you are paired up with loves the Chrysler, so you'll drive her down there in that and get her all excited. You know that your girl is going to get naked with you, no question about it."

"I hope so," Marino said, letting Butler teabag his ego a little.

Butler then went into his self-loathing mode, telling Marino how it won't be as easy for a puffy PI to trick a decoy into getting naked. Butler asserted that his plan would be to sexually harass the decoy into giving him some action.

"In order for this girl to even think about getting a job, she has to do everything she is asked, and then some," Butler told Marino.

Butler then fantasized about hooking the rest of his crew up with easy sex.

"Norm's gotta get laid," Butler told Marino. "We gotta make Norm happy."

Marino and Butler reached an auto body shop where Butler's Honda had been getting its windows tinted. As Butler got out of Marino's beater Mazda, the PI fired a cheap shot at his director of operations, "With all this money we're making [dealing stolen drugs], you could get yourself a nice car stereo," Butler said.

18
The Last Supper

ON SATURDAY, FEBRUARY 12, Carl Marino spent the morning and afternoon doing extra casting work on the Steven Soderbergh movie *Contagion*, filming a fight scene with Jude Law. That evening, Marino and his wife drove to the East Bay retirement community of Rossmoor, located very close to the supermarket parking lot of his first drug deal as an undercover informant. The Marinos were headed to the One Hundred Club Crab Feed, an annual fundraiser for families of fallen police officers and firefighters in Contra Costa County.

I knew about the event, which is a veritable who's who of local law enforcement, and it would not have been out of the ordinary for *Diablo* to cover the event for our society pages. I decided to stay away because I did not want Butler to see me so deep into the investigation. Also, I was hosting a screening of *Breakfast at Tiffany's* that night in a nearby cinema.

Chris Butler bought two tables at the crab feed. Butler's guests at one table were Norm Wielsch and his wife, Diane; Carl and Ilona Marino; and retired FBI agent Max Noel, whose stellar law enforcement career included arresting Ted Kaczynski, better known as the Unabomber. Noel, a weapons expert, had been introduced to Butler by his colleague

Chuck Latting, and offered firearms training to the PI Moms during filming of the reality show.

At the second table, Butler sat with two cast members of the *PI Moms* show: Linda Welch, the decoy involved in the gypsy psychic scam, and Sharon Taylor, the platinum blonde whose specialty included setting up unsuspecting husbands by hooking up with them in front of hidden cameras (as seen on *Dr. Phil*).

Another attendee was a representative from Glock firearms who had helped secure a product-placement deal to have Chris Butler distribute ten Glock 19s to his staff, with the understanding that whenever the cameras were filming, Butler and the PI Moms would always refer to their guns as Glocks. Another Glock 19 was donated to the One Hundred Club of Contra Costa as a raffle prize for the event.

The evening's other big raffle prize was lunch and a helicopter ride with Contra Costa Sheriff David Livingston, who had held the office of sheriff for all of forty-three days, and had no idea that the highest-ranking narcotics agent in the county had designs on stealing a big bag of crystal meth out of the sheriff's office evidence locker the following Tuesday.

"I have both the dirtiest and cleanest cops I know sitting with me for dinner," Marino wrote me in his recap of the night. "We actually had a great time. I always get along great with Norm (cop humor goes a long way), as much as I despise him."

Norm's wife, Diane Wielsch, who also had no idea that Butler and her husband were under investigation, later told me Marino spent much of the dinner talking about being a police officer in Manhattan on 9/11, and all the horrors he had witnessed on that infamous day.

By February 14, the team of Department of Justice investigators had plenty of evidence against Chris Butler after Marino had recorded purchases of several pounds of marijuana, as well as containers of steroids and ephedrine. The DOJ also had Wielsch on wiretap, talking about the plan to sneak a pound of meth out of evidence. But the team of investigators still needed to catch Wielsch in the act of selling drugs to go ahead with a bust.

Wielsch provided the investigators with a Valentine's gift when he convinced a local judge to sign a destruction order for a pound of crystal meth that had been sitting in the Contra Costa Sheriff's Office evidence locker waiting to be destroyed. The stash had been sitting in evidence for a while; Wielsch let the guy he arrested for selling it escape prosecution in exchange for some CNET informant work.

The morning of February 15, Butler picked Wielsch up in his Hummer and took the CNET commander to the evidence storage locker in Martinez, California, where Wielsch checked the crystal meth out of inventory and put it in a bag in the back of Butler's vehicle. From there, they drove to a nearby dump, where they disposed of some weed and hashish and then drove the meth back to Butler's office in Concord to sell it to Carl Marino.

Little did Butler and Wielsch know, the DOJ was following their felonious adventure with a small airplane.

Just after 12:30 PM, Carl Marino was waiting at Butler's office with $10,000 in cash when Butler and Wielsch arrived in the Hummer.

Marino had received a head's up from the DOJ that Wielsch was en route with the meth, which made Marino understandably nervous. Until this point, Marino had only dealt drugs with Butler; Wielsch might be familiar with the recording equipment that the DOJ had given him.

Marino was also excited to get the meth deal done because he had an appointment in San Francisco to do a television interview, with a CBS affiliate reporter, to talk about his role in reuniting the missing teenage girl with her family.

As Wielsch and Butler came into the office, around 12:47 PM, Marino activated the hidden camera in his keychain.

"What's up?" Marino said to Wielsch, shaking the CNET commander's hand while filming him. At the same time, Butler showed Wielsch a coffeemaker that also had a hidden camera in it, which Butler used to sting prostitutes. As Wielsch looked at the coffeemaker, Marino volunteered information about his upcoming TV interview.

"CBS wants to interview me today," he told Butler.

Butler was surprised, as if he had already forgotten about the disastrous situation that led to the end of his TV show. “Who [wants to interview you]?” Butler asked Marino.

Marino explained that a local news reporter wanted to talk about the missing teen, without mentioning that it was the case that pulled the plug on *PI Moms*.

“Are they coming here or are you going there?” Butler asked, no doubt wondering if he could get some camera time. Marino said he was going to the CBS station on Battery Street in San Francisco.

“Do you have a Butler & Associates shirt you can wear?” Butler asked.

Wielsch pulled out the plastic Baggie filled with crystal meth, which Butler placed on his digital scale.

“Holy shit, this is a lot,” Butler said, looking at the toxic narcotic and measuring its weight. Wielsch, anxious about the severity of the crime he was committing, inquired about Marino’s fictional drug connection.

“This guy has never been arrested or anything like that?” Wielsch asked Marino.

“My cousin has been buying weed from this guy for like fifteen years,” Marino assured the CNET commander.

“I’m just kinda worried, because this is like a big step up,” Wielsch said nervously.

Wielsch calmed down a little when he saw the fat wad of cash Marino was willing to hand over for the meth.

“This is more comfortable to me, because cops never give the money ahead of time,” Wielsch said, incorrectly. The longtime drug agent started counting the nearly $10,000 in marked bills.

Butler, wearing rubber gloves, offered to give Marino the package. “Let me give you the burrito,” said the PI. “One pound, one ounce.”

“That’s probably perfect,” said Marino, taking the meth.

“Beautiful,” said Wielsch.

Marino excused himself from the office, saying that he would go call his connection and arrange a meeting nearby to get rid of the meth, without letting the buyer know where he got it.

“I’ll get rid of this as quick as I can,” said Marino. “I got the guy hanging out nearby.” Butler asked Marino to hustle back from the meth drop-off, so they could go out to lunch.

Marino drove away, calling the DOJ as soon as he was out of sight to arrange a meeting spot. He drove for about ten minutes, then met the DOJ in an undisclosed parking lot.

"Hey, buddy," an agent said to Marino. "Were you getting a little nervous there?"

Marino said that he did not expect Wielsch to show up, hand over the meth, and count his cut in person. "He counted out the money in front of me," Marino said. "I'm not going to lie, I got a little nervous."

"Unbelievable," said a DOJ agent, explaining how they had been watching Butler and Wielsch go get the meth and bring it back to Butler's office. "Un-be-lievable."

Immediately after meeting with the DOJ, Ronald Rutherford wrote me the following:

> It was another nerve racking, crazy day of undercover work. Got some stuff today that we weren't even expecting. It made the DOJ's job even easier. More on that later. CBS5 wants to interview me about [the missing teenager] at their studio now. I will write later...

A few hours later, Rutherford wrote again:

> I think after today the DOJ could make a move any time. Meth reared it's [*sic*] ugly head today in a big way...with both Norm and Chris being videotaped by me...very scary situation, but I trust the DOJ boys with my life right now. Things are really crazy now and I have had terrible dreams about alternate endings.
>
> Today was one of the most stressful days, but probably the most rewarding for the DOJ. They don't have to add 2 and 2 to show 4 anymore. They got concrete proof.
>
> I am a little scared (as is my wife) about any backlash from "their friends in low places"...and they both have many. I believe I will be looking over my shoulder for a long time after this. This is going to affect a lot of people when things go down.

The next morning—Wednesday, February 16—Rutherford gave me the biggest news since asking for my help getting to law enforcement, thirty-six days before:

"It happened this morning. Call me for details."

On the morning of Wednesday, February 16, Dean Johnston and his team had an early morning meeting to discuss the strategy for arresting Butler and Wielsch.

With the evidence in hand that Wielsch indeed had been stealing and selling narcotics from CNET's busts, the DOJ did not need to wait any longer to slap the cuffs on the task force commander. They still needed to figure out a way to take him down safely, as Wielsch always carried a weapon.

So, Johnston had an agent Wielsch knew call him with a request to come to a meeting at the police department in Benicia, California, to listen to an unknown female make a complaint against a DOJ agent. Wielsch was there bright and early, and checked his firearm with an officer before going into a holding cell, expecting to find one more citizen in trouble for selling drugs. Instead, Wielsch found Dean Johnston and another DOJ agent waiting to arrest him.

Wielsch broke down and started crying and, for the most part, admitted his crimes to representatives of the Department of Justice agency, where he had worked for the past thirteen years.

According to the DOJ report about the arrest, Wielsch said he would cooperate with anything that law enforcement needed, and that he had made a big mistake. After going through the events of the past few weeks, since the DOJ started tapping his phone and watching his every move, Wielsch called his wife, Diane, to let her know about his arrest.

"I'm in jail," Wielsch said. "I've been arrested. The police are coming to our house with search warrants. I've told them you will meet them there to let them in, and open the safe."

Diane, completely stunned, said she would go straight home. Within a few hours, DOJ agents had seized several thousand dollars in cash that

Wielsch had received for the meth deal the day before, as well as some illegal steroids that Wielsch had stolen from evidence for personal use.

Wielsch was taken to the Contra Costa County jail and booked on numerous felony counts, including possession, transportation, and sale of marijuana, methamphetamine, and steroids, as well as burglary and embezzlement charges. Wielsch's shoelaces were taken from his shoes and he was immediately placed on suicide watch, standard practice for cops who get hooked after breaking their oath to protect the community in such an egregious fashion.

As Wielsch was being arrested in Benicia, Chris Butler went to the UFC Gym in Concord for his morning workout. Just a few days before, Butler was meeting several PI Moms and Carl Marino at the gym each morning to work out, free of charge, with the UFC people expecting plenty of product placements on the Lifetime reality show.

By the morning of February 16, Butler only had one staff member left to work out with: Heather, the unpaid intern he had given some stolen weed to for sampling. Butler was expecting Carl Marino to be at the workout as well, but received a text message that morning from Ilona Marino saying that Carl would not be coming to the gym.

At approximately 8 AM, agents from the DOJ followed Butler from his office in Concord to the UFC Gym. They watched him park his Hummer and go inside, and waited for him to complete his last workout as a free man.

The DOJ had arranged for two uniformed officers from California Highway Patrol to wait outside the gym to arrest Butler in the parking lot. Just like Wielsch's arrest, the DOJ's strategy was to approach Butler at a time when he was unlikely to be packing a gun.

At approximately 9:35 AM, Butler came out of the gym and headed for his Hummer. He was contacted by one of the CHP officers and told to take his hands out of his pockets. Butler complied and was handcuffed. The officer asked if Butler was armed and Butler said no. When asked if he had a weapon in his Hummer, Butler said, "I don't have one here."

A team of agents converged on the PI from tactical positions, and Butler was informed that the DOJ had a warrant to search his vehicle and office. Butler then admitted that he had a gun in the Hummer.

Butler told a DOJ agent he would answer any questions after he had a chance to consult an attorney, and let the investigators know that they would find what they were looking for in the trunk of the Cadillac parked at his warehouse office.

When the DOJ searched the Hummer, they found a Glock 19—one of the firearms given to Butler as a *PI Moms* product-placement freebie—hidden in a green canvas bag. The gun was loaded with fifteen bullets in the seated magazine, with one more in the chamber. A search of the state's automated firearms system showed the Glock was registered to Butler.

The agents also found prescription vials and a stack of five-dollar bills that matched the serial numbers of the cash that Carl Marino gave to Butler on one of the weed deals.

Over at Butler's office, DOJ agents seized $5,500 in cash, three handguns (two more Glocks and a Smith & Wesson, all registered to Butler), and an illegal Sub-9 assault pistol, for which there was no record in the state's automated firearms system. The agents also seized nearly two hundred bottles of anabolic steroids, 106 codeine tablets, 1,956 ephedrine tablets, four bags packed with hundreds of prescription Xanax pills, almost ten pounds of marijuana, and 141 grams of methamphetamine.

Butler was transported to the Contra Costa County detention center and booked on twenty-eight felony counts. Butler immediately hired one of the area's most prestigious defense attorneys to guide him through the river of shit that he had waded into.

Needless to say, the story made the news.

The last email I received from Marino as Ronald Rutherford arrived on February 16 at 12:53 PM, just after Butler and Wielsch were arrested.

The email read, "It happened this morning. Call me." The phone number attached was from the 585 area code, the prefix for the Rochester area of New York State.

It had been forty-five days since I first heard from Ronald Rutherford, telling me that the ride-along I had been taken on was a hoax. It took me less than a day to figure out that Ronald Rutherford was likely Marino, even when Marino played dumb and perpetuated the lie about the ride-along being real, three days after emailing the initial tip-off to the editors of *Diablo*.

The previous seven weeks had been a surreal roller coaster of adrenaline and mystery, with secret meetings with law enforcement, warnings that Butler had designs on setting me up, and cliff-hanger messages from my secret source, giving me the inside scoop on a confidential investigation of a dirty cop and the private investigator who had the pulled the wool over the eyes of national TV producers and journalists and played himself off as a good guy when he was really a sociopathic criminal.

During this drama, I felt I had formed a unique friendship with this inside source who had told me he was a former cop in Rochester, and now an actor, model, and part-time PI turned undercover informant in one of the biggest corruption investigations in East Bay history.

Now I could finally get to chat with the real Ronald Rutherford. I dialed the 585 number.

"This is Carl," Marino answered.

I introduced myself again, starting from scratch. Marino went right into information-dump mode, recapping the arrest updates he had just been given by the DOJ agents a few minutes before.

"Norm broke down and admitted everything," Marino claimed. "But Chris lawyered up."

I was surprised at how nonchalant Marino sounded. I expected him to be in full-on sigh-of-relief mode, but he was very matter-of-fact about the arrests. Honestly, I expected a warmer tone from the guy I had safely connected to law enforcement in his hour of desperation.

Over the phone, Marino sounded considerably colder than Ronald Rutherford had come across in so many emails, thanking me for helping him when he did not know what to do. Looking back on the events through the prism of hindsight, I suspect Marino was somewhat sad that his adventures as an undercover informant had come to an end. He had been able to go to top-cop fantasy camp with the big boys, and now that was over.

As we were chatting, the other line buzzed on my iPhone. I recognized the number as that of Sharon the Client's real boyfriend. Marino had sent me the number in one of his information dumps before letting me know about the drug dealing. I had held off contacting this fellow (who I will call Quincy) for a while, so as not to draw any more attention from Butler about my investigation. Finally, I started calling and leaving the former fiancé messages asking to speak with him about a story I was writing for *Diablo* magazine.

"Carl, I'm going to call you back in a little while," I said to Marino. "I have [Sharon the Client's ex-fiancé] on the other line and I don't want to play phone tag with him."

I picked up the call from Quincy and introduced myself as a writer for *Diablo* who was working on a story that might be of interest to him.

"I don't know what you're talking about," said Quincy, sounding angry. "You need to tell me exactly what you are doing, and how it involves me."

"Have you ever heard of Chris Butler, or the PI Moms?" I asked.

Ex-Boyfriend was silent for a few seconds and said, "Come over to my house right now." He gave me his address, which I scribbled in a reporter's notebook and entered into my car's GPS.

"I'll be there in fifteen minutes," I told him. "I'm looking forward to speaking with you."

As I drove east on the freeway, my mind started to race about all that had happened in the past hour—first and foremost, the fact that Chris Butler and Norm Wielsch had been busted.

With Butler and Wielsch sitting in jail, it was time for me to stop being the secret email pen pal of Ronald Rutherford and start writing my story for *Diablo*, one that would certainly get more attention than my guide to the East Bay's best burgers, or even my feature profile on local boy turned *Saturday Night Live* star Will Forte.

Thinking of the Will Forte piece reminded me of Charmagne Peters and how she had raved about the article. I wondered what Charmagne would say about the ride-along now that Butler was sitting in a jail cell for selling stolen drugs. As I parked on the street outside Quincy's house, I sent Charmagne a text: "We need to talk."

I gathered a file of notes, walked up to the house, and knocked on the door. Quincy, a thin, bald, fiftyish fellow—who looked nothing like the crew-cutted beefcake the PI Moms and I had followed all over Napa—opened the door and invited me inside.

Quincy did not seem happy to see me. We walked into his home office and he sat down at his desk.

"You mentioned something about a private investigator," said Quincy. "Now, what is this all about?"

I pulled out a Facebook page I had printed out, showing a smiling Sharon the Client.

"Do you recognize this woman?" I asked.

"Yes, she's my girlfriend," he answered, his face turning red. "Or, she was my girlfriend. She broke up with me. How do you know her?"

"It's very complicated, but I will explain everything," I said, trying to sound as soothing as I could be. I pulled out the *People* magazine from March 15, 2010, the issue that had featured a four-page feature about the PI Moms. I pointed to the full-page photograph on the opening spread.

"Do you recognize any of these women?" I asked, showing Quincy a photo of Charmagne Peters, Michelle Allen, and another investigator, Julia Kostina, holding walkie-talkies, video cameras, and binoculars while posed like *Charlie's Angels*.

Quincy recognized Charmagne and Michelle, and looked like he was going to have an aneurysm.

"What the hell is going on here?" Quincy asked me, his eyes dashing wildly from me to the magazine picture and back.

I took a deep breath and explained who the PI Moms were and how they had received considerable media coverage and a reality show deal from Lifetime during the past year. I told him about my ride-along and how Sharon the Client had come into Butler's office to meet me and talk about why she needed to hire the PI Moms to investigate her fiancé. I said that I had spent an entire day following a man who was supposed to be her fiancé around Napa, and that the guy appeared to be on a date with a buxom, tattooed young woman.

I pointed at the *People* magazine story again and asked how he knew Charmagne and Michelle. Quincy said that he started receiving new notifications from a dating website a few months ago. He said that somehow the account had been reactivated without his knowledge, and he started getting mash notes from someone who was single and ready to mingle. He pointed at Charmagne's picture in *People*.

"It was her," he said. "It was that woman right there."

Quincy said he met Charmagne on two occasions. The first meeting was in Walnut Creek, when Charmagne and Michelle showed up to chat with Quincy over margaritas at the patio bar of a Mexican restaurant. I explained that I believed Chris Butler was sitting nearby, filming the encounter.

"What the hell?" Quincy was pissed. "He was filming me?"

"That's what he does," I told him, hoping he would calm down. "Tell me about the second meeting."

Quincy said that he had hoped to pick Sharon the Client up at the airport the night she returned from Europe, but was told that one of Sharon's girlfriends would give her a ride home. Quincy, disappointed that his relationship seemed to be in the ruts, then received a follow-up email from Charmagne, saying what a nice time she had getting to know him.

So, Quincy agreed to meet Charmagne again and scheduled the date for the same night that Sharon the Client was supposed to get back from Europe. Which was all very convenient, of course—Quincy to be caught snuggling with a PI Mom, when Sharon the Client and her girlfriend came waltzing into the wine bar on their way home from the airport. Despite the overwhelming coincidence, Quincy had no idea that he had been set up until I walked him through the sting.

"Why would they do this to me?" he bellowed. "Who are these people?"

I said that I thought the PI Moms were just suburban housewives lured into business with a scam artist, but Chris Butler was a more insidious character.

"He was arrested today for selling drugs," I said. I did not mention the fact that I was the one who had notified law enforcement about Butler's criminal behavior.

It was strange to say this out loud for the first time, to tell someone this news. But it felt appropriate to tell one of Butler's victims that the King of Stings was behind bars.

Quincy picked up his phone and started to dial Sharon the Client's number. I warned him not to say too much, as I still needed to confront her myself. I was hoping we could all sit down in a Starbucks and go over everything face-to-face.

"Just say you need to talk to her about something important, and that you want to meet face-to-face," I whispered a warning, as Quincy punched at the buttons on his desk phone.

My warning did not register. At all.

"Sharon, it's me," Quincy hissed into Sharon the Client's voice mail. "I know all about Chris Butler and his PI Moms and all the trouble he's in with jail and drugs. You need to call me back, Sharon. You're in big trouble."

He slammed down the receiver and looked at me with a look of demented satisfaction.

"Dude, I told you to take it easy," I said. "That was not easy."

Done with Quincy, I headed back to my car. I wanted to get over to Sharon the Client's house right away. Maybe I could ring her doorbell before she checked her voice mail and lost her shit.

As I drove to Sharon the Client's house, I got a text message from Charmagne.

"I just heard Chris got arrested today!! What's going on??" she wrote.

"We need to talk," I replied. I did not get a response.

I exited the freeway in Lafayette and headed for the same neighborhood that Charmagne, Denise, and I had parked in at the start of the ride-along. The area's spacious family homes were all a million dollars and up, with lots of yards and trees. I got to Sharon the Client's driveway, which dipped into a steep ravine. As I was headed down the driveway, I saw a white Mercedes driving up. It was the same car we had followed all around Napa a few months before, but this time there wasn't a ridiculously muscular man behind the wheel. This time, it was

Sharon the Client, who had a worried look on her face. I hit the brakes and blocked her path out of the driveway, and rolled down the window.

"Hi Sharon, I'm Pete Crooks from *Diablo* magazine," I said. My attempt to sound friendly came across as the kind of goofy that requires medication. Sharon the Client blanched as she recognized me from Butler's office, and the parking lot where she gave the dramatic performance of her life, following the "discovery" of her "fiancé's infidelity."

"What's going on?" she asked, petrified. "I just got a message that Chris Butler is in jail."

"That's right," I said. "He was arrested today for selling drugs."

"But how does Quincy know about that?" she asked.

"Because I was just over at his house," I said. The look on her face said, "You have got to be kidding me."

"We need to talk about that ride-along I went on," I told Sharon the Client. "Because it was not a real case. I said I would not use your name in the article, but that's when I thought I was watching a real case."

"But it was a real case!" Sharon said, looking terrified. "That was what really happened with [Quincy]."

"Look, you told me on September 9 that you were in a three-year relationship with this guy Al, and you weren't," I said. "I rode around in a van for ten hours on September 11, following a guy Chris Butler had hired for the day—a guy you had never even talked to until that morning when you gave him the keys to your car. It was *not* a real case."

"You're right," Sharon admitted, after a moment of "when you put it that way" clarity. "It was fake."

Sharon the Client said that she needed to pick up her daughter at a nearby BART train station, and would come right back and talk to me. I told her I would wait right there in her driveway until she returned.

As I waited for Sharon to come back—I assumed she would return, knowing that I was staked out in her front yard—I thought about my approach to reporting the rest of the story for the magazine. Certainly, the Bay Area's local TV, radio, and daily newspapers would be off and running with the story as soon as they heard that the highest ranking narcotics agent in the county had just been arrested for selling drugs.

I had the inside scoop on how these events came to be, of course, but the question was: Could I publish a story in a monthly magazine in time to keep the scoop? As Ronald Rutherford, Marino had promised me that he would be an exclusive source—but I wasn't sure if I could even name him as a source at all, due to his confidential informant status in the legal case against Butler and Wielsch.

I decided the best way to tell the story was to go after everyone who had played a role in setting me up in the ride-along, get them to admit it was a big fake, and then attach that to the information about how I brought the allegations about criminal activity to law enforcement. That way, *Diablo* could expose Butler as a lying attention whore who went to great lengths to con me, hoping I would publish a story about his business and reality show. I would give Ronald Rutherford credit for tipping me off about the hoax, and explain how that led to the exposure of a spectacular corruption scandal.

Just as I was beginning to worry that Sharon the Client had skipped town, her Mercedes coasted down her steep driveway. Sharon the Client, her college-age daughter, and another woman in her early fifties got out of the car. I introduced myself to the daughter and the woman, and explained that I was writing a story about Chris Butler, who had been arrested for serious felony crimes earlier that day. It was an awkward introduction, but Sharon opened the front door and we went to sit around her kitchen table.

I pulled out my iPhone and turned on a recording application, and let everyone know that the conversation would be on the record. I asked Sharon how she knew Chris Butler, and listened to her very nervous explanation.

Sharon said that she had been involved in a relationship with Quincy for a few years, and they were engaged but had not set a wedding date. A few months before my ride-along, Sharon had used her fiancé's laptop computer and noticed the browser history showed heavy activity on a website called MillionaireMatch.com. I recognized the website as the one Butler had mentioned in my first phone conversation with him, and realized that Butler's original pitch for a ride-along case had been a more faithful re-creation of Sharon the Client's actual case.

Sharon went on to explain that she knew her relationship was doomed, but did not know how to confront Ex-Boyfriend about her discovery. As she hemmed and hawed over the situation, she came across a big feature story in the *Contra Costa Times* newspaper about Butler and the PI Moms, and how they help housewives catch adulterous husbands.

The *Contra Costa Times*' story, which ran in April 2010, featured Charmagne Peters and Denise Antoon following a cheating husband taking a woman out for a date in a black Mustang. Later, I would discover that the article was based on a case that was just as fake as the one I had witnessed—the man who was driving the Mustang and pretending to be a cheater in the *Times*' story was a friend of Butler's, a local sheriff's deputy, Steve Tanabe.

Tanabe was also the arresting officer in the two Dirty DUI setups that Carl Marino orchestrated on January 9 and January 14, 2011.

Butler's main purpose for stinging the *Contra Costa Times* (and *Diablo* magazine via yours truly), was to lure in new business via the area's top publications. The *Times* sting worked like a charm: Sharon the Client read the article and thought Butler and the PI Moms might be able to help her out of her unpleasant situation. So, she hired Butler to work his magic on Quincy while she took her daughter on a European vacation, before the daughter went off to her first year of college.

The sting worked. Quincy took the bait and replied to emails he thought were coming from Charmagne Peters. (Chris Butler was actually the one sending the lovey-dovey messages, such as, "You look like that actor whose name I can't remember.") While the Client was in Europe, Butler, Charmagne, and Michelle Allen had stung Quincy at the Mexican restaurant—he showed up and acted as if he was single and interested. Sharon the Client showed me the video of the meeting: Quincy sitting at a patio bar, listening to Charmagne talk about her interests and hobbies, while Chris Butler sat at a nearby table, filming with a hidden camera.

Sharon the Client said she received an update from Butler while in Europe with her daughter, and was very upset to learn that her fiancé had taken the bait so easily. She told Butler that she wanted to witness Quincy out with Charmagne when she got back from Europe. Butler said no problem, and they set up Quincy again, this time letting Sharon the Client catch him canoodling with Charmagne while seated at the downstairs bar in Oliveto, one of Oakland's most acclaimed restaurants and a perennial favorite of *Diablo*'s readers.

After being busted, Quincy chased Sharon the Client out of Oliveto, trying to explain his way out of the situation. Butler, witnessing all of this from a tactical position, made a quick phone call to one of his police buddies. In just a few minutes, a uniformed police officer arrived at the scene to break up the skirmish.

"That was very odd," Sharon the Client told me. "The police officer asked all kinds of personal questions, and I explained that [Quincy] had been seeing other women on MillionaireMatch.com. The officer asked if either of us were millionaires, and we said no. Then, [the cop] asked if I would date him, because he wasn't a millionaire either."

I asked Sharon the Client why she went along with setting me up with a fake story. She was extremely embarrassed as she explained that, following the sting on Quincy (for which she paid Butler $3,500), Butler had invited her to become a part of the PI Moms operation.

"He told me that once the show began, he was going to start opening satellite offices around the country, and thought I might be able to manage the San Francisco office," Sharon the Client told me. She said that she agreed to shadow the PI Moms around the office for a while to see if she would be interested. She did go to staff meetings and workout sessions at the UFC gym for a few weeks, but quickly lost interest when she got a sense of the kindergarten-ish culture at Butler & Associates' Concord office. Still, she felt that Butler had done a very good job on her case. He did exactly what he said he would do in the initial meeting.

Soon after Sharon the Client stopped shadowing the PI Moms, Butler called her with a request for one favor: Let *Diablo* magazine write a story about her case. Butler told Sharon that the article would be helpful to many, many women who were in the situation that she had been in—stuck in a dead-end relationship with a cheating husband or boyfriend. Sharon the Client agreed to let Butler tell *Diablo* about her case, as long as she was not identified.

However, the project kept shape-shifting from the original proposal. Soon, Butler was requesting that Sharon come meet with the *Diablo* writer, and act as if she was in the process of hiring the PI Moms.

"I told Chris, 'This isn't what we talked about,'" Sharon the Client told me. "I said, 'Why don't we just tell the writer what you and the Moms did for me?' Chris answered, 'Because he won't write the story if we approach it that way. He has to believe what he is seeing is real. And it will make the story so much more interesting.'"

Sharon the Client began to cry as she described Chris Butler's skills as an acting coach.

"That day up in Napa, when we were driving up to meet you, Chris coached me very carefully," Sharon told me. "He said, 'When you look in the trunk of the car and see the gift bags, I want you to think about how you felt when you saw Quincy out on a date with another woman. And, remember how many women are in your position: They know their husbands are cheating and they don't know what to do.'"

Sharon looked at me, red-faced, and said, "When you saw me crying in Napa, those were real tears. I was really right back in the place when I remembered seeing my fiancé, out with another woman. That was a very painful experience to have to go through again."

"Maybe Chris Butler can direct plays with the other inmates in prison," I replied. "Sounds like he is missing out on his true artistic calling."

I told Sharon that I would talk to *Diablo*'s editor-in-chief about whether or not we would need to identify her by first and last name. After several hours of conversation, I believed that Sharon was a nice woman whose biggest mistake was believing that the private investigators she had read about in the local paper were honest, decent, and caring professionals. I did not feel she had played a role in my sting for any malicious or self-serving purpose.

I stopped by Sharon the Client's house on the way to *Diablo*'s office the next morning, and told her I would advocate for not using her name in the story. Sharon was relieved, and invited me in for coffee. She had been reading about Butler's arrest on the front page of the *Contra Costa Times*, and wanted to know what caused his downfall.

"Do you think Carl Marino turned him in to the police?" Sharon asked me. I wanted to respond that I was the one who brought the information about Butler's drug sales to law enforcement, but bit my tongue. I asked why she thought Marino may have been the informant.

"He's quoted in the story," Sharon told me. I asked to see a copy of her newspaper. Sure enough, Marino was quoted throughout the article.

"He was a master of deception," Marino said of Butler, in the *Contra Costa Times*' February 17, 2011 article, "Fallout from Contra Costa's Top Drug Agent's Arrest Begins." Marino added, "I felt like his whole business was deception, and he didn't care who he hurt in the process, and ended up hurting a lot of people. He kind of got what he deserved."

That was quick, I thought. *There goes Rutherford's promise of being an exclusive source.*

I went outside and called Marino.

"Hey, you promised to be an exclusive source," I told him. "Then you give a quote to the *Times* the day they were arrested? Now, your name is out there and everyone is going to be calling you."

Marino vehemently denied breaking his promise of exclusivity. He claimed that the *Contra Costa Times* reporter tricked him into giving that quote, and it was printed out of context.

Marino explained that the reporter was supposed to be writing a story about finding the missing teenage girl, and then asked at the end of the interview, "By the way, Butler was arrested today. Whaddya think about that?"

Marino's explanation was not believable. I told him that I was disappointed he broke his word about being an exclusive source. Even though I helped Marino for non-journalistic reasons—my concern about the CNET commander selling drugs that someone else might have gone to jail for possessing, along with the public safety threat of C-4 getting into the wrong hands—I certainly expected Marino to honor his promise.

I also told Marino that we should meet in person to talk about everything we had been through during the past few weeks—him on the inside and me on the outside of this incredible true-crime story. Marino agreed, and I offered to take him and his wife to lunch on the following Saturday afternoon.

Then I drove to *Diablo* to tell my bosses that we had a big story, with a unique angle, and I was ready to write it.

Just after I got to the office, I ran into *Diablo*'s publisher, Barney Fonzi, who I had kept up to speed about the ride-along story and the Ronald Rutherford emails claiming it was a fake. I've worked with Barney for years and love the guy, and was excited to tell him the big news.

"Pete!" Fonzi said as soon as he saw me. "I heard Chris Butler was arrested for selling drugs! It was the first story on the news."

"I heard something about that," I said. "Can we go somewhere to talk about this?"

The publisher and I went into an empty office and I gave him the full download: I had been in regular contact with Rutherford since his initial email, when all of a sudden he asked for my help getting to law enforcement about the drug sales. I had a meeting with my old friend Cindy Hall, who got the ball rolling by calling her supervisor, and eventually the Department of Justice was brought in to investigate.

Fonzi, also a fan of noir films, such as *Chinatown* and *L.A. Confidential*, sat wide-eyed as I went through the details of this true-crime melodrama in *Diablo*'s sunny suburban neighborhood. He said he understood why I had to keep such a tight lid on the information about the criminal investigation during the past few weeks.

The next meeting I had was with *Diablo*'s president Steve Rivera. Rivera, who had come up with the *Columbo*-style approach to confronting Chris Butler about the ride-along, was extremely excited about the story's potential.

"I want this story to get national attention," Rivera told me, via Skype. "This needs to get coverage on the *Today* show, or a show like that."

Rivera's next directive was almost as ambitious as the *Today* show request: Finish writing the story for the next issue—otherwise the area's other publications and news programs would inundate the public with so much coverage, *Diablo*'s story would not pop. Because we were already deep into production of the April 2011 issue, I was under the gun to write the biggest story of my life in the next few days.

So that's what I did. I pulled all-nighters through the weekend, and by Tuesday, February 22, I had banged out a ten-thousand-word feature that was ready to roll for *Diablo*'s April 2011 issue.

19
Halfway on the Record

ON SATURDAY, FEBRUARY 19—three days after Butler and Wielsch were locked up in jail—I finally got to meet "Ronald Rutherford" in person for the first time since he reached out to let me know that the ride-along was fake.

I picked up Carl and Ilona Marino outside their apartment in San Francisco, and drove them to lunch at a waterfront café in Sausalito. Ilona thanked me for helping put her husband in touch with the right people.

We talked about Butler and Wielsch's chances of making bail, and what would happen if they did hit the streets again. The Marinos were worried about retaliation.

"Let me put it this way—they both have lots of friends in low places," Carl said.

I asked Carl if he knew what happened to the C-4 that Butler had offered to sell. Disgusted as I was at the thought of the CNET commander selling drugs, it was the explosives that had been giving me horrific nightmares for the past few weeks.

Carl had asked his contacts at the DOJ about the C-4, after the arrests. He told me that the DOJ said that the material Butler thought was C-4 was actually duct sealant. Whoever had been supplying Butler with his explosives had been ripping him off.

Ilona and Carl Marino attending a 2011 Oakland A's baseball game, following the arrests of Chris Butler and Norm Wielsch. *Photo by Pete Crooks.*

As concerned as Carl seemed to be about his safety, when I mentioned the article I was writing for *Diablo*, he enthusiastically volunteered to go on the record.

"Even though the story has become this much bigger exposé, the problem I might have is with demonstrating that the ride-along was a fake," I told him. "Chris Butler certainly isn't going to talk, the PI Moms aren't returning my calls, and you're a confidential informant. All I have is [Sharon the Client] explaining how she got sucked into playing a role, and I'm probably not going to identify her by name."

"You have Carl Marino. And you have Ilona Marino," Carl replied, immediately and confidently. "I can talk about how the ride-along was staged. I just can't talk about any of my work in the investigation."

I was pleased that the Marinos would admit they played a role in duping me during the day in Napa. I assumed they felt that it was the least they could do to help me with the article, after all I had done to help Carl get in touch with law enforcement.

Besides, they had willingly played a role in setting me up, two months before Carl learned that Butler and Wielsch wanted to sell stolen drugs. I felt that their dishonesty still required an apology, or at least some explanation. I was hungry to write the story, and the clock was ticking fast—the *Contra Costa Times* and *San Francisco Chronicle* had run front-page stories about the case every day since the arrests.

Still, I did not want to do anything to jeopardize the case against Butler and Wielsch, who had committed insidious crimes. I did not want them to walk on a technicality because of public statements with Marino, and then have to look over my shoulder, knowing that they knew I was the one who turned them in.

"Are you sure you can do that?" I asked Carl. "Do you want to run that by the DOJ?"

Marino insisted that he could proceed with the interview. "I just can't talk about the investigation," he said. "I can talk about anything else."

Throughout the next few days, I reached out to Charmagne Peters and Denise Antoon repeatedly, requesting that we meet for an in-person interview to discuss the ride-along and the recent events. While I hoped they would admit that they had lied to me and the other publications and programs that did PI Moms stories, I also wanted to give them a chance to distance themselves from the heinous crimes that Butler was charged with, because I did not believe they knew anything about the drugs. But I wasn't going to tell them that I was the one who went to law enforcement in the first place; they could read that when the article came out.

Unfortunately, both PI Moms dodged my request for any kind of interview. I exchanged a few messages back and forth with Denise, who advised me that she was going to consult an attorney about whether or not she could speak to me.

The last email I received from Denise said:

> What you don't seem to understand is Chris is a very scary guy. I quit several weeks ago and have heard he was out to seek revenge on me for doing so. My son has been fearful as to what may happen to me since then. My family is afraid. My children are my priority. I work hard to take care of my family. I went to work

> [the day of the ride-along] to do what I was instructed to do by my boss. I don't understand why you want to hurt moms when the criminal is Chris not us!

I replied with the following:

> Believe me, I know how bad and scary a guy Chris Butler is. My intention this whole time has been to let you know that I know the ride-along was fake—to let you get as far away from him as possible. I am not out to hurt any moms, or sensationalize anything. It's just about telling a truthful story. I believe you that you were following Chris' orders. Hope we can talk, even if we can't, you won't be editorially ravaged for participating in a staged ride-along.

I never heard from Denise again.

Similarly, Charmagne Peters walked back on her promise to talk to me about the ride-along. She called me the evening of February 20 to say that she had spoken with an attorney about a nondisclosure agreement she had signed when she went to work for Chris Butler, which said she could not talk to the media about any cases for twenty years. I found this to be an infuriating excuse to not admit to the fake ride-along—first, because she had been very chatty about various cases during the ride-along, and second, because the person she had signed this alleged twenty-year confidentiality agreement with was now sitting in jail on charges for selling stolen drugs.

"Charmagne, you can't hide behind a confidentiality agreement with Chris Fucking Butler," I said, taking a totally unprofessional tone. "The guy is looking at twenty-eight felony counts for selling crystal meth that he stole out of a police evidence locker!"

My aggressive approach in getting Charmagne to fess up was ineffective. Charmagne started yelling at me about the confusion she was feeling.

"I don't know who to believe!" Charmagne said. "I didn't know Chris was involved with any of this, and now I have Carl Marino calling me and telling me he was working undercover for the last two years and that he secretly recorded everything that happened in that office! I feel like I'm the victim of all this!"

I certainly didn't pity Charmagne as any kind of victim—she participated in more staged PI Mom media stings than anyone, and she had lied to me from the day I met her. But I was startled by her claim that Marino had claimed to be a deep-cover agent for two years.

"Wait, what did Marino tell you?" I asked. "He said he was undercover for two years?

"Yes, he called me and told me that he was some kind of secret agent for the Department of Justice and that he was recording everything that happened there the whole time he worked for Butler," Charmagne told me. "He said that there was enough C-4 in the office to blow up a school and we never knew it. I don't know what C-4 is, but I could have been killed!"

I told Charmagne that I would be happy to speak to her lawyer and explain why she should tear up any confidentiality agreement she had with Butler, but it looked futile. She was not going to meet, and neither was Denise.

That night, Carl Marino sent me an email that demonstrated that he knew the PI Moms were gossiping about his role in the investigation:

> They know I am the under cover that provided the evidence to the DOJ . . . At this point, they don't know exactly who I am and I am letting them go with that. I am a mystery to them. They think that it is possible that I have been working with the DOJ since I first started at Butler and have been deep cover the entire time. I am letting them run with that for now.

I wrote back:

> I'm sorry I'll need to bust your two-years-deep cover image with my story.

On Monday, February 21, I went back into San Francisco to meet Carl and Ilona in their small apartment in the pricey Marina District. We agreed that I would interview the Marinos about the roles they played in the ride-along on September 11 and how Butler organized my sting with hopes that I would write a favorable story in *Diablo*. I would not ask any questions on tape about Carl Marino's role as the confidential informant in the DOJ's investigation.

When I asked about my initial visit to Butler's office, when Sharon the Client tearfully shared her suspicions of infidelity, Marino quickly threw Butler under the bus.

"That was all scripted by Chris Butler," Carl Marino said. "Everything about it was planned out. And everything about the day you spent with Charmagne and Denise was planned out in advance: We even had a staff meeting about it. I drove up to Napa with Chris Butler to scout the whole trip. We picked that Holiday Inn because it had the right parking lot for [the make-believe adulterers] to walk right through the lobby and get in a car that we had driven up the night before, and drive home."

I asked about how the ride-along ended with Butler's decision to drive off in Sharon's Mercedes, which had seemed like such an irresponsible decision. "That was scripted too," said Carl. "Chris thought that would be exciting for your story. Look how he left this cheating fiancé hanging at the Holiday Inn without a ride home."

I told Ilona that I spoke with Carl the same week the first Ronald Rutherford email arrived, and that he had told me, when I asked him about it, that he had always assumed it had been a real case. I had not reached out to Ilona, assuming that she would be on the same page as her husband.

"So that week, if I had asked you if the ride-along was real, would you have lied to me again?" I asked.

Ilona looked very nervous, or possibly ashamed. She chose her words carefully.

"At that time, I was being coached," she said. "So, I guess...yes, I would have been coached to tell you that it was a real case."

Ilona said that she "only occasionally" assisted Carl on Butler & Associates cases. She made no mention that she had assisted her husband on two Dirty DUI setups, on January 9 and 14, respectively, including one in which Carl lured a man into a meeting by claiming to be a reporter from *Diablo* magazine. I discovered that little gem more than a year later, via court documents from a civil lawsuit that the victim filed against Butler, the arresting officer, and Contra Costa County, which was employing Sheriff's Deputy Steve Tanabe at the time of the conspiracy.

Carl also claimed that Butler was very brash about his media fraud. "In the office, Chris was always saying he's the guy who stung his way into *People* magazine and *Dr. Phil.*"

That brought me to a question that had been bothering me since the day "Ronald Rutherford" contacted me about the hoax in his email. If Marino really felt that a con man like Chris Butler did not deserve free publicity in a classy magazine like *Diablo*, then why did he play a role in planning and executing the sting?

"So, why did you two even take part in setting me up?" I asked.

Carl grinned from ear to ear, seemingly totally unashamed. "That's what we had to do to promote the business and the TV show," he replied.

I was not satisfied with Marino's response and felt a bit irritated by his smug tone. Of course, I knew he was actually the guy who wore a wire and helped expose a much bigger scandal. But he didn't know about Wielsch's drugs when he was setting me up—he had willingly and enthusiastically participated in a fraudulent case.

"It's not OK to lie to a reputable magazine," I contended.

"We were working for Chris Butler at the time," Marino said, still cocky. "Our boss told us we had to do it."

"You told me you were a police officer for seventeen years," I said, challenging Marino's ethical compass. "You know the difference between right and wrong. Why didn't you tell your boss to go fuck himself?"

Marino didn't respond like someone who had spent most of his adult life enforcing the law. Again, Carl deflected to the "Butler made him do it" defense.

"Look, I do feel badly about a lot of things Chris Butler asked us to do. Things that were not in my character or my wife's character," Marino said. "Your sting was one of our more pleasant assignments. It was just a day where we went to Napa and tasted some wines."

I had given the Marinos enough chances to apologize, or say, in hindsight, they should have walked away from Butler long ago, when they realized what a con man he was. If Carl wanted to respond to my questions with douche bag answers, that was his choice. (Before going to print with it in *Diablo*, I told him, "I think your identity as the confidential informant will be intact. The way you answered those questions about planning the ride-along was so douchey, I doubt anyone will think that you were actually the guy who did the right thing.")

After the interview, I showed the Marinos the DVD of Butler and the PI Moms on *Dr. Phil*, to see if they could identify any fakeries on the show. Marino insisted that the case in which Butler sent a male decoy into a hotel room with a hidden camera, to investigate possible prostitution, was staged.

"I know that case was scripted because Butler wanted me to play the decoy who goes in for a massage," Carl said. "I never wanted to do it—and I got a job on *Trauma* instead. Obviously, I'm really glad I didn't go on *Dr. Phil.*"

As Carl and I were chatting, I noticed a picture on his bookshelf. The picture showed a young man with a crew cut, wearing a formal military uniform. The picture looked like it could have been a young Carl Marino, but it also could have been a nephew or brother or other relative.

"Is that you in the picture?" I asked.

"That's from when I was at West Point," said Marino.

My mind went for a quick spin.

"West Point is... Marines?" I asked.

"No, West Point is Army," Marino corrected.

I felt a little stupid. Of course, West Point is the US Army's elite military academy. I knew that graduates from West Point had an obligation to enter the Army with a minimum service requirement.

"Did you serve?" I asked.

"Yes," said Marino, looking me right in the eye. "I was in Desert Storm."

No wonder this guy wouldn't put up with a couple of greedy clowns like Butler and Wielsch selling stolen drugs, I thought. *This guy has served his country and been through the horrors of war. The Shit.*

Since Marino and I were approximately the same age, I considered the difference in our life experiences. While I was watching *Network* in mass media classes at UC San Diego in the early 1990s, I imagined that Marino must have been watching oil derricks spray apocalyptic columns of fire into the sky, hundreds of feet above a desert in the Middle East, and living through other similarly intense experiences like the ones I had seen in the movie *Jarhead.*

20
The Case of the Candyman

WHEN BUTLER AND WIELSCH were arrested on February 16, they were each charged with twenty-eight felony counts. I was relieved that they were behind bars—I never stopped worrying that Butler was going to try to set me up again, as Marino said he had threatened to do.

I was also exhilarated by their arrests, as I had been keeping such a tight lid on sensational information for what felt like an eternity. Actually, the arrests had happened very quickly—less than four weeks from the day Marino gave the DOJ two pounds of shrink-wrapped marijuana, three Xanax pills, and the allegations that the drugs came from Butler via Wielsch.

As the Bay Area news media chased the story and I worked furiously to prepare my feature for *Diablo*'s April issue, Marino and I wondered if Butler and Wielsch would make bail.

Wielsch was the first to get out. His elderly father put up Wielsch's bond after a judge reduced the bail amount from $1 million to $400,000.

Butler had to stay in the slammer awhile longer. On March 3, I went to Butler's bail hearing in the Contra Costa courthouse in Martinez. The hearing had a circus feel, with dozens of reporters packing into the courtroom alongside Butler's family and friends.

I cruised through the crowd like an invisible man; no one knew that I was the one who had blown the whistle on Butler's dirty business. Later that month, they would know who I was, when the new issue of *Diablo* hit newsstands.

Defense attorney William Gagen made an appeal that the court reduce Butler's bail, providing a letter of reference from local police officer Don Lawson. Lawson had known Butler since high school, and was the arresting officer in a 2008 Dirty DUI sting of an aerospace engineer. There was also a local priest in attendance to support Butler's bail appeal.

A member of the Contra Costa District Attorney's Office, Jun Fernandez, argued that Butler's bail not be dropped from $900,000 because of all the criminal behavior being discovered about the private eye. There were the Dirty DUI arrests—which the public was hearing about for the first time—and there was also a truly disturbing video of a setup in which Butler and his associates made an illegal arrest of a teenager who had been lured into bringing drugs to a meeting with a pair of pretty decoys. The boy was ordered from a car at gunpoint, bound in plastic flex-cuffs, and read his Miranda rights. Then Butler and Wielsch (who "supervised" the takedown) took the boy back to his home in the suburbs, searched his house, and stole his drugs.

After hearing all of that, Judge Nancy Davis Stark rejected the request that Butler's bail be lowered. I saw Butler's wife, Rose, break down in tears at the decision, and on my way out of the courtroom, I held the door open for the elderly priest who was there to support Butler.

"Thank you, my boy," the priest said to me as he walked through the door. "I can't believe they did not lower the bail."

"Yeah, that's a shame," I replied. As the priest passed by, I tried to get a closer look at his collar, and wondered, Was he was truly a man of God, or just an actor in a rented priest's costume?

Outside the courtroom, I called Carl Marino on my cell phone to let him know that Butler's bail reduction had been denied. Marino sounded relieved at the news and wanted to hear all the details about the court appearance.

I tried to recap as much as I could, and then described the video that the DA had cited showing Butler conducting a false arrest on a teenager.

"Oh, I gave them that video," Marino said proudly. "I made sure to keep my original copy. Do you want to see it?"

"Hell yes, I want to see it," I replied, and made plans to visit Marino's apartment again the next morning to watch Chris Butler in action.

I arrived in the Marina District just after 9 AM on Friday, March 4. Marino, wearing baggy basketball shorts and a blue gym shirt, let me into his apartment.

Marino had a DVD copy of the teen drug dealer takedown that had been discussed in court the day before. Butler had made a copy for him following the event, which took place in early February 2009, just a few weeks after Marino had moved from New York to California. The obscenely illegal operation was one of Marino's first assignments at Butler & Associates.

The Candyman Case started when a suburban mom came to his office and told Butler she was worried that her nineteen-year-old son spent too much time smoking weed with his friends at a local junior college. The mom feared her son wasn't just smoking the odd joint but selling narcotics to his friends. Terrified that her idiot teen would get caught, get arrested, and ruin his life, the mom turned to Butler for help.

Butler told the mom not to worry, and explained that he had a colleague who happened to run the Central Contra Costa Narcotics Enforcement Team. Butler said that he and his law enforcement colleague, CNET commander Norm Wielsch, could teach the teen a lesson he would never forget by slapping his wrists for selling illegal drugs, without making him face any real consequences. If the Candyman took the bait, Butler and his team would stage a phony drug raid and slap some flex-cuffs on him, which presumably would terrify the kid back onto the straight and narrow forever. Butler convinced the mom that Wielsch and Butler's team of bandits would perform a fake arrest—at which point the teenager would throw his hands up in the air, shit his pants, and promise never to sell drugs again.

The mom, believing the operation would be legal and supervised by CNET, gave Butler $3,500 and her permission to do his worst. Operation Candyman was a go.

For the "scared-straight sting" to work, all Butler had to do was trick a nineteen-year-old boy by enchanting him with a couple of sexy decoys. Stage one of the sting involved the mom sending the Candyman to the grocery store to purchase some poultry, where he happened to run into two beautiful young women in the chicken aisle. They began a conversation with the kid, and asked for his phone number. Soon after that, the two decoys attended a party at the kid's house, where the teen and his friends pounded beers and smoked joints dipped in codeine cough syrup. Just kids having fun.

A few days later, the decoys met the Candyman again, this time for dinner at a Macaroni Grill restaurant. The girls cooed about an upcoming lingerie party with their hottest friends, and invited the Candyman to attend. Just after he RSVP'd, one of the decoys got a cell phone call with some bad news: The Ecstasy connection for the party had fallen through. The decoys asked the Candyman that age-old existential question: Without a bunch of Ecstasy, what's the point of having a party?

The Candyman, of course, saw this as his chance to be the decoys' knight in chemical armor. He quickly told his new best friends that he would have no problem securing thirty Ecstasy pills in time for the party. The decoys purred with delight.

The next stage of the sting played out on the video that Marino showed me. Butler made sure to videotape the entire operation with two cameras, so he could later edit the footage into his reality show sizzle reel.

During the first half hour of the video, Butler was at his badass best, running a tactical planning session in front of Wielsch, Marino, several female operatives, and a bread truck deliveryman who would be posing as an armed police officer for the evening.

Wearing a mesh Antioch Police tank top over a dark t-shirt, Butler stood in front of a whiteboard and spelled out the mission. Due to the size of the operation—and no doubt the knowledge that what was about to happen was totally illegal—Butler and Wielsch explained that the safest place to bust the Candyman was in the Contra Costa Narcotic Enforcement Team parking lot.

Of course, depriving a teenager of his civil rights in the parking lot of the area's undercover narcotic task force sounds outrageous. But when I later visited the parking lot where the fake bust went down, it made sense. Due to its high walls and lack of escape routes, the back of the CNET parking lot was a clandestine spot to corner the Candyman.

In the video, Butler explains that he, Marino, and Bread Truck Guy will be hiding in the bushes when the Candyman and the two decoys arrive in the parking lot. Another decoy—the Ecstasy buyer—would then drive into the lot to meet the three partygoers. When the Candyman handed over the drugs, Butler, Marino, and Bread Truck Guy would leap from the bushes with guns drawn. Norm Wielsch would drive up in Butler's Hummer, with strobe lights in full force. After that, Marino would pretend to arrest the three females and escort them away from the Candyman, leaving Butler and Wielsch free to fully fuck with the young man.

Of course, this all had to happen on the down-low.

"As soon as [the Candyman] is in the Hummer, we shut the lights down, because we don't want to make it look like there's a lot of police activity," Butler warned his associates. "Because right across the street is Pleasant Hill PD."

"What happens if the Pleasant Hill police department comes over?" asked one of the decoys, one with a conscience and some common sense.

"Norm deals with them," was Butler's immediate response. Wielsch provided more details.

"If that should happen, I'm just going to tell them that I'm basically training you guys on stops," Wielsch explained.

Then Butler described how his associates could avoid getting popped for the felony crime of pointing guns at a young man during the fake drug bust arrest.

"As soon as this kid is cuffed and in the Hummer, put the guns back in the holster and cover them up," Butler said to Marino and Bread Truck Guy. Butler also attempted to ease any anxieties in the room by explaining that Marino and Bread Truck Guy would use unloaded guns, and Wielsch would be the only one carrying a loaded weapon.

Another decoy asked an interesting question about the ethics of luring the Candyman into such a dangerous situation.

“The kid has a DUI on his record and a suspended license,” said the decoy. “He’s really not supposed to be driving and he’s embarrassed about it.”

Butler looked irritated by the decoy’s suggestion that the kid shouldn’t drive with a suspended license, and instructed her to do her best to make sure the Candyman drove his own car to the setup.

“Tell him you two are gonna get shitfaced on Smirnoff and you need him to drive you around,” Butler commanded. Both Butler and Wielsch reminded the women it should be easy to convince the Candyman to drive to the party if he had the impression he would be getting laid.

“Tell him you’ve got a California King mattress,” Wielsch suggested.

“Yeah, tell him you’ll all be sleeping in a California King and you guys will be on either side and he’ll be in the middle,” Butler snapped, enjoying a ripple of laughter from the decoys and police impersonators in the room. “Light his fuse!”

After the planning meeting, Butler and his team set up their gear in the CNET parking lot and filmed several practice runs of the Candyman takedown, so when it was time for the real fake arrest, the fake cops would be ready.

The takedown went down without a hitch. With the decoys in his car, the Candyman pulled his Cadillac into the parking lot right on schedule. The trio met up with the third decoy, who handed over $600 for a Baggie containing 30 Ecstasy pills.

Right on cue, fake cops Butler, Marino, and Bread Truck Guy came jumping out of the bushes with guns pointed at the Candyman, yelling, “Police department! Put your hands on the steering wheel! Slowly!”

Even though the video is shot at nighttime, it is clear that the scheme was an adrenaline thrill ride for Butler and Marino, as they pretended to be undercover drug cops in front of a real DOJ agent. I looked over at Marino, who was grinning as he watched his performance. He told me that it was his job to whisk the decoys away from the scene as the Candyman was being escorted to the Hummer by Butler.

“Get ready for some of the worst acting you’ve ever seen in your life,” Marino said, nodding at the TV, while one of the decoys sobbed ridiculously fake tears as she was detained by Fake Officer Marino. The other decoy screamed, “We didn’t do jack shit!”

The Candyman, who believed his evening's agenda had just been changed from slam-dunk three-way to trip-to-jail, was visibly terrified as Butler illegally read him his Miranda rights. Even so, the Candyman had enough composure to notice that the situation was weird. "Why are they videotaping?" he asked, nodding at the women operating cameras and filming the fiasco.

For the final stage of the sting, Butler and Wielsch did not take the teenager to jail but drove him back to his mom's house in the nearby town of Danville. That's where they played good cop (Wielsch) and bad cop (Butler) in front of the kid and his mother for a while. At the end of the charade, Wielsch "brokered a deal" with the mom, agreeing not to arrest her son that evening in exchange for her promise of cooperation with CNET. Butler pretended to be furious with Wielsch for letting the kid off the hook.

"I have years to file these charges on you," Butler warned the terrified teen.

Then Butler went upstairs and tossed the Candyman's room, finding Baggies filled with several thousand Xanax tablets, which he promptly stole along with the Ecstasy from the drug raid. (Butler later told Marino on one of the wire recordings that he sold the Ecstasy to an employee.)

The end of the video shows Butler back in his office, delightfully describing the look on the Candyman's face as he was terrorized and robbed by police-impersonating bandits. One of his employees brought a bottle of champagne so they could all have a toast to celebrate the successful sting.

After viewing the video, I told Marino that I was running late to get back to *Diablo*—which was true, as we were in full production crunch on the April issue. I was fascinated by what I had seen, but frankly, a bit too astonished to interview Marino about what on earth possessed him to take part in such a nasty scheme. At the very least, a guy who had been a police officer for seventeen years had to know that impersonating a cop—and pointing a gun at a kid while making a false arrest—was a no-no.

Much later, Marino would claim that he was not responsible for any crimes because Wielsch's authority nullified any conscience that he should have demonstrated.

After his arrest, Butler gave a statement to law enforcement saying that he did not realize the operation was illegal, and that Wielsch's participation had misguided his conscience from realizing it was a crime to impersonate a cop and to hire Marino and Bread Truck Guy to do the same.

Butler's statement, of course, was total bullshit. He knew the operation was illegal the whole time, as did Marino. In fact, Marino showed me an email sent by Butler a few weeks after the setup, in which Butler wrote: "If the 19-year-old ever finds out it was a sting, we're all in very big trouble."

The day Chris Butler was arrested, Contra Costa Sheriff's Deputy Steve Tanabe got a very uncomfortable feeling about the fact that the DOJ had been investigating his former "PI buddy" for the past several weeks. Tanabe and Butler had known each other since the mid-1990s, when they both worked for the Antioch Police Department. (Both left Antioch PD under less-than-stellar circumstances.)

Tanabe, who had been the arresting officer in the Dirty DUI arrests of January 9 and 14, realized that Butler's phone must have been tapped—which meant the heat could have been listening to any phone calls between Tanabe and Butler during the past few weeks.

Concerned that such phone conversations would not sound favorable, Tanabe called a reserve sheriff's deputy who had been on duty with him the evening on January 14 and asked if he could come over for a visit. The reserve deputy, a volunteer for the Contra Costa Sheriff's Office named William Howard, said OK.

Tanabe drove to Howard's house in an agitated state, and asked Howard if he had heard the news about Butler and Wielsch's arrest. Howard had no idea what Tanabe was talking about, and started getting nervous when Tanabe repeatedly insisted that there was nothing wrong with the DUI arrest of a certain Livermore winemaker that had been conducted on January 14.

Howard's discomfort grew exponentially when Tanabe went out to his car and came back with a long black bag. Howard later told investigators that he took the black bag and did not open it, in order to get Tanabe out of his house.

Turns out, Tanabe needed to stash an illegal AR-15 assault rifle, in case the cops were going to search his home.

After shooing Tanabe away, Howard had to figure why Tanabe was so insistent that there was nothing fishy about the January 14 arrest of the Livermore winemaker.

One week later, Howard reported the incident to a supervisor and was quickly interviewed by two investigators. Howard's statement led to an affidavit, a search warrant, and Steve Tanabe's arrest on March 4. Tanabe, then forty-seven, was charged with possession and transferring of an illegal assault rifle and conspiracy to possess and sell controlled substances (steroids).

Tanabe would later be prosecuted for taking a bribe for the Dirty DUIs of January 9 and 14, and for playing a role in another such setup in November 2010. Prosecutors alleged that Butler paid Tanabe with cocaine and one of the Glock 19s slated for product placement on *PI Moms*.

Tanabe adamantly denied being given any cocaine and claimed in court that the Glock that Butler gave him had no quid pro quo attached to it—his argument was that Butler was giving free guns out like candy and only attached the bribery allegation to shift the responsibility for the Dirty DUI setup over to the guy who was wearing a badge and making the arrest.

21
Butler Squeals

BUTLER'S FAMILY eventually gathered the 10 percent of his $900,000 bail, and pulled the PI out of the slammer to await his trial. During his time behind bars, Butler realized that he was going to be spending a good chunk of his life in prison for the crimes that Marino filmed him committing with Wielsch. Butler, with ample legal advice no doubt, quickly realized that the most productive way to start digging himself out of the cavernous hole he was in would be to start throwing every criminal conspirator under the bus, especially those wearing a badge.

On March 17, 2011—three days before my exposé in *Diablo* was published—Butler gave a lengthy interview to investigators from the DOJ and Contra Costa District Attorney's Office. The interview began with the DA making Butler and his attorney sign documents that said Butler was in no way being offered any kind of special treatment for giving the interview.

"I'm here because I want to tell the truth. I want to, if at all possible, assist the District Attorney in learning the truth," Butler said. "I'm hoping it will help my position. My case. I know that there's no guarantee that it will."

From there, they were off and running. One of the first things Butler presented in the interview was an award that was given to him by Norm

Wielsch around December 18, 2010, for all the work Butler did assisting CNET with cases. The award was presented just a few days after Butler gave Wielsch a split of the cash that Carl Marino had paid for the first pound of stolen marijuana.

"I was very touched by [the award]," Butler told investigators. "I was very happy to receive it and it struck a chord with me."

Butler went on to describe how he knew Wielsch at Antioch PD, where they both worked in the late 1980s and early '90s. Butler said that they weren't especially close friends at Antioch PD, because Butler tended to hang out with the guys who were more athletic than Wielsch.

It's clear that during their time at Antioch PD, Butler and Wielsch were headed in different directions, careerwise. From interviews I've had with various sources, Butler did not have a good reputation in Antioch. Not that he was evidence locker–thievin', meth-dealin' dirty—just more of a self-serving prick who liked to take as much credit as he could, whenever he could, and stab his coworkers in the back all the time.

Butler also had a reputation as a philanderer and fame whore. One former colleague told me that, in the late 1980s, Butler was infatuated with the Chicago Bears star quarterback Jim McMahon. Butler would cut his hair like McMahon and wear wraparound shades and a McMahon Bears jersey when off duty. Once, the source told me, Butler came into the Antioch PD locker room wearing the jersey before a shift, laughing and boasting that he had been at a local shopping mall signing autographs as Jim McMahon for naive young children.

Butler's time in Antioch ended badly, when he was reprimanded repeatedly for inappropriate behavior. By Butler's account, he was eventually given a choice of "quit or be fired," when he was involved in a high-speed pursuit that ended in a car crash. Butler said that he applied to be a cop in the Southern California community of Thousand Oaks, but was not hired because of his reputation in Antioch.

Wielsch, on the other hand, had a decent enough reputation as a young cop in Antioch. As he worked his way up through the ranks, he did well with narcotics investigations. In 1998, Wielsch applied to the state's Department of Justice and was hired to work for the Bureau of Narcotic Enforcement.

By 2002, Wielsch was running the Central Contra Costa County Narcotics Enforcement Team. Butler said he was very eager to help CNET whenever possible, and worked as a confidential informant on numerous drug and prostitution cases.

During the interview, Butler told investigators that, sometime in 2009, Wielsch gave him a bag of approximately four hundred Oxycontin pills to sell to one of his decoys. Butler said he thought the assignment was some kind of initiation test to get in tight with CNET, something he claimed he desperately wanted to do. Butler claimed that he did sell the pills to the decoy, but Wielsch was upset that he didn't sell them for more money.

Butler also said Wielsch wanted him to unload a huge cache of Ecstasy tablets, but he wasn't able to move those. Butler claimed that, sometime later, Wielsch complained that another police officer who worked with CNET, Lou Lombardi, had taken the Ecstasy stash and sold it, but hadn't given Wielsch a cut.

Butler told the investigators that he was terrified of Lou Lombardi. Butler claimed that when he got to know Lombardi through Wielsch, Lombardi was always making scary threats about having a confidential informant who would kill on command.

What Butler did not tell the investigators that day was that Scary Lou Lombardi played the cheating husband in the PI Moms story that ran on NBC's *Today* show. How terrified could Butler really be of a man who would help him set up Matt Lauer's crew?

Next on the laundry list of crime and corruption admissions was the marijuana that led to Butler's arrest. Butler claimed that Wielsch called him in October 2010 to say he had obtained multiple pounds of weed, and it was Butler's job to sell it. Even though this opportunity arose just a few days before Butler was scheduled to start filming *PI Moms*, he agreed to do his best to sell pot for the commander of CNET, and gave samples to three female decoys, to see if they would be interested. Butler claimed that Lombardi was also going to be giving samples to one of his confidential informants to try to sell, but that Lombardi's informant and Butler's three decoys all said that the weed was garbage. Unsmokable and certainly unsellable.

Butler choked up when he told the investigators about his next decision, which was a tipping point toward his spectacular downfall.

"It's just hard to talk about. Okay, so anyway, I got to Carl [Marino] and I ask Carl, 'Do you know anyone who smokes marijuana?'"

Butler paused to clear his throat and said, "I don't know if I'm getting emotional because of the betrayal on his part, or because it was just plain stupid for me to do it, but I asked Carl if he knew anyone who smoked marijuana, and he said, 'Yeah, I do.'"

Butler's account of what happened next was pretty close to what Marino had told the DOJ two months before: Butler showed Marino a box with about eight shrink-wrapped pounds of marijuana, said they came from Norm Wielsch, and invited Marino into a conspiracy to sell stolen narcotics.

Then, Butler told the investigators that Marino's goal was to get a role on the reality show, and that he had even threatened to blackmail Butler with the weed.

"[Marino] had told me out in the parking lot that if [Marino] didn't get on the show, he was going to, like, tell about Norm and his marijuana and go and talk to my clients about undercover stings and all of that stuff. So, I couldn't fire him," Butler told investigators. In a statement that Butler wrote, he claimed that Marino told him that Butler "had better figure out a way to include him in the show or he would make [Butler's] life 'a living hell.'"

Butler told investigators that he went to great lengths to get Marino a role on *PI Moms*, but any chance of that happening disappeared when Marino sabotaged one of the cases being filmed for the show.

"I loved Carl like a brother," Butler said. "I tried my hardest to get him on that show."

Butler kept talking for hours, emphasizing how loyal he had been to Marino and how dirty Steve Tanabe and Lou Lombardi were, and especially how corrupt Norm Wielsch was. Butler said that he didn't sell the drugs for the money, but because he wanted to help the Narcotics Enforcement Team.

"I just wanted to be around CNET. I thought CNET was the coolest thing," Butler told the investigators. "It's kind of like... God, how can I say this? It's like when you're around somebody that's famous, you know, or somebody that you want to be. You'll do anything for whatever they ask you to do. Even if you know it's morally wrong."

Butler, who was talking to career narcotics officers and district attorneys, knew he had overreached by speaking in second person and shifted gear back into first.

"I'm telling you how I would react," Butler said. "I did bodyguard assignments for celebrities and famous people, and if they had asked me, 'Hey, will you go purchase narcotics for me?' I probably would have done it. Just because I wanted them to be happy. You know? They were what I wanted to be. I wanted to be like them. I wanted to be, you know, rich and famous."

At that point in the interview, DOJ agent Dean Johnston called bullshit and reminded Butler that he had listened to all the wire recordings of Butler boasting to Marino about how much money they could make selling stolen drugs. So Butler didn't need to sprinkle "all I really wanted was to be a reality show celebrity who was helping CNET" fairy dust over his documented criminal activity.

Once Butler was arrested, I never had a chance to catch up with him again about the ride-along. I did see him in court a few times, where I would receive icy stares from Butler, his wife, Rose, and various other family members.

At one appearance, Butler's defense attorney saw me standing outside the federal courtroom. He approached me, extended a hand, and said, "Well, if it isn't the devil incarnate."

I was taken aback by the remark, to say the least.

"I'm the devil?" I asked.

"Those are not my words," said the attorney. Behind him were Butler and Butler's family, grouped in a small circle outside the courtroom. I assumed they were the ones comparing me to Lucifer for exposing Chris Butler as a criminal con man and ruining the reality show celebrity dream.

I soon found out that there was more to expose than the drug sales and the media setups. It's kind of a shame that Lifetime's cameras did not fully capture what was going on in Butler's world, because they would have had one hell of a reality show.

Turns out Butler also robbed prostitutes, posed as a porn producer, and even ran a brothel for a few months. Can you say sweeps week?

22
The Case of the Porn Princess

ALTHOUGH CNET'S FOCUS was on investigating narcotics trafficking, Norm Wielsch's crew also took down prostitutes in Contra Costa County from time to time.

Just like any community, Contra Costa has its share of brothels—from rub 'n' tug massage parlors to full-penetration whorehouses. Wielsch used Butler as a confidential informant from time to time, letting Butler go into a massage parlor to see if the services being offered went beyond legal limits.

On several occasions, Butler accompanied Wielsch on outright robberies of prostitutes. The scam worked like this: Butler would make an appointment for a massage from women advertising in the adult services section of Craigslist, then go knock on the door of a local hotel. When the women answered, Wielsch would barge in with his badge out and shake down the hookers for their cash, cell phones, and computers.

The robbery victims were Asian women without US work visas; sex slaves forced to live in the shadows of American suburbs. The cash these women earn for jacking off johns certainly doesn't fund a down payment on the American Dream—the money goes to pimps, who sneak these women into the country and shuttle them to shitty hotel rooms and strip mall massage parlors. Who knows what happened to the hookers when they had to report to their bosses that two men claiming to be cops robbed them of the day's income.

Wielsch also helped Butler with the PI's dirty business, when hookers were involved. Take, for example, the Case of Luscious A.

That one went down in June 2010, when a wealthy North Bay client met with Butler about setting up a North Bay-based prostitute who advertised services under the name Luscious A, a blonde siren with 36Cs. Her will-do spirit earned rave reviews on a prostitution website and numerous dates, including an all-expense-paid trip to New York with a well-to-do executive, much to the chagrin of his wife—Butler's client.

Butler devised a scheme to get Luscious A arrested, using the law enforcement resources of Contra Costa County's Narcotics Enforcement Team, led by commander Norm Wielsch. In late June 2010, Chris Butler and two employees made a dinner date with Luscious A at a San Francisco restaurant. Butler introduced himself as a successful producer of pornographic videos, and said he saw star potential in Luscious A.

Butler explained that the newest market in porn was shooting sex videos featuring extremely wealthy businessmen getting it on with porn stars, and that stars were paid extremely well for their performances—five figures per night, easily.

Luscious A took about two seconds to say, "I'm interested," and was paid $560 for her time at the dinner, ending the easiest date she ever had as a hooker. Butler's assistant kept in touch with Luscious A via email and proposed another meetup several days later, this time to take the merchandise for a test run. Luscious A was invited to come visit and play escort at the Walnut Creek Marriott Hotel, where he was staying in room 211.

Next door, in room 213, Chris Butler and CNET commander Wielsch had improvised a command center of video screens. One of Butler's PI Moms brought a pizza for the team to enjoy while they waited to watch Luscious A's life get turned upside down. Butler's case file gleefully records the sting minute-by-minute, complete with still photos from the surveillance cameras. Here's what went down:

1. Luscious A knocked on the door of room 211, came into the room, and sat next to Butler's male decoy on the bed. Luscious A then went to the nightstand and picked up an envelope containing $600.
2. Luscious A lit scented candles and went into the bathroom to change into lingerie and spiked heels. She came back to the bedroom and straddled the decoy, who was lying face down on the bed. Luscious A rolled him over, groped his oncoming hard-on, and started to peel a condom over his tumescence.
3. Wielsch, and several other officers from CNET, burst into the room and arrested Luscious A.

For Butler, the sting was a great success. He got to orchestrate and conduct a complicated operation, which worked perfectly. Butler also got to help CNET bring in a collar, which gave his broken inner cop a perverse surge of pride. And best of all, he was paid for his trouble by his client.

But for Luscious A, being set up by Chris Butler wasn't much fun. The twenty-three-year-old sex worker had been dodging an outstanding warrant for a probation violation, and when the CNET officers rushed into the room to arrest her, she let them know all about it.

"I told them, 'I want to make this easy on you and go easy on me…I have a warrant,'" Luscious A explained, three years after the incident.

Luscious A told me that she was flex-cuffed by the police officers while Chris Butler and his team revealed themselves from the control room to gloat about the setup. After being read her rights, Luscious A asked one of the police officers if she could put on the casual outfit and comfortable shoes she arrived in, but the officer refused her request.

"He said, 'No, you're wearing those [spiked heels],'" said Luscious A. She shuddered at the memory of her clumsy perp walk through the crowded lobby of the Walnut Creek Marriott.

The outstanding warrant for Luscious A simplified the paperwork for the arresting officers. Wielsch did not file new prostitution charges against Luscious A for the two-second rub 'n' tug she gave to the male decoy. He didn't need to—Luscious A's probation violation was enough to lock her up in the slammer, and Butler's client was content that her husband's favorite hooker had been busted. Win-win.

After his own arrest, I quizzed Norm Wielsch about the Luscious A incident during an interview in his attorney's office. Wielsch was noticeably confused when I brought it up.

"Wait, a minute, that was real...she really was a prostitute," Wielsch told me. "There was even a warrant out for her arrest."

I asked Wielsch about the propriety of using his using CNET resources to help Butler bust someone for the satisfaction of a rich client from a neighboring county, reminding Wielsch that Luscious A wasn't even working in his area. She was invited by Butler to come to Contra Costa County, and walk right into a setup—the reason the sting had to happen in Contra Costa County was that Butler needed Wielsch to make the arrest.

Wielsch nodded. "When I think about the crazy stuff Butler asked me to do, I can't believe what I went along with," he said. "Butler would explain some idea he had, and your first reaction would be, 'No, that's a terrible idea.' Then [Butler's] golden tongue would come out, and he would justify it, and you would drive home thinking, 'That was a really good idea.'"

Luscious A did not understand why she had been set up until I explained it to her in person. Her probation violation, and some undisclosed previous legal jeopardy, was serious enough to get Luscious A sent away for three years of incarceration. After being released from state prison, Luscious A agreed to meet me at a Starbucks in Vallejo. As I explained the setup, she reacted with a cocktail of confusion, anger, and sadness.

Luscious A told me that her son was three years old when Wielsch busted her. Now her son is almost seven, and still has no idea what made mommy go away for such a long time. Luscious A was particularly frustrated that she hadn't been able to figure out Butler's sting as it was happening—despite the red flags—a reaction I could very much relate to.

"When they first met me at that restaurant, they told me they were these high-roller porn producers. But they all ordered only salads," Luscious A said. "I should have known something was up with that."

According to Butler, the Asian hooker shakedowns also served as an entrepreneurial inspiration—he realized that he could open his own sensual-massage parlor, staff it with sexy decoys, and make some serious pimping money. Also according to Butler, the beauty of the business plan was that their brothel could never get busted—if anyone complained, Wielsch could provide protection with his CNET status, for a kickback.

Wielsch has always denied having any knowledge of or connection to any sensual-massage parlor. But there absolutely was such a business, and Butler oversaw its operations.

Sometime in 2009, Butler leased a business office in Pleasant Hill, located about four miles away from his Concord office, then spent about $2,300 at an IKEA store on furniture for the business, and put security cameras around the building.

Butler assigned one of his decoys—Madame DD, the woman who introduced Ryan Romano to Butler—to be in charge of managing the business and staffing it with sexy masseuses. Butler gave very specific instructions to Madame DD about how the masseuses were supposed to conduct themselves so as to avoid legal peril should an undercover cop happen to get through the force field that Wielsch could provide.

The parlor was to provide hand jobs only—masseuses were told they could never provide oral sex or intercourse, even if the clients offered to pay extra. Condoms were never to be kept on the premises, as they would be obvious evidence of full-service activity.

The problem with Butler's brothel was that it did not turn out to be the cash cow he had expected. Each masseuse was expected to pay $500 per week for the privilege of having a place to jack guys off, and Butler collected the cash every Friday. But the weekly envelope was always lighter than he expected and, after a few months, Butler said he realized he wasn't even clearing enough to pay the rent on the building.

When a neighboring business complained repeatedly that the business appeared to be a house of ill repute, Butler decided to pull the plug on the massage parlor. Just like his reality show, the brothel did not blossom into the booming enterprise that Butler had dreamed of.

"I really took it in the shorts on that one," Butler told investigators.

As soon as Butler was behind bars, I worked furiously to finish my story. I let the editor and publisher know that Carl Marino was Ronald Rutherford and that Marino was willing to go on the record about the ride-along. As for the role Marino played as a confidential informant, we would protect his identity by referring to Ronald Rutherford as a mysterious figure, a Deep Throat–style do-gooder who helped bring down the bad guys.

"This guy was a former cop in Rochester, New York. He's also a West Point grad and a Desert Storm veteran," I told the editor, vouching for Marino's credibility, based on the background Marino had provided.

Just before I finished writing the story, I invited Carl and Ilona to my house to have dinner and watch the Academy Awards. It was the only time that my wife, Tamara, met the Marinos in person.

As *The King's Speech* and Christian Bale won Oscars, Carl and Ilona and Tamara and I sat in our living room and talked about Butler and all the crazy experiences that Carl had been through during the past few weeks—wearing a wire and watching Butler, the King of Stings, get set up and taken down by the big guys.

Carl and I were excited to talk about the story, but Ilona was quiet for most of the evening. Tamara listened closely as Carl told tale after tale about Butler's dirty deeds. We got to the DUI setups, and Carl described how he lured the marks in under false pretenses, using the name "John Brownell" as his cover.

"Who is John Brownell?" I asked Carl. "Where does that name come from?"

"He was a kid I went to school with," said Marino, smiling out of the right side of his mouth. "I never really liked that kid very much."

Marino failed to mention the fact that "John Brownell" lured one DUI victim into thinking he was being interviewed for *Diablo* magazine, or that another DUI victim was led to believe that Brownell worked for a Bay Area–based production company called ArtistFilm. ArtistFilm was the first company to ever hire Marino as an actor—for *Sedona's Rule*, a tiny-budgeted thriller; Carl and Ilona met on the set of the film.

When I contacted Josh Gillick, the founder of ArtistFilm, to let him know that his business' identity was used as a false pretense for a Dirty DUI sting, the filmmaker was horrified to realize what Marino had done to an unsuspecting mark.

Before I learned of this behavior, and some other ugly truths, I saw Carl as a heroic figure in the story—the guy who stepped up and did the right thing. My wife, however, saw right through the good guy veneer that Marino was so proudly presenting. Toward the end of the evening, she asked the million-dollar question.

"So, Carl, why did you come to Pete for help?" Tamara asked, recognizing that of all the people to share top-secret information with, a journalist might want to make that information public, rather than to keep a lid on the scandal while the DOJ did its job.

Marino smiled confidently. "I didn't know anyone in the area, and I figured [Pete] might know someone who could be trusted. And he did."

Marino said that he sent the early Ronald Rutherford messages as a test, to see if I could pass his confidence tests. According to Marino, I proved myself trustworthy and that's why he asked me to help him get to law enforcement. At least, that's what Marino said on February 27, 2011—less than two weeks after Butler was arrested.

Marino's answer made me feel good. I felt a strong bond with his Ronald Rutherford persona. He was like "the Shadow" from the old radio mysteries, a good guy who helped the community though his covert takedowns of villainous criminals.

The Shadow never sought credit for his efforts. He busted the bad guys because it was the right thing to do.

PART FOUR

A BRIGHT WHITE SPOTLIGHT

23
Breaking the Inside Story

ON MARCH 20, *Diablo* published my article on the magazine's website. I did a long interview with an NBC news station just before the article ran. The Bay Area NBC affiliate promoted the story all weekend.

The cover of the April 2011 *Diablo* magazine showed Butler's face and had a grabber of a cover line: "Exclusive Report: The True Life Case of the Dirty P.I." A subhead read, "Chris Butler was ready for his reality show close-up, and then he made his big mistake: He asked *Diablo* to write about him."

I was proud of the story, as the ten thousand–word exposé gave our East Bay readership the inside scoop about how the incredible scandal was exposed. I credited Rutherford and Cindy Hall (who was identified by the alias Cortez, a handle Cindy had used in previous undercover investigations) as the heroes who deserved credit for doing the right thing and bringing down the bad guys.

I sent an advance copy of the article to a representative of the DOJ to read in advance of publication. I wanted to make sure the representative felt it was accurate and there was no information in the story that could jeopardize the case against Butler and Wielsch.

The day the article ran, I received an email from Kent Shaw. He wrote:

> I am the assistant chief of the DOJ, Bureau of Narcotic Enforcement, and I have been overseeing the investigation of Norman Wielsch and Chris Butler. I want to compliment you on this well-written story, but I especially want to compliment you for your tenacity in this matter and your professionalism. You did right the thing by facilitating our investigation even though you had the scoop on all your colleagues. Thank you.

I forwarded Shaw's message to Marino, thinking he would like to see that the DOJ had shown appreciation for my role in the investigation. Marino replied almost immediately.

> Wow . . . that is fantastic. The story is great. Ilona and I both read it. I still flinch a little reading the quotes attributed to me. Even though they are all true, knowing he is out there reading them also still scares me a little. As far as scooping your colleagues, the timing of everything favored you. It seemed as though it was fate and everything played out perfectly. It was a gamble that I had to take and I obviously picked the right person. Who knows what would have happened if I had gone a different route. Congrats again on the article.

Just before the *Diablo* story ran, I made sure to contact *People* magazine, the *Dr. Phil* show, and the *Today* show, as I wanted to let them know that the article was going to mention that they had all run positive PI Moms stories based on fraudulent cases. I received a "no comment" from *People*, and no response at all from *Today*. I spent a half hour on the phone with a representative from *Dr. Phil*, explaining what parts of the hour-long *PI Moms* episode were fake and how Butler and his minions set me up as well. I asked if I could get a quote from Dr. Phil himself about the situation. That call never came.

When the *Diablo* article came out, I received responses from some major media outlets dazzled by the story's twists and turns. One producer from a news magazine program called to ask some questions about my experiences reporting the story, and told me it would make a great subject for prime time, but was missing one crucial component: There was no homicide.

The producer asked if I would agree to be interviewed on camera, saying that when I found out that Butler had plans to set me up, I was certain he was going to try to kill me.

"No, I can't say that, because it's not true," I replied. "I was worried for sure, but I thought he might try to plant drugs on me or set me up in a compromising situation with one of his decoys. I didn't think I was going to hear a click and have the lights go out... so I can't say that now just to get on TV."

The producer sounded disappointed but promised to check in again after running the story by the network bigwigs. I never heard from the producer again. No murder, no story, I guess.

The same day, I received a call from a writer named Josh Bearman, who had contributed several stories to the acclaimed public radio program *This American Life*. Bearman told me he thought my story would make for an interesting episode of the show. The call was a great thrill for me—like so many fans of *This American Life*, I've found myself driving around in circles on Saturday mornings, riveted to the broadcast. In my opinion, Ira Glass' program represents the high bar in American media and journalistic storytelling, and to be considered for the show was an incredible honor.

I told Bearman that I would be delighted to be on the show and would do all I could to help him put the radio story together.

I also received calls and emails from people who claimed to have been wronged by Chris Butler. A woman who saw me on TV called repeatedly to say that Butler and his crew kept breaking into her house to steal the recordings taken by surveillance cameras that she kept around her house. Another woman claimed to have worked briefly for Butler, only to find out that her boss was burglarizing neighboring businesses. A guy called to let me know that the Concord police had inserted a chip into his neck, and monitored his every move. Yet another claimed that Wielsch and other CNET officers had tried to murder him on numerous occasions.

Some of the callers had legitimate experiences with Butler; many were wackos who craved attention or needed medication and counseling.

The most disturbing call came from another victim of Butler's: a former client who had hired Butler to help with a domestic issue. The client was actually the person who came up with the "concept" of the PI Moms, telling Butler that his staff of female investigators could help counsel women going through the stress of divorce and custody issues.

Not only did Butler allegedly steal the client's concept, he convinced this woman to invest in his company, promising riches and adventure. In federal court, Butler admitted that the client invested "somewhere in the neighborhood of $700,000" in his business, enough for Butler to buy his Hummer and tricked-out Mustang.

After a few phone calls with this client, I finally met her in an East Bay recreation area. The client was extremely thankful that I had exposed Butler as a criminal and con man, but was still convinced that he "had eyes on her at all times." When a man parked a pickup truck nearby, she pulled at my arm to walk the other way, claiming that the man was one of Butler's spies.

After chatting with the victim for an hour or so, and listening to her tales of Butler's manipulation and exploitation, I realized that there was nothing much I could do other than to tell her how sorry I was that she had been sucked into his world.

I drove away from the meeting feeling heartbroken over this woman's obviously disturbed state. She had been easy pickings for Mr. Cool, and even Butler's inevitable prison sentence wasn't going to bring her $700,000 back.

Not long after the *Diablo* article was published, Marino called me to say he had some good news about his acting career.

"I auditioned for a new show on Investigation Discovery called *Homicide Hunter: Lieutenant Joe Kenda*," Marino said. "I got the part—I play Lieutenant Joe Kenda! I'm going down to L.A. to start filming in April."

Marino told me that Joe Kenda was a retired homicide detective from Colorado Springs, Colorado, who had solved more than 350 murder cases during his storied career. The part sounded like a huge opportunity for Marino, and I offered congratulations. I was happy that Marino was getting such a big break in his acting career, especially after all he had just been through as an informant.

A few weeks later, I was in Los Angeles to talk to more sources who had worked for Butler. Since Marino was shooting *Homicide Hunter* nearby, I asked if I could stop by the set for a visit. Marino sent me the address of his shoot, an outdoor setup in Los Angeles' Griffith Park.

I found the location when I saw a police car with Colorado Springs markings. Marino, who was wearing a suit and a detective's badge, was waiting around between shots. The camera crew and set decorators were staging a gruesome murder scene nearby, and Marino was waiting for the call to come take his mark.

After catching up on some details about Butler and Wielsch's legal situations, I told Marino that I had received an email from an aspiring screenwriter who had read my story in *Diablo* and was interested in adapting the material into a screenplay. The writer saw my article as a modern-day *Chinatown*—high praise, of course, for a film noir geek like myself.

The most surprising part of the writer's pitch was that he claimed to know Rutherford's actual identity. The writer later told me that he had met Carl and Ilona Marino in a San Francisco bar, and that Carl claimed to be a retired police detective from New York who was working for a PI in the East Bay. When the writer read the *Diablo* article, he put two and two together and confirmed that Rutherford was Marino by making a call to the bar owner.

I told Marino I was concerned that someone was able to confirm his identity so easily, as Marino was still supposed to be a protected confidential informant for the eventual trials of Butler and Wielsch—it was probably something a bar owner in the Marina District did not need to know, let alone disclose to people calling there out of the blue.

I also told Marino that this was not the first person to reach out about pitching a movie based on the material. I had been contacted by several producers and aspiring screenwriters.

"I'm writing a book about all of this," I told Marino. "But if someone wants to turn the story into a movie, I'd love to work on it with you. I think it would be fun."

Marino stared at me with an odd and intense gaze, his eyes piercing and angry.

"I've been contacted also," Marino said, "by people who want to make a movie with me."

I wondered how movie producers would know to contact Marino. Maybe they all hung out in the same bar in San Francisco. I was getting the impression that he was letting the confidential part of his informant status slip.

I was also confused by Marino's angry vibe when I told him I was thinking of taking the story to Hollywood. All of our interactions to that point had been very friendly—and despite the fact that Marino had broken his promise of exclusivity, I still believed he was grateful for all the help I gave him in contacting law enforcement.

Hey man, remember me? I thought, as Marino continued to stare daggers. *I'm the guy who put you in touch with the cops when you were sitting on two pounds of stolen weed without a clue of who to call.*

The *Homicide Hunter* production crew called for Marino to return to a make-believe murder scene, so he could be filmed pretending to look for clues. Marino headed off for his close-up, leaving me standing by a phony Colorado Springs police car, wondering whatever happened to my old pal Ronald Rutherford.

In late April, I attended one of Butler's court appearances in Contra Costa County. Butler and Danville Sheriff's Deputy Steve Tanabe both pleaded not guilty to charges that they conspired to set up Dirty DUI arrests. Butler and I locked eyes as he was exiting the courtroom; he was the first to look away.

During the court appearance, Butler's attorney requested that Marino's status as a confidential informant be dropped, because Marino had been giving quotes to the *Contra Costa Times*, and because a picture of him on the ride-along had been shown in *Diablo*. The Contra Costa District Attorney agreed that Marino's confidential status was no longer necessary.

I quickly stepped outside the courtroom to call Marino and let him know that he was no longer a CI. Marino was surprised and disturbed by the news, and demanded to know why the DA would do such a thing. I explained that Butler's defense attorney had demonstrated that

Marino had been giving quotes to the local newspapers, which disqualified his confidential status.

Marino was furious, but because he had told me on several occasions that he had been granted immunity from prosecution by the Department of Justice, I did not think he should worry.

"Of course it won't be pleasant if the defense attorneys attack your character, but at the end of the day you've got immunity," I told Marino.

24
Mystery Date and Madame DD

AS EXCITING AS breaking the big Butler story had been, it was quickly time to put out the next issue of *Diablo*. As I worked on stories about Oakland-based *Good Morning America* correspondent Becky Worley and an Alameda resident who wrote the first *Friday the 13th* movie for the May issue, I had to do all my follow-up reporting about the Butler story in my spare time.

While pushing deadline on my May stories, I received a message from Ryan Romano, the woman who played the role of the tattooed mistress during my ride-along. I had reached out to her many times, but this was the first time she had responded to me. Romano sent me a note through Facebook, saying she had seen me on the news and had read the *Diablo* story.

"I figured now is a good time to talk, if it's not too late," she wrote.

I set up a meeting immediately and drove to Danville to meet Romano in her friend's clothing boutique. Romano apologized for dodging my contacts, explaining that she had been instructed by Butler not to talk to me.

"I had no idea that he was involved in all the stuff he was busted for," Romano told me. "And when I read your article, I realized that you got

Ryan Romano, aka "Mystery Date," ducks behind a copy of the April 2011 issue of *Diablo* magazine. Photo by Pete Crooks.

it exactly right—you were set up and then turned the tables on Butler to take him down. That's when I thought that I owed you a call."

Romano explained that she had been introduced to Butler by another decoy, Madame DD. Romano was a live-in nanny who worked in the gated community of Blackhawk, and her access to the privileged side of the gate was seen by Butler as an asset during a case he was working a few weeks previous to my ride-along.

Romano told me that Butler was investigating a divorced man who lived in the gated community. The man was having a big party at his house, and his ex-wife suspected that there was going to be copious cocaine use at the party. Butler's decoys were instructed to crash the party and get the man to give them cocaine—or, even better, do some cocaine in front of them.

So Romano, Madame DD, and a PI Mom went to the party and had no problem getting in. The decoys also had no problem meeting the man they were supposed to sting and asking if he had some blow. The mark's response surprised the trio.

"He said that he used to have a problem with cocaine, and he wasn't using it anymore because he was trying to be a good dad to his kids," Romano told me. "Which made us feel badly that we were there to get him in trouble."

Romano and Madame DD reported back to Butler that the alleged cokefest was a bust. I asked Romano what other cases she had worked for Butler, and she told me about a man in Sausalito. She and Madame DD had been assigned to stake out a breakfast restaurant the guy ate in every Saturday morning, hoping to reel him in with their sex appeal. The approach did not work, however, because the mark never showed up when Romano and Madame DD staked out the café.

Finally, I asked about my ride-along. Romano told me that Butler hired her to play mistress for the day and confirmed everything Carl Marino had told me about a staff meeting the day before the event, during which the PI Moms were instructed about how to string me along and get me to believe it was a real case.

Romano said she thought I was onto the hoax when I sat at the same table as she and her mark did while at the Rutherford Grill in Napa.

"I looked up, and you were right there. I thought you were just going to call us out," Romano told me. "I freaked out. When one of the PI Moms got up and left the table, I followed her into the bathroom and said, 'What the hell? The writer is sitting right at our table!' She told me, 'Don't worry, you're doing great—he's not going to suspect a thing.'"

I went back to my office and wrote an online follow-up story to my big exposé, and called it, "Meet Mystery Date." I knew that *Diablo*'s readers—who had reacted to the original story with unprecedented enthusiasm—would be interested in another angle and more lurid details.

I sent the story's URL link to Marino, assuming he would get a kick out of Romano's side of the story as well. However, Marino did not find the article amusing at all. He replied:

> I'm a little confused as to why you would give so much press to someone of such little importance and basically an afterthought. She is basically a whore that we used that could have been substituted with about a dozen different girls, and she

> actually didn't even do that good of a job. I think you are spending too much time on the likes of Romano and [Madame DD] and are missing the big picture. They are, and need to be shown as, small fish in all of this.

I was startled by Marino's response. Especially when he went on to make veiled threats about going to go on a media campaign with other journalists:

> This is on the cusp of me coming forward in the press with the biggest story and quotes of this entire saga so far (approved of by the DOJ). Possibly in the next week. This will make all of the other stories and players pall [*sic*] in comparison, and will possibly contradict other stories that are out there. I have not lied yet and will not. You, of anyone, know that I am not afraid of the truth, no matter how dirty it may be... I've been through too much in my past already.

Marino then claimed that he had planned to contact the Department of Justice on his own, without my assistance. Most bizarre was his claim that he had done a background check on me before reaching out, and that he factored my love of film noir and crime fiction into his decision to tell me about the drug activity:

> You have to realize and understand that I did my homework also and investigated you before I "blindly" put my trust in you. I was aware of (and appreciated) your love of film, noir, and the detective stories, which fit into the equation well, and I took a shot. I think you know that I'm not stupid.

Marino's main complaint seemed to be that, by writing the exposé in *Diablo*, I was stealing his spotlight and taking away the attention he deserved for his heroic actions as a confidential informant. He also suggested that he had been involved in even more criminal activity with Butler, as if that was some kind of badge of honor:

> Many people who are following your stories and who know the truth are worried that my interests are not being protected and that things are being misrepresented. They know what I gave to you. There is a much bigger story here, and I (who lived it for over two years) think you are approaching it from the wrong angle for personal reasons. I sometimes think you forget how close I

> was to Chris Butler and everything I was responsible for. I legitimately know him better than anyone, and know about every nasty thing he was involved in, most of which I was a key player.

As insulted as I was by Marino's response, his aggressive, accusatory tone was also hurtful. I considered him to be a friend, believing that we had been through a uniquely intense experience together. I updated the "Meet Mystery Date" story to make sure it was very clear that were it not for the information sent to me by Ronald Rutherford, I would not have realized that my ride-along had been a hoax. I went back and re-read my original *Diablo* story, which said the same thing.

I told Marino that I had duly noted all of his concerns and wanted him to receive credit for his valiant efforts as an informant.

I also told him that I was going to be doing an interview for *This American Life*. Marino had never heard of the show, so I told him about its acclaim. I let Marino know that, because his confidential status had been dropped, I could let the show's correspondent know that Ronald Rutherford was ready to go on the record—as long as the Department of Justice did not feel that his appearance could damage the cases against Butler and Wielsch.

Marino immediately said he wanted to be on *This American Life*.

As the Bay Area media chased every lurid thread of the Butler and Wielsch scandal—the Dirty DUIs, the stolen meth, the staged cases for the media—the unholy grail was the brothel. The allegations that the CNET commander was giving protection to Butler's illegal massage parlor while raiding the competition were just too outrageous.

The origins of the illegal massage parlor were all centered around one of Butler's decoys, the mysterious Madame DD. When Ryan Romano came clean about her role in the ride-along, she told me that she would reach out to Madame DD to see if she would meet with me. ("I wouldn't count on it," Romano told me. "She's pretty horrified by everything that's happened.")

To my surprise, I received a phone call from Madame DD at my work desk. She told me that she had been dodging phone calls from local TV and newspaper reporters, and was dreading the day that her name and role in the scandal was going to come out in the media.

As we chatted, I thought about the first conversation that I had had with Chris Butler, six months before. Butler had told me about Madame DD, and made it seem like no man could resist her sex appeal. Butler's description of Madame DD made me think of Linda Fiorentino in *The Last Seduction*, a femme fatale who could make a man suck on a spray can of poisonous mace and then ask for more. But talking to her on the phone did not give me that impression at all—she seemed like a nice person, who was horribly embarrassed by the situation. And she was more than a little frightened that Chris Butler was out on bail.

I told Madame DD that I wasn't in the kind of rush that the other reporters were in to put her name in the paper that day. I told her that I was working on a book, which would be published long after Butler was in prison, and convinced her to meet me in person, the next day, at a diner near her house in the East Bay city of Hayward.

I went to the meeting feeling a little nervous, wondering if she was going to flash me a coquettish wink or wiggle and nuke my marriage to hell. I drove to the diner straight from another TV interview about my reporting, and arrived half an hour before Madame DD and I were scheduled to meet. Madame DD showed up right on time, wearing a blue sweater and white slacks. She was certainly very pretty, in a girl-next-door way, but I had been overhyped by Butler's buildup of a be-all, end-all *femme fatale*. She recognized me from TV, approached, and shook my hand.

We found a booth in the diner and chatted over steak fries. I caught her up to speed with Butler and Wielsch's bail situations and court dates. I asked if she was worried about being prosecuted for anything that went down at the massage parlor and she shook her head no. She told me that she received a letter of immunity in exchange for her willingness to assist the investigation, and to testify when the time came.

"I wouldn't be surprised if that never happens," I told her. "Butler and Wielsch are buried under a mountain of evidence. They're on tape counting out ten thousand dollars cash, and selling a pound of crystal meth that came out of the evidence locker. I don't see how they're going to plead not guilty at the end of this."

"I hope so," Madame DD said.

I asked Madame DD to walk me through her time with Butler. She told me that she answered the infamous Craigslist decoy ad that Butler would post. Her first assignment was to go to a bar and flirt with a man Butler had identified as a wealthy CEO, the husband of a client.

"The man turned out to be Carl Marino. The whole thing was a trick. Or, they said it was a test, and I passed. After the 'test' was over, Carl and I went out to have a drink," Madame DD told me. "He told me that he used to be a cop in New York and he was there at Ground Zero on 9/11. He said the reason that he moved out to California was that he saw such horrible stuff on 9/11 that it really messed with his head."

Marino hadn't ever mentioned anything to me about being a first responder on 9/11, just that he had been a police officer in New York. I had the impression that he had been in cop in the Rochester area, hundreds of miles from Manhattan.

Madame DD said she distanced herself from Marino when he showed up, unannounced and uninvited, to see her at her night job bartending in San Francisco.

I asked Madame DD about the other decoy work she did for Butler. I was curious about the alleged cocaine party that she and Romano had been instructed to crash in the gated community of Blackhawk. Madame DD's story was the same as Romano's: They were supposed to see if the guy would use cocaine in front of them, and he didn't.

"He seemed like a really nice guy," Madame DD told me. "And then [Butler] said that he was going to plant some cocaine on him, and I thought, 'There's no way I'm doing that.'"

Madame DD explained that the man from the party had asked her to dinner and she had gone, but never told him that she had been hired by a private investigator who had been hired by the man's ex-wife.

Meanwhile, she lied to Butler, telling him that she never heard from the man again.

According to Madame DD, it wasn't the only example of her needing to offer subterfuge during one of Butler's attempted setups.

"Just before Chris got arrested, he had me staking out this breakfast restaurant in Sausalito," she told me. "The husband of one of his clients ate there every Saturday morning, and it was my job to see if he would flirt with me."

Madame DD described how she got up early for several Saturdays in a row to drive to the North Bay café to see if a man in his mid-fifties would put the moves on her.

"The guy didn't even look at me the whole time, and went out to his car to drive away," she said, blushing. "I ran out into the parking lot and literally knocked on his car window. He rolled down the window, and I said, 'I'm sorry to bother you, sir. I'm new to this area, and was supposed to work at a friend's massage studio, but that fell through. You wouldn't happen to know anyone who needs a masseuse in the area, would you?'"

The approach wasn't subtle, but it worked. (Not a huge surprise, the mark was the same guy who had been courting Luscious A, the prostitute from Butler's porn-producer sting.)

"He said, 'Do you want to come over to my office right now?'" she said. Madame DD declined, but told the mark she would love to get together for an appointment in the near future. They exchanged cell phone numbers, and Madame DD reported back to Butler that she had finally made contact.

"That's when Chris got really scary," Madame DD told me. "He kept talking about how he was going to make me have sex with [the unsuspecting man] and videotape it and then he would own him. I was very scared of Chris, and did not know what he would do if I backed out. But I wasn't going to be a part of blackmailing someone. I wouldn't do that to someone."

Just like in the Case of the Dad Who Wouldn't Do Cocaine, Madame DD wanted to have nothing to do with blackmail, although in the latter case, the mark wasn't such a sweetheart. Soon after giving her digits to the unsuspecting horndog, Madame DD started receiving a flurry of unwanted X-rated text messages.

"He'd text stuff like, 'I'm going to fuck you with my big donkey dick,'" said Madame DD, cringing. "I wouldn't reply. But then I had Chris calling and asking, 'When are you going to meet this guy?' I kept telling him, 'He hasn't returned my messages, so he must not be interested.'"

I sat there, listening and nodding, and thinking, *Little does Donkey Dick know, she did him the biggest favor of his life by not returning his texts.*

25

They're Not Booing, They're Yelling "Lou"

SAN RAMON POLICE CHIEF Scott Holder was as astonished as everyone else in the Bay Area law enforcement community by the news of Norm Wielsch's February 16 arrest. Holder, a longtime East Bay cop, worked closely with Wielsch as a CNET administrator, and told me he had no idea what Wielsch was up to until he got nabbed. Holder was fascinated by my article in *Diablo*. But it was the NBC11 news story that ran the same night we published the Chris Butler exposé that really caught his eye.

The NBC piece had used footage from Butler's *Today* show appearance as B-roll; the footage worked perfectly as a visual tour of what I experienced, because it had so closely mirrored my ride-along. What Holder noticed in the video was that the "cheating husband" in the *Today* story was San Ramon police officer and former member of CNET Louis "Lou" Lombardi. Lombardi had been Wielsch's second-in-command while working at CNET.

Butler had thrown Lombardi under the bus in his statements to the Contra Costa District Attorney and the Department of Justice, but his statements had to be taken with a grain of salt—Butler had clearly lied to *People, Dr. Phil, Today*, the *Contra Costa Times*, and *Diablo* to make himself look honorable enough to get a reality show, so it stood to reason that he would lie to help his case after his arrest as well.

Nonetheless, the *Today* show tape didn't lie. There was a face-blurred image of Louis Lombardi, on national TV, pretending to be a cheating husband to help Chris Butler get some free publicity. Not a cool thing for a cop to be doing, even off-duty.

Lombardi's association opened up a new tributary of investigation, which led to some unsettling discoveries. Lombardi was involved in stealing and selling drugs via a confidential informant in Arizona. Lombardi was also found to be robbing people who were served with a warrant: designer sunglasses, jewelry, and top-shelf liquor had gone missing on searches of homes that Lombardi conducted.

So why was Lombardi ripping off citizens on search warrants? Because he was a tough-guy cop who thought he could get away with it because he was the guy wearing a badge? Maybe.

More likely, however, was that Lombardi's moral compass had been obliterated by his addiction to narcotics. The husky officer had on-the-job injuries, which led to painkiller addictions, which led to harder stuff obtained through the same outlets that junkies go to: street slingers.

As a former CNET cop, Lombardi had more access to shady sources than the standard doper. According to a statement given to investigators, Lombardi went to one of his confidential informants to buy cocaine, then went home and blasted it up his nose.

At first, the CI thought the purchases were for official police business. The coke-selling snitch grew suspicious when Lombardi bought small amounts just before the weekend and never asked for information about where the blow came from. Lombardi's only request was that the CI made sure that it was good shit.

According to one statement, the CI told investigators that dealing with Lombardi felt like being in a movie about a bad cop.

Louis Lombardi, thirty-eight years of age, was arrested on May 4, 2011, and charged with a range of crimes, including grand theft and possession of stolen property, as well as accessory charges for aiding and abetting and conspiracy, and for possession of an illegal assault rifle.

This time around, I broke the story of Lombardi's arrest on *Diablo*'s website—although my scoop only lasted about two hours, at which point every Bay Area newspaper and TV station was all over it as well.

26
Let's Make a Federal Case over It

ON JUNE 3, 2011, I attended a press conference at the Contra Costa District Attorney's Office. District Attorney Mark Peterson announced that the US Attorney's Office and Federal Bureau of Investigation were taking over the investigation of Chris Butler, Norm Wielsch, Stephen Tanabe, and Louis Lombardi; all had pleaded not guilty to their respective charges in the scandal.

Peterson's statement in a press conference about the case discussed the scope of the investigation, which encompassed multiple police officers, multiple police agencies, and had crossed state lines.

"The 38 criminal charges filed to date include conspiracy, the sale and possession for sale of methamphetamine, illegal steroids, and marijuana," Peterson's statement said. "The charges also include possession of assault weapons, embezzlement, receipt of stolen property, and bribery. Some of these criminal activities were committed under the 'color of authority.'"

Citing budget concerns, the manpower that would be required to continue the investigation, and the possible conflicts of interest involved in the investigation of police officers in the jurisdiction of the Contra

Costa District Attorney, Peterson announced that he was requesting that the cases be handed over to federal authorities.

"After a full and careful consultation, and deliberation, it is my belief that the interests of the people of this county are best served if we enlist the resources of the United States Attorney's Office and the Federal Bureau of Investigation," Peterson's statement concluded. "They have kindly offered to provide that support and we have gratefully accepted that offer."

Once the feds took over the case, I stayed out of their way—the FBI and US Attorney have a reputation for not commenting on active cases, even to reporters who kick-started an investigation by bringing allegations of criminal activity to light.

Even years later, after all the criminal cases had been prosecuted, it was tough to get comments of substance. I sent questions about Butler, Wielsch, other police officers involved, and victims of Butler's setups to the FBI and the US Attorney's Office.

When I finally sat down for an interview with Assistant US Attorney Hartley West—who was able to spend a great deal more time interviewing Chris Butler than I was, following his arrest—she responded to many of my questions about criminals and victims and the prosecutorial process with, "I can't comment." Other questions were answered in very general terms, without specifics to the case.

One topic West could discuss, however, was the job that Kent Shaw, Dean Johnston, and the team from the California Department of Justice did on their investigation of Butler, Wielsch, and others, long before the feds took over.

"I think they did a great job," West told me. "A lot of people worked really, really hard at the outset of this, and then when our office took it over, a lot of those people worked very, very hard to bring us up to speed. I have nothing but praise for the work they did."

27
Face-to-Face with Norm Wielsch

EVEN AFTER THE CASE hit the news, my lingering questions were all about Wielsch: What made this career cop cross the line, betray his badge, and sell the same drugs that CNET had taken off the street? As the weeks went by following his arrest, I found myself thinking about Wielsch all the time.

In mid-June, I contacted Norm Wielsch's defense attorney, Michael Cardoza, requesting an interview. Cardoza returned my call and listened to my pitch. I told him that I wanted to hear Wielsch's side of the story—I had been pulled into this bizarre story by writing about Butler's reality show and ended up exposing one of the biggest police corruption scandals in the area's history.

Cardoza sighed, and told me that his client was extremely remorseful about his crimes. Cardoza told me that he would ask Wielsch if he wanted to talk to me.

To my surprise, Wielsch agreed to talk on the record.

On June 30, I met Norm and Diane Wielsch at Cardoza's office in Walnut Creek. Wielsch, who looks like the actor Ron Perlman with a goatee, handed me a piece of paper after shaking my hand. "As long as you put this in this story," Wielsch said, "I will tell you about what I did."

Wielsch handed me a typed statement that said, "I want to sincerely apologize to: All past and current CNET agents and commanders. All agencies participating in CNET. The California Department of Justice. All law enforcement officers. All citizens that trusted me with my position. I violated their trust. I'm sorry."

I looked over Wielsch's apology and asked him if he thought most people would read it and say, "Sure he's sorry—now that he's been caught."

Wielsch nodded and said, "Of course they will. But I need to say that, to get my apology out there, to start to heal myself. I need to let people know that I am not a monster."

I told Wielsch that printing the apology sounded reasonable, and we sat down and started the interview. Wielsch told me about growing up as an only child to his German immigrant parents, Ernie and Linda. The family settled in the East Bay and he spent much of his teen years racing cars and working in his father's auto shop. His dad, Ernie, expected his son to take over the shop after high school. But Norm had other plans. He wanted to be a cop.

"The whole police lifestyle was so intriguing to me—not just the cliché of helping people," Wielsch said. "In 1983, I put myself through the police reserve academy and became a police reserve at Pleasant Hill PD. I worked a couple of years as a police reserve and I just loved it."

Despite Norm's desire to be a cop, Ernie Wielsch gave his son a hard time about being a public servant.

"It broke my dad's heart," Wielsch told me, in one of many references regarding his father's opinion of him. I sensed that Ernie Wielsch's approval meant more to his son than anything in the world, but Norm was not able to connect to his dad on an emotional level.

"My father [was] a workaholic kind of guy," Wielsch said. "He always taught me that men are strong; men don't cry; men don't show their feelings."

Wielsch married his first wife, Lisa, right after high school. After working as a reserve officer for the Pleasant Hill Police Department, he was hired by Antioch PD in the mid-1980s, and Wielsch went to work as a full-time cop. During his first few years at the Antioch PD, Wielsch and his wife had two daughters. When their youngest daughter, Jennifer, was a newborn, she was diagnosed with aplastic anemia, a condition in which the bone marrow does not produce enough blood cells. Jennifer needed a bone marrow transplant. Wielsch's marrow was a match, so he became the donor.

"I think I handled Jennifer's illness a little better than Norm did," Lisa told me, when interviewed separately. Lisa has remained Wielsch's close friend despite their divorce after ten years of marriage. "I always tried to stay positive and hope she would be OK, but Norm feared the worst, and thought her illness was his fault. He was relieved that at least he could share his bone marrow; do something to help her."

As we discussed Wielsch's twenty-five years in law enforcement, there were clearly dramatic highs and lows—the lows often showed up in his personal life, with family stresses and Wielsch worrying that he was not making his father proud. The highs came from his cop career, as Wielsch did well at Antioch PD and then joined the California Department of Justice's Bureau of Narcotic Enforcement in 1998. Wielsch told me he saw drug enforcement as his calling.

"Early in my career, I saw that narcotics and alcohol are the root of all evil. They affect almost every crime," Wielsch said, adding that he wrote an instruction manual, *The Patrol Officer's Guide to Narcotics Enforcement*, to help cops deal with drug users and narcotics protocol. Wielsch performed well for the DOJ, and by 2002, he was running the CNET task force in Central Contra Costa County.

But as Wielsch's career flourished, he was plagued by injuries and physical disabilities. Around the time he started working for the DOJ, Wielsch started having symptoms of peripheral neuropathy, a progressively debilitating condition that destroys nerve endings in the extremities.

"I've had fifteen surgeries on my feet. [Doctors] had to remove all these bones from behind my toes," Wielsch said. "I would get infections and they would have to remove pieces of the bone. They did not have to give me [anesthesia] while operating, because I could not feel my feet."

Wielsch showed me his feet, which were grotesquely misshapen. Wielsch said that he hid his illness from his superiors in the DOJ, and

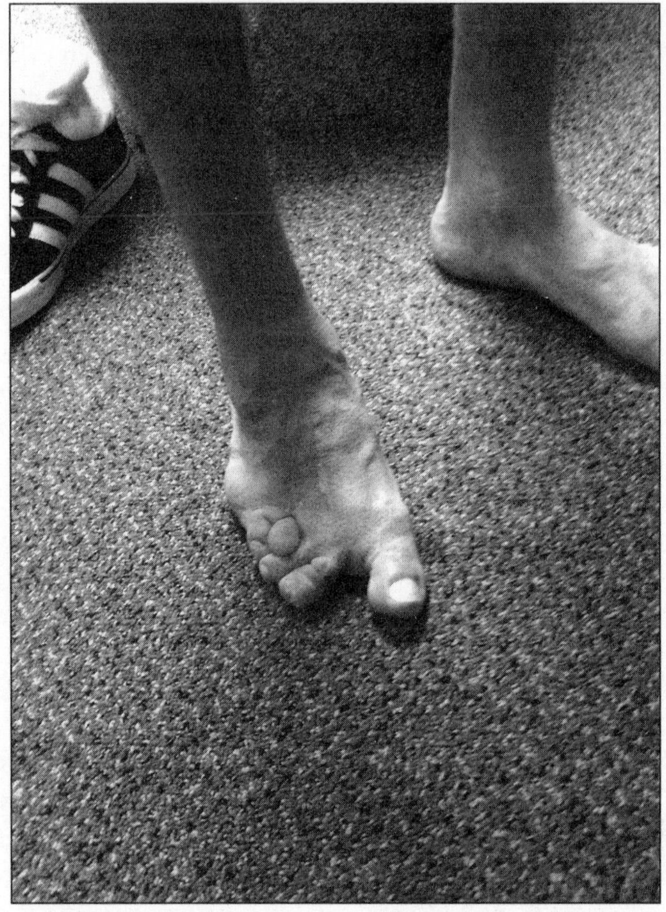

Norm Wielsch's feet, seen inside of his defense attorney's office. *Photo by Pete Crooks.*

also hid the fact that the neuropathy affected his ability to fire his gun. Wielsch told me that the realization that his neuropathy would eventually cause him to stop working in the field was so depressing that he became suicidal.

Wielsch described driving his work vehicle on the freeway at ninety miles per hour, explaining that he fantasized that a car crash might mean he could retire with an injury, rather than end up sitting at a desk.

Another side effect of Wielsch's neuropathy was impotence. Wielsch told me that Viagra and other erectile dysfunction medications were no help, and the only way he could get an erection was by self-injecting medicine into the base of his scrotum.

"I was not a complete man at work and even less of a man at home," Wielsch said.

Diane Wielsch chimed in to say that she had found her husband's syringes and erection blasters hidden in the refrigerator drawer where she kept her mini-Snickers and Milky Ways.

"I was so startled to find these needles, because no one uses that drawer but me," Diane told me. "I was afraid he was using hard drugs. He explained what they were, but looking back, I realize he was secretly crying out for help. Because there were a million places he could have hidden the needles, where I never would have known."

Eventually, Wielsch's neuropathy became so disabling that he decided to retire. Then, his father—who had grown to like the fact that his son held such a powerful position—shot that plan down.

"My father told me 'No, that's stupid. You're only fifty years old, what do you expect to do?'" Wielsch said, shrugging.

During all of this, Wielsch was in contact with his former Antioch PD colleague, Chris Butler. Despite the fact that Butler's and Wielsch's career paths had gone in opposite directions, the two had remained friends. When Butler started speaking about reality shows and sexy decoys, Wielsch was impressed. Or, at least, he was distracted from his depression.

It's my opinion that Butler's bullshit world of fancy cars and sexy decoys was a kind of virtual Viagra to Wielsch, a fantasyland where powerful cops made women's panties melt.

I asked Wielsch about the drug dealing. He told me it all started with a marijuana seizure in the fall of 2010, which contradicted Butler's claim that Wielsch had first given him seized Oxycontin pills and Ecstasy tablets to sell. (In reference to selling stolen drugs, it was Butler who was heard on a wire recording, telling Marino, "[Norm] is nervous. He's never done anything like this before.") Wielsch claimed that the drug-selling conspiracy began in November 2010, during the first month of production for *PI Moms*.

Wielsch said Butler told him that the much-anticipated show was ruining his real business by sucking up all the time that he would normally need to take actual cases. According to Wielsch, Butler convinced him to hand over about ten pounds of weed that CNET had confiscated from a shipping store. Since the drugs were intercepted but not tied to an arrest, the marijuana was going to be scheduled for destruction. Butler, who Wielsch said had previously sought his consult about how to legally open and operate a grow operation to harvest medical marijuana, asked Wielsch if they could try to sell the pot instead of destroying it.

"My right and wrong switch just didn't work anymore," Wielsch said. "I wish I could say he conned me, but I can't, because I made my own decisions. I wish I could just tell you I was greedy and I did it for the extra money. But that's not it. I don't know why I did it."

I believed that Butler got a thrill from his connection to Wielsch, and had no moral dilemma with selling stolen drugs. But for Wielsch to suggest that Butler smooth-talked him into selling marijuana, independent of any other corruption, simply wasn't true. Wielsch had also given a sample of the dope to his former CNET colleague, Lou Lombardi, to sell.

"Lou took out about an ounce, and he said that he was going to show it to one of his informants to look at [and judge its quality]—to see if his guy could sell it," Wielsch admitted.

Wielsch said he agreed to split whatever money Butler could get for the pot. And in the middle of December, Carl Marino gave Butler around $1,200 for the first pound of weed, and the Butler-Wielsch pot business was off and running. By late January 2011, Marino was in touch with the DOJ while telling Butler "his guy" loved the garbage weed and wanted more, more, more. "Also, what about those steroids and that C-4 you mentioned? My guy wants those as well."

"Chris would say, 'The guy's got cash, I've never seen so much cash in my life. Don't worry, I'll take care of everything,'" Wielsch said.

Wielsch said that when he told Butler about the meth cache, Butler was very excited. "Chris was rushing me and rushing me. But, you just don't go in and take it. There's a process. You have to get court orders and contact the sheriff's department. Chris would get mad [that it wasn't happening fast enough]. I take my dad to Cache Creek every couple of months, and he plays on the nickel machines. I was at Cache Creek and Chris called me twice to see what was going on with the meth. I said, 'Chris, I'm with my dad... I can't right now.'"

Wielsch said Butler's arm-twisting didn't take long.

"A few days later, I wrote a court order and had it signed by a judge," Wielsch admitted. "And then I picked a day [Tuesday, February 15] where the whole CNET team was out on a training exercise. I did not know that [DOJ investigators] were following by plane and watching the whole thing.

"When I went to get the evidence at the sheriff's department. I took Chris with me. We took evidence that was ready to be destroyed," Wielsch continued. "Instead of dumping it where I should have dumped it, we kept it. We kept the steroids and the meth; we dumped the other stuff."

I asked how the meth evidence had been seized on the street, originally.

"It was from a case where we did an undercover buy," Wielsch said. "The guy we purchased it from ended up becoming an informant. We did not charge that case. The guy had fulfilled his obligation in the informant arena, and so that meth was ready to be destroyed."

I asked what happened to the cases against the drug dealers who had first sold the pound of meth that Wielsch and Butler had tried to recycle back into the black market.

"The cases [on those arrests made from tips from the informant] were pending at the time of my arrest," said Wielsch. "I do not know what has happened to them since."

I spent hours interviewing Wielsch that day, and set up a second interview a few weeks later with Josh Bearman for *This American Life*.

By the time we were done with both interviews, I found Wielsch's story to be more tragic than sinister. He seemed like a broken man, who started out as a good cop and went dirty in the twilight of his career.

Both Wielsch and his wife told me that one of the reasons they agreed to the interview was to spread the word about the incredible pressure that law enforcement faces, and that there are not appropriate resources for stressed-out cops to get help. Which, true or not, does not excuse any of Wielsch's crimes.

I did hit a wall when Wielsch started to complain about how much jail time he was looking at, and compared his crimes to other police-corruption cases in the Bay Area. He told me that the US Attorney was asking him to plea to sixteen years in federal prison.

"There was a cop in San Jose who molested kids, and he only got three years," Wielsch said. "I didn't do anything like that. I didn't kill anyone."

I stared at Wielsch for a few seconds and said, "Norm, it doesn't matter what someone in San Jose did. You were trusted by this community to get drugs off the street, and you took a pound of crystal meth out of the evidence locker and went out and sold it. Meth that had been taken off the street—you put it right back on the street. That's what you did."

Wielsch stared at me and his eyes filled with tears. His whole body began to shake.

"I know, I can't even reconcile it in my mind. There is no way to ever justify what I did," he said, sobbing. "I did it, I regret it, and I don't know why I ever did something so stupid. I gave up a $100,000-a-year job for what amounted to about twelve thousand dollars. I'll plead guilty when the time comes."

For the most part, I believed that Wielsch was straight with me during the interviews. There was one exception: In both of my interviews with Wielsch, the former CNET commander adamantly denied having any involvement with the massage business.

Wielsch said that the first he heard about it was when a neighboring businessman complained to the Pleasant Hill police that the salon appeared to be a house of prostitution. Wielsch said one the CNET officers looked up the business license and saw Butler's name, so Wielsch gave the PI a call. Wielsch said Butler claimed the business was an auxiliary office to conduct decoy interviews and PI business from, and then he emptied the place out "a week-and-a-half to two weeks later."

Wielsch did admit that, just days before his arrest, he called Madame DD to warn her that CNET was about to start a series of raids on massage parlors in the Tri-Valley.

"I did call her with my own phone," Wielsch told me. "It was the wrong thing to do—but she was a nice person, and if she was doing something wrong, I didn't want her to get in trouble."

Wielsch had arrested Madame DD once before, when he raided another sensual-massage parlor in the area. Madame DD answered Butler's Craigslist decoy ad soon after that, and let Butler know that she had a recent arrest on her record. When Butler realized that it was Wielsch who had made the arrest, the PI went to buy furniture at IKEA with which to open an illicit massage parlor, and put Madame DD in charge of managing the place.

"I only dealt with Chris about the salon," Madame DD told me. "He had me refer to Norm as 'Ed,' and tell the other girls working there that a guy named 'Ed' was protecting us."

After Madame DD told Butler that Wielsch had arrested her for giving sensual massages, Butler kept insisting that she would need to "be nice to Norm" and "finish that massage someday." Because Wielsch had helped Madame DD get her charges reduced from solicitation to disturbing the peace, she believed that Wielsch had, in fact, done her favor, and she would need to return the favor behind closed doors.

A date was coordinated for Wielsch to meet Madame DD and another woman at an East Bay hotel for an evening of three-way fun. According to Madame DD, Butler was very aggressive about setting the date up.

"Chris said, 'This is your chance to pay Norm back for everything he did for you,'" Madame DD told me.

By all accounts, the date began like something out of a *Penthouse Forum* letter, with Madame DD and the other masseuse undressing in front of Wielsch. But Wielsch's impotence cut the party short. The threesome shifted gears and watched a movie on television.

Wielsch's eyes bugged when I told him that I knew about his secret three-way with two of Butler's masseuses and admitted that the date did occur.

"I thought that maybe these two sexy girls could make me feel like a man," Wielsch said sheepishly. "I was so embarrassed that night."

Madame DD told me that Wielsch was very shy throughout the experience, and told her repeatedly that she did not need to be there on his account. It was Butler who insisted that she give Norm a good time. But, during the evening, Madame DD said she mentioned the code name "Ed" to Norm, in reference to the person who was protecting the massage parlor from getting busted.

"Norm said, 'You don't need to call me 'Ed,'" Madame DD told me. "And I knew that he knew about [the massage parlor]."

28
Summer of Carl

I SPENT THE SUMMER OF 2011 in close contact with Carl Marino. We would talk almost daily about the proceeding prosecutions of Butler, Wielsch, Tanabe, and Lombardi, the reporting that Josh Bearman was doing for *This American Life*, and my plans to write a book that would tell the inside story about Chris Butler's reality show house of cards getting knocked down.

The more I discussed the book, the more Marino wanted to be a part of it. My idea was to pull back the curtain on Butler's world: the stings, the setups, and the quest for fame that led to the production of a Lifetime reality show. Then I would tell the inside story of the DOJ's investigation, which I had not been able to share in my original article for *Diablo*, due to Marino's protected confidential status.

Marino insisted that the narrative should be told from his point of view. ("This is a fantastic, tragic, awesome, horrible story, that needs to be told. It needs to be told the right and most interesting way," he told me.) I didn't entirely disagree; Marino had been extremely close to Butler, so his perspective made a great entry point to Butler's quest for his fifteen minutes.

But Marino took offense at my wanting to include peripheral characters, such as Ryan Romano and Madame DD or the retired FBI agents whose careers and reputations Butler had exploited to build up his own reputation.

The more time I spent with Marino, the more I realized that we had much different ethical compositions.

At one point Marino and I met in a Berkeley cocktail lounge to discuss outlining a book proposal. When Marino arrived to the meeting, he gave me an ear-to-ear grin.

"I have a gift for you," he told me.

Marino handed me a pen. It was a symbolic present, a tool to start writing a bestseller with. I took the pen and looked at it closely. It was a heavy, quality ballpoint, with small, all-caps letters printed on the side that read: BUTLER & ASSOC. INVESTIGATIONS.

I feigned excitement. "Thanks, man!"

Marino beamed. "I took that from Chris' Mustang the day of your ride-along," he told me.

Well, that's something to be proud of, I thought. *Here's a stolen pen from that day I helped set you up. A small token to remember how we met.*

"I took another one that works a little better," added Marino. "I'm keeping that one for myself."

You do that.

During that summer, I also took Marino to three Oakland A's games to talk about the story. (I've always felt that a baseball game is a good place for a long chat, and have taken other interview subjects to games before.)

During the third game, Marino told me about the "decoy test" scam that he and Butler would run on young women who answered the Butler & Associates Craigslist ad.

The sting was pretty simple. Young women would come in and meet with Butler for a preliminary interview, and if they possessed the right qualities of attractiveness and naivety, Butler would tell them he had a case to give them: A make-believe client was concerned that her husband was cheating, for example, and had hired Butler to find out for sure.

Butler would show the young woman a photo of Marino and explain that he was a rich CEO who always hung out at a certain bar at a certain time. He would instruct the decoy to approach Marino in the bar and start flirting.

Butler would tell the first-time decoy that the point of the assignment was to see how far this cheating, rich, handsome CEO would go on a bar hookup. Especially after doing some tequila shots.

"Don't worry, I'll be there observing and filming," Butler would tell the decoy, assuring her that she would not be taken advantage of.

I asked Marino if Butler told him the decoy tests were really just a way to take advantage of young women. Marino replied that at first he thought the tests were legitimate PI training, but after four or five experiences, he started to realize that Butler was really just exploiting young women. Wink.

For his part in the scam, Marino didn't really seem to mind fooling them into thinking he was a rich, horny CEO. "Hey, I was a single guy who had just moved out to California," he told me, cocking his side-grin.

I felt a hot tickle of vomit in the back of my throat as I contemplated Butler and Marino, two men in their forties, going to such great lengths to hook up with very young women. Marino described the decoy test as a sicko three-way, with Marino getting the physical action while Butler played voyeur puppet master, recording the setup with a hidden camera.

"Did you tell Ilona about these decoy tests?" I asked Marino, wondering what his wife was going to think when she read this lurid tell-all section of the book.

"I told her that there were some things that she wasn't going to like reading," Marino replied.

Marino described the most elaborate decoy test that he and Butler conducted. There were three decoys who had come in for interviews during the same week. The first two hotties were best friends who came in together, and would be "assigned" to hook up with Marino. The third would be Butler's plaything.

Butler told all three decoys that Marino was a hotshot Silicon Valley millionaire who frequently dined in a restaurant located in the same strip mall as a rent-by-the-hour hot tub business. Of course, the best friend decoys had no problem "picking up" their CEO mark, and the sting was off and running.

"We had some drinks in the restaurant, and then I said, 'Hey, I like to go to soak in the tubs in this mall—you guys up for it?'" Marino told me. "Once we got to the hot tubs, I had two girls all over me, and things quickly got sexual."

It wasn't enough for Marino to proudly describe his virile performance in the three-way. He had to deride Butler as well.

"I look over and see Chris' flabby naked ass in the shower area," Marino said, laughing. "He's groping at [his decoy] and whispering, 'Come on, we have to make this look real!'"

The scenario Marino described was so date-rape ugly that I started to feel woozy; the afternoon sun was baking my bald spot, and I thought I might puke onto the back of one of the Oakland Coliseum's plastic seats.

I turned to Marino and told him how I felt about the decoy tests and their place in the book.

"Carl, obviously there are guys who lie to women to get them into bed. But this—you pretending to be a CEO, and Butler videotaping the setup—it's above and beyond," I said to Marino. "If you want to come across as a good guy in this book you need to either apologize for those decoy tests or not tell those stories."

Marino stared at me icily.

"I don't think that any female readers are going to think you're a hero after reading about you tricking young women and then having sex with them," I said, wondering if the decoy tests could legally be defined as sexual assaults. "Even when they get to the part about you wearing a wire to help bust a dirty cop."

Marino looked very irritated that I missed the entire point of his story, which was, apparently, to boast about how much pussy he was getting while running scams with Butler.

I would later discover that, during an elaborately constructed decoy test, Marino had hooked up with a nineteen-year-old stripper at one of Butler's setup parties. According to both Carl and Ilona Marino's Facebook timelines, this hookup took place exactly two weeks after the "Real Mr. and Mrs. Smith" got engaged.

The Case of the San Fernando Valley Hot Tub Party and Decoy Test is a perfect example of the kind of planning and dedication Chris Butler put into manipulating and exploiting people, just to be able to do it.

Phase One of the decoy test occurred in late December 2009. After placing a decoy recruitment ad on Craigslist Los Angeles, Butler rented

Carl Marino frolics with a nineteen-year-old woman in a hot tub during one of the infamous "decoy stings."

a business suite at a Southern California hotel, drove to the Valley, and spent a day interviewing about twenty women. Butler told the candidates that he was working with California's Department of Justice on an upcoming narcotics investigation.

Butler made sure to get head shots of the top candidates and prepared a document that he distributed to Wielsch, Marino, and a friend who worked in Contra Costa County's probation office.

Some of Butler's notes on the prospective decoys included: "She is a tad bit heavy, but she has a tremendous fun, party attitude"; "A 19-year old who strips at Cheetahs in Hollywood full-time . . . wants to be assigned to interact with the drug dealer character"; and, "If we asked her to jump in the pool or hot tub naked and stay that way for the entire evening, she would. Hell, if I asked her to blow me during the interview, she would have."

On January 14, 2010, Butler invited the hottest and most naive Craigslist candidates to a hot tub party at his brother's house in the

San Fernando Valley. Butler instructed the Craigslist decoys to act super horny and get into the hot tub with some high-level cocaine dealers who were coming to the party. Norm Wielsch attended, as did a number of cast members of *PI Moms*.

Another of Butler's employees, who was writing a book about her year as an apprentice investigator, believed that the situation was a real investigation and intended to write about it. The case certainly appeared authentic when Wielsch introduced himself as a DOJ agent to Butler's staff and the unsuspecting Craigslist recruits, and gave a briefing about how the bullshit operation would go down.

Before long, Marino arrived at the party with two friends he had met on the show *Trauma*, pretending to be hipster cocaine traffickers. Butler ordered pizzas, because the only thing coke dealers love more than loose women in a hot tub is pizza.

Butler's cub reporter introduced herself to *Trauma* Extra #1, an actor who, later that year, would be a groomsman in Carl and Ilona Marino's wedding. *Trauma* Extra #2 found himself being courted by Sharon Taylor; she of many a cheating-husband sting. The Cheetahs stripper made a beeline for Marino.

For the next few hours, those three women hooked up with the *Trauma* Extras and Marino in the pool and hot tub.

"I definitely thought it was a real case, and I thought it was going to be a good chapter in the book," the writer told me. "I have this very clear memory of Chris Butler kind of hanging around the hot tub, wearing a creepy smile while he watched me make out with this guy."

The writer wasn't the only person being deceived that night. I interviewed both *Trauma* extras about their role in the sting, long after Butler and Wielsch were arrested. Both told me that they had no idea there was a DOJ agent present; and both said they were recruited by Marino, who assured them the decoy test was standard operating procedure for the PI office.

"I figured Carl, who told me he was a former cop, was being straight with me," *Trauma* Extra #1 told me. *Trauma* Extra #1 had no idea that the woman he kissed in the hot tub was a writer, and that the experience was intended to be reported in a book.

As for the nineteen-year-old Cheetahs stripper who frolicked all night with Marino, then forty-one years old, I've never been able to track her down. According to Marino, after the party wound down, he drove the young woman back to her apartment in Hollywood in Butler's leased Mercedes for more fun.

"Carl came back to the hotel room we were staying at the next morning, bragging about the night he spent with that girl," *Trauma* Extra #1 told me.

Marino told me the same story, in graphic detail, during one of our baseball game conversations. "Her apartment was just as dirty and disgusting as you would expect a stripper's place to be," Marino recalled, flashing a particularly gross side-grin.

Throughout late July and August, I helped Josh Bearman with the reporting for the story he was preparing for *This American Life*. I made several trips to the KQED FM radio station in San Francisco to record hours of interviews, and I drove Cindy Hall to a recording session on the UC Berkeley campus.

Marino also went into the KQED station to tell his side of the story on Ira Glass' beloved program. In the meantime, Marino and I continued to discuss a book collaboration. I had my fingers crossed that the issues I was having with Marino's self-centered storytelling ideas would work themselves out.

In late August, I took a trip to the island of Molokai, as I wanted to write a travel story about the one Hawaiian island that wasn't packed with hotel high-rises, golf courses, and ABC stores. After checking into Molokai's one hotel—a beach bungalow resort that would be right at home in an early Elvis movie—I checked my work email and found that I had been contacted by a representative of the F/X television network, inquiring about the availability of story rights for my exposé of Chris Butler and the PI Moms.

I had been contacted by several producers and screenwriters at this point, and had every intention of seeing if there would be a Hollywood ending to my take on Butler's weird world. It might make a nifty twist at the end of the *This American Life* episode; something like, "Chris Butler's story might still end up on cable TV, just not the way he thought it would."

Author Pete Crooks recording for *This American Life. Photo by Pete Crooks.*

I sent Bearman a note about the F/X contact and received an immediate response. Bearman wanted to speak with me about film rights, and said that *This American Life* was already interested in exploring the possibility of developing the story into a feature film. Bearman let me know that many of the magazine articles and radio stories he had recorded had been optioned by Hollywood for film and TV development. In fact, one big piece he wrote for *Wired* was just about to start filming. That movie turned out to be *Argo*, which would go on to win the Oscar for Best Picture in 2013.

The episode of *This American Life* was scheduled to air on September 23, 2011, on the show's hometown public radio station in Chicago, and on September 24 nationwide. As of September 20, however, Bearman and his producers still had much work to do. I drove into San Francisco to meet Bearman in a coffee shop and show him one of Butler's statements to law enforcement, which Bearman wanted to check for some timeline information.

In the statement, Butler claimed that Marino had volunteered to sell marijuana and had tried to blackmail him with the weed when Marino did not get to be on the reality show. Marino claimed that Butler was revising history as a defense strategy; it was the King of Stings playing smoke and mirrors, trying to make everyone else seem dirty to shift the blame.

Bearman had asked me repeatedly what I thought about Marino's motives for tipping me off about my ride-along, and he raised the question about Marino's method of contacting law enforcement: If Marino was a former cop, why did he have to go to an entertainment reporter to get in touch with the police about Butler and Wielsch's drug dealing?

These were questions I had asked myself many times, and I told Bearman what I had been telling myself: Who cares if Marino may have been motivated to turn in Butler because of a reality show snub? In the end, Marino did do the right thing—and his performance as an undercover informant was helpful to the criminal investigation. Bad cops were exposed and Butler's criminal activity shut down.

I still wanted to believe that Marino was a good guy, despite his shifty behavior following the arrests.

Then Bearman passed along an interesting fact.

"You know," Bearman said, "Carl didn't graduate from West Point."

Marino had told me, very specifically, that he had graduated from the military academy. That's why I wrote, "Marino is a West Point graduate and a retired police officer from New York who moved west to be closer to his family in San Jose," in the original *Diablo* exposé.

In fact, the West Point reference was a last-minute addition to the story. In my initial draft, I only mentioned that Marino was a former police officer, but when I told the editor that he was also a West Point grad and Desert Storm vet, it reminded her of the honor code that West Point cadets are instructed to uphold.

"Those West Point guys don't lie," she said.

So, we put the West Point graduate comment in the story, just before sending it to our printer. Bearman seemed certain that Marino wasn't a West Point grad, but I wanted to believe Marino had been truthful about his military background.

"Marino told me he graduated," I told Bearman. "He said he was in the Army after West Point, and he fought in Desert Storm."

Bearman asked, "Did he go into the Army as an officer?"

West Point graduates have a six-year service obligation and enter duty as a second lieutenant.

I had no idea. I had asked Marino about his service at least six times since February 21, when he told me he fought in Operation Desert Storm. Despite mentioning his Desert Storm duty many times, he had been otherwise vague about the details of his service.

I had intended to refer to his deployment in my book, as my feeling was that a war vet did not deserve to be dragged down by Butler's dirty business later in life, and that Marino's military experience had been a catalyst for coming forward about Butler and Wielsch's criminal conspiracy.

Bearman and I were interrupted by a phone call from the producer in New York for *This American Life*, who was scrambling to put all the sound together on the very complicated story. Bearman went outside to take the call, and I dialed Marino to ask him some questions that had been raised by Butler's statement.

Marino picked up, and I asked him first about a plaque that Norm Wielsch had given Butler in recognition of the help Butler had given CNET. Marino confirmed that he had seen the plaque.

Next, I asked Marino if he remembered the exact date he had first met with the DOJ. It was something I could have easily looked up in my notes and cache of Ronald Rutherford emails, but I did not have them with me at the time.

The question made Marino freak out.

"Why? Who cares? What does it matter?" he asked angrily.

"It matters because we're looking at the timeline that Butler gives in his statement," I replied.

Instead of just checking his calendar, Marino suggested that he might just go on the record with the *San Francisco Chronicle*, so *This American Life* would not get his exclusive media debut.

Marino had made comments like this to me several times since I had posted the story "Meet Mystery Date" on *Diablo*'s website a few months before. Marino claimed that both Justin Berton, a reporter at the *San*

Francisco Chronicle, and Joe Vazquez, a reporter for CBS5 news, were champing at the bit to tell Marino's story.

"I can snap my fingers and be on the front page of the *Chronicle*, or the lead story on the evening news," Marino told me on several occasions. Marino's defensiveness was bizarre, and I reminded him that *This American Life* was not looking to do some kind of hatchet piece about his character.

Then came the question that had prompted my call.

"Oh, one more thing," I started, in *Columbo* fashion. "Carl, you *graduated* from West Point, right?"

"YEAH!" Marino snapped.

I wanted to believe him, but knew I would have to check with West Point as well. Which I should have done in the first place.

Bearman had finished his call and come back to our meeting, so I wrapped up my call with Marino. Bearman looked extremely stressed, as he had much work to do condensing Butler, Marino, the PI Moms, Wielsch, and me into an hour of public radio broadcast time.

It was nearly noon, and I had planned to meet Marino for lunch near the city's Marina District. I told Bearman to call me if he needed any help.

As I walked to the car, I received an email on my phone. It was from Marino, who was quite agitated by our phone call from a few minutes before.

Marino wrote:

> Honestly, I'm thinking about going on the record with [the *Chronicle*] before [*This American Life*] even airs. I am the only one who did the right thing at great cost... if there is even a mention of a question of my intentions, I will give a full detailed statement of how everything REALLY happened, and provide all of the documentation. [The *Chronicle* reporter] seems to be the only one who sees the big picture of what I did and knows the others are full of shit. I know he will be fair and accurate. How in the world can any attack on me be taken seriously after everything that has transpired is beyond me. There would be no *Diablo* story or [*This American Life*] story if I hadn't of [*sic*] done what I did... and I get attacked instead of any credit. I've lost thousands of dollars... and my own TV show because of this... and I went into it knowing that, because it was the right thing. I have a sense of Honor that was instilled in me many years ago by my father and even more so at West Point... and I live my life by it, unlike many others.

There was much to unpack from the diatribe—that Marino was giving up "his own TV show" was just wacky. The "show" was *The Real Mr. and Mrs. Smith*, which had been a pipe dream. The "thousands of dollars" that Marino gave up would have likely come from setting up more dirty DUIs, or Candyman stings, or whatever shady and illegal business would have come Butler's way if he had not been exposed.

The line that really stood out came at the very end, when Marino claimed to live his life with the sense of capital-*H* honor that was instilled in him at West Point. Cadets at the US Military Academy are expected to uphold a formalized honor code throughout their entire lives. The Cadet Honor Code simply states: "A cadet will not lie, cheat, steal, or tolerate those who do."

Looking back, I had witnessed Carl Marino break every part of that code.

I drove across San Francisco and met Marino at his apartment. He had cooled his jets, possibly because I had replied to his diatribe with another message that said he should not expect to be treated like a villain in the *This American Life* story.

Marino and I drove a few blocks to the Presidio, a former Army base that had been turned into a national park. The area also houses *Star Wars* creator George Lucas' business offices, as well as other high-end businesses, including the investment company where Ilona was working that day. Carl had mentioned its cafeteria as a place where we should convene to discuss our book collaboration, and that we could eat whatever we wanted for free as guests of Ilona.

I ordered a salad and Carl stocked up a pile of sushi. Ilona joined us briefly to card-swipe our lunch bill, then hustled back to her office, as she was organizing a company-wide Vegas retreat, which was departing that evening. Carl was tagging along as her "plus one."

Carl and I went back to talking about our ideas for the book: a big picture telling of the events that led to Butler's arrest. I had an outline for the narrative as I saw it, which would begin with Carl entering Butler's office for the first time, in response to the Craigslist decoy ad. Because Butler and Carl hit it off—and Butler immediately insisted that

Carl take a screen test for a reality show sizzle reel—this seemed like a good place to bring the reader into Butler's wacky world.

Then Carl pulled out a stack of pages and announced, "I've already written five thousand words. This still needs some work, but here's chapter one."

I felt another link in our partnership dissipate. Due to the writing style I had observed in the hundreds of emails I had received from both Ronald Rutherford and Carl Marino during the past six months, I knew that I needed to be the person composing the manuscript. This impression was enforced tenfold as I read Carl's take on "chapter one" of the book.

Marino's story was, as expected, *All About Carl*: A young boy who grew up in a small town in western New York, got good grades in school, and excelled at sports. He loved his hometown and it loved him back. After his red, white, and blue childhood, Carl went to work for the sheriff's office in his hometown, and he was proud every time he put on his duty uniform.

I finished reading and looked up at Marino, who was waiting expectantly.

I gathered my inner creative writing teacher.

"Well, Carl, you're a good writer. This is colorful and descriptive," I told Marino. "The problem is that there is no narrative structure. Chapter one needs to hook the reader into the narrative, tease them a little with the promise of mystery. Get the pages turning, you know?"

Marino scowled. I tried again.

"This reads a little like the "about us" section of a website," I told him. "Once the reader realizes that chapter one is about you getting good grades and being a track and field star in high school, they won't want to read chapter two."

"I disagree," Marino insisted. "I think the reader needs to know exactly who I am, right from the start. That way they know exactly who they are dealing with."

Ugh, I thought. *This is not going to work.*

I shifted gears to get back to the topic of the day.

"I noticed you jumped straight from high school to working for the sheriff's office," I said. "Why didn't you put in anything about Desert Storm?"

Marino mumbled that he just hadn't gotten around to writing about his military service yet. I realized that his evasiveness was consistent each time we discussed his Army days. I had been concerned that the stories were too painful for Marino to talk about. *Band of Brothers* and whatnot.

"What division were you in?" I asked. "What did you do in the Army?"

Marino looked me in the eye. "I was in the 82nd Airborne," he told me. "Army Rangers."

"Oh, wow," I said. "You jumped out of planes?"

"Yep," Marino stated.

"Well, there you go—there's something for chapter one," I said, suggesting that we draw a comparison of jumping out of a plane into battle to wearing a wire around Butler and exposing his criminal activity.

Internally, I thought that I was long overdue to reach out to the US Army records office to ask a few questions.

Marino and I talked for a few hours, until we were the last patrons in the cafeteria. As we walked back to the car, he told me that he had been contacted by several other writers who wanted to publish his story. I wasn't sure if Marino was bluffing, but I was kind of excited by his claim.

I should say, 'Why don't you work with another writer, and I'll just keep working on my own book.' I thought. But, I didn't.

Marino kept talking, describing the book he had in his mind.

"I was having lunch with a couple of Ilona's friends, and telling them about everything I did with the DOJ, and about Chris Butler," Marino told me. "Ilona's friends all said, 'We don't want to read a book about this scumbag Chris Butler, who was setting people up. We want to read a book about the hero who took him down.'"

"I treated that lunch conversation like a focus group," Marino told me. "They want to hear the story of the Hero. They want to hear my story."

Carl and Ilona flew off to Las Vegas, and I drove back to the East Bay to work on a long-past-deadline story for the October 2011 issue of *Diablo*. The story was right in my wheelhouse: Brad Pitt was playing Danville resident Billy Beane in the movie *Moneyball*, based on Berkeley writer Michael Lewis' book about the Oakland A's. A home run *Diablo* story would have been an interview with Pitt, but I was happy to settle for a double off the wall by running a Q&A with Beane, then putting together a lineup of East Bay players who helped make the movie.

Meanwhile, *Diablo*'s marketing team had written a press release to promote the weekend's broadcast of *This American Life*. The presser read: "Peter Crooks, senior editor of *Diablo* magazine, will be featured on the acclaimed documentary program *This American Life*. The program will air *Diablo*'s inside story of Concord-based private investigator Chris Butler and his now-infamous efforts to get a reality TV series, as well as the shocking police corruption connection to this wild and scandalous story."

The press release was intended to draw attention to *Diablo*'s brand. As in: Check out this community magazine getting national buzz!

I proofread the copy and signed off on it, satisfied that I had fulfilled my boss' directive of getting national media attention for the Butler exposé.

The press release was sent to an agency that distributes such promotional pieces to media outlets across the country. We hoped it would be picked up by as many outlets as possible so *This American Life* fans across the country would be introduced to *Diablo*, visit our website, and subscribe to our magazine.

I went to bed around midnight on Thursday, September 22, exhausted from the week's circus of activities. I hoped to get a full night's sleep, because I was driving to Ojai the next day, where I was scheduled to host a screening of *One Flew Over the Cuckoo's Nest* and interview Louise Fletcher about her Oscar-winning performance in the film.

The *Diablo* press release hit the wire sometime after my head hit the pillow that night. The *San Francisco Chronicle*'s website was one of many publications to pick it up; and because Marino had his smartphone set to Google Alerts to notify him anytime the names "Chris Butler" and "Norm Wielsch" (and "Carl Marino") were mentioned in any media, he received a ping about *Diablo*'s Pete Crooks being featured on the upcoming episode of *This American Life*.

Marino, whose Facebook page revealed that he had been indulging in a bottle-service bender of Grey Goose and Red Bull, was unable to differentiate the press release from a news article and proceeded to completely lose his shit.

At 3:37 AM, I awoke to my buzzing iPhone and saw it was an incoming call from Carl Marino. Concerned that there must be an emergency—why else would he be calling at such a ridiculous time?—I answered the call.

Marino greeted me with a tidal wave of profanity, with "motherfucker" receiving the most usage.

"I read the article, motherfucker!" Marino screamed. "Did you think I wouldn't see it, motherfucker?"

I tried to shake the fuzz out of my brain and took the phone out of the bedroom so as not to disturb my sleeping wife. I also grabbed my pad and pen to take notes on whatever crazy lecture I was about to endure.

"Carl, what are you talking about?" I mumbled. It took me a few seconds to put together the press release–news article equation.

"Don't you dare okey-doke me, motherfucker," Marino screamed. "I've fucking had it. I just read this big bullshit article where you are taking all the credit for everything I did again. I'm going to the *Chronicle* and they are going to print the Carl Marino Story. [The *Chronicle* reporter] is foaming at the mouth to tell my story and expose your bullshit."

"You're mad about *Diablo* sending out a press release? Is that it?"

I was figuring it out, through my sleepy fog. Marino saw the presser as another shot at the spotlight, and he had been cut out. Again.

It got worse.

"You are Chris Butler!" Marino accused me, screaming insanely. "You're taking all the credit for something you didn't do. You're taking *my* credit!"

As insulted as I was by the absurd suggestion that a con man like Butler and I were the same breed of cat, I took a deep breath and attempted to talk Marino off the ledge. I explained that it was in *Diablo*'s interest to promote the fact that their writer was being featured on a national radio show. My explanation of this simple and practical reality shifted Marino's drunken state from violent rage to intense despair.

"I never should have turned in Chris Butler! What am I getting out of this?" Marino screamed. "You're getting an award-winning story. I gave up my own TV show and thousands of dollars to turn in Chris Butler. What am I getting for it?"

Marino continued to howl.

"I'm worried that the DOJ is going to come slap the cuffs on me when they hear my interview tomorrow," he said.

"Wait, what?" I asked. Marino had told me many times that he had been given immunity from prosecution by the DOJ because of his undercover work. "You have immunity."

"Some of the stuff I did, they can come slap the cuffs on me," Marino admitted. "Some of that stuff was illegal."

"What are you talking about?" I asked. "What kind of stuff? You told me you had immunity."

Marino's cell phone died before I could get an answer.

29
A False Complaint

WHEN MARINO ADMITTED that he had taken part in illegal activities, he could have been referring to any of a number of incidents. At the time of that extremely uncomfortable conversation, I still did not know that Marino had been falsely representing himself as a *Diablo* reporter during a Dirty DUI setup.

He could have been talking about the Candyman incident, in which he impersonated a police officer and pointed a gun at a terrified teenager, and then assisted in the teen's false arrest. But again, I thought he had immunity from prosecution for all of that, because he had turned over a copy of the Candyman DVD and spilled the beans on Butler and Wielsch.

Or Marino could have been referring to his role in the diabolical setup of a lieutenant in California's Richmond Police Department. This one is a doozy—the bizarre Case of the Richmond Police Explorers, Inc.

The hot mess started when two Richmond beat cops, Danny Harris and Ray Thomas, decided to run a private security business within city limits to make extra cash, despite the obvious conflicts of interest and official department policies against such an enterprise. Even more egregious than the brazen disregard for department policy was the way that Harris and Thomas staffed their security business.

The two cops recruited their security guards from the ranks of the Richmond Police Explorers, a program sponsored by the local Boy Scouts of America council that gave inner-city teens a chance to learn about law enforcement; in fact, Harris had been an Explorer before becoming a cop.

Harris and Thomas oversaw the Richmond PD's Explorers program, and even created a 501(c)(3) nonprofit called Richmond Police Explorers, Inc., which they used to soak up donations from corporations that thought it was good PR to throw some money at a police-sponsored program helping youth in one of the country's most violent cities.

Hiring inexperienced teenagers to patrol housing projects in Richmond's most dangerous neighborhoods was a questionable approach to running a security business, and made more questionable by the fact that Harris and Thomas provided handguns for some of their young staff. This was totally illegal, not to mention insanely dangerous.

When young Explorers would question Harris and Thomas' methods, the two cops would threaten to boot them out of the program, or to inform immigration officials about their family members.

A Richmond police lieutenant, Michael Booker, had gotten wind of Harris and Thomas' scam and reported the cops to his supervisor. Looking for retribution, Harris and Thomas made an appointment to meet with Chris Butler at that infamous warehouse office in Concord, where Butler outlined a plan to set up Lieutenant Booker.

So, one day in September 2010, soon-to-be *PI Moms* cast member Linda Welch contacted Michael Booker. The buxom decoy told Booker that she was a San Jose State University student and wanted to interview him for a paper about law enforcement. Welch later texted Booker, telling him how excited she was to have met him and inviting him to come meet her in San Jose for a follow-up interview.

If the sting had worked as planned, Booker would have ditched work for the day and driven out of Richmond in his squad car—a violation of department policy. Booker did meet Welch for lunch, but took time off from work to do it and drove his own car to the meeting.

During the lunch, Welch flirted with Booker while recording the conversation with a hidden wire in her purse (one the gypsy psychic didn't swipe). After the meal, Welch walked Booker back to his car, then kissed him openly, so Carl Marino, parked nearby, could videotape the smooch.

For the next part of the scam, Marino called the Richmond Police Department and demanded to speak with Chief Chris Magnus. Marino told Magnus that he wanted to meet in person to discuss the behavior of a certain Richmond lieutenant. Magnus agreed to meet, and brought along a representative from Richmond PD's Internal Affairs. Marino, using his John Brownell alias, handed over a DVD showing Welch kissing Booker. Marino told the chief he had found text messages from Booker on his girlfriend's cell phone, so he hired PI Chris Butler to follow her.

Marino demanded that Booker be reprimanded or he would take the video to the media. Despite the fact that knowingly making a false complaint against a police officer is a crime, Marino seemed proud of pulling the wool over the police chief's eyes.

After Marino left Richmond, PD, he sent Butler a text: "On the way to the office. One of my finest pieces of acting."

When I interviewed Chief Magnus about the event, Magnus said Marino was very convincing, and the official complaint required an internal affairs interview with Booker.

It should be pointed out that Magnus had more than enough to worry about as chief of police in Richmond, a city with its fair share of crime and violence, without having to deal with Marino lodging a false complaint against his staff.

"Policing Richmond can be a bit like being a short-order cook with one hundred burners, with all of them turned on HIGH all the time," Magnus told me.

Lieutenant Booker did not know that he had been caught on video kissing Welch, but he told the truth when interviewed about the incident. He told internal affairs that Welch had come into Richmond PD to meet him, which was confirmed with a review of security camera footage. He explained that the decoy had invited him to lunch and kissed him as he approached his vehicle to go home.

If Booker had lied about the incident—even though it was a setup—he would have been out of a job. Instead, he was cleared of the investigation.

Since that sting didn't work, Butler met with Harris and Thomas again. This time, the two cops wanted to get the guns they had sold to two teenagers back, and to get them in trouble while they were at it. So

Butler devised a scam to have two hot decoys try to set the teens up for a DUI arrest, hoping to also get them caught in possession of the firearms.

The sting was thwarted when Marino made up a Facebook account under the name Suzy Smith and then tipped off the teens about the setup. The teens didn't show up for their date with the hot decoys, who had waited at a Chevys bar until closing time for the Boy Scouts to arrive.

I noticed that the same Suzy Smith went on *Men's Health*'s Facebook page to post an accusation that a modeling competition for a line of grooming products was fixed. Regardless of Marino's petulance about not getting picked to model scented shaving creams in Las Vegas, the tip-off that Marino gave to the two young men to help them avoid the legal peril they could have faced was a pretty cool thing to do. However, Marino's lying to Richmond's police chief to set up and smear a lieutenant was absolutely a dick move.

Marino's maniacal 3 AM wake-up call obliterated any chance of getting some sleep the night before *This American Life* was scheduled to air.

In the morning, I drove to *Diablo*'s office in a daze, took care of some odds and ends, and faxed off my signed life-rights agreement to *This American Life*'s production office in New York. The agreement was to attach my personal story rights to any movie that was developed out of the material that aired on the radio show.

I knew that Marino had been given a similar agreement. Based on his insulting and frightening phone call a few hours earlier, I didn't really care if he signed his agreement or not. I was fed up with his bullshit and was done giving him the benefit of the doubt.

It was my understanding that no movie could be developed without additionally obtaining the story rights to my original reporting about the Chris Butler scandal, because my reporting broke the story and the *This American Life*'s episode followed my original story very closely.

I wrapped things up at the office and hit the road for Ojai. During the summers of 2010 and 2011, I hosted an outdoor classic film series at the gorgeous Ojai Valley Inn and Spa to benefit local charities. The events began at twilight, when I would introduce an iconic actor from a Hollywood classic—Rita Moreno from *West Side Story*, Tippi Hedren from *The Birds*, Mary Badham from *To Kill a Mockingbird*—and we would sit down for an in-depth conversation about the film. When it was dark enough, we projected the movie on a giant outdoor screen.

These screenings were very special. I fell in love with classic Hollywood at a young age, so talking to silver-screen legends about what it was like to win an Oscar or to work with Alfred Hitchcock or Gregory Peck is a thrill.

I looked forward to the six-hour drive from the Bay Area to Ojai for each event, because it always helped to clear my head of the anxiety I had been dealing with during the Butler scandal. But this time, the drive to Ojai was different. I got a late start and did much of the drive after dark; I was painfully exhausted, and my mind was still spinning about the bizarre call I had received from Marino early that morning.

I could not stop thinking about Marino's claim that he might be arrested after the show aired. He made the decision to go on *This American Life*, but I did not want to see him facing prosecution because he had finally talked about his experience as an informant. Then again, at this point, I still did not know about much of the shady behavior Marino had been a part of before he decided to blow the whistle—I did not realize Marino had posed as a *Diablo* reporter until nearly a year later.

Looking back, I realize that my feelings had been deeply hurt by the way Marino kept revising his story about how I helped him get out of the biggest jam of his life. I found it deeply unpleasant to see this person, who I had considered to be a friend, change his tune from "Thank you for helping me" to "You are Chris Butler."

During the final stretch of the drive, a spectacular lightning storm lit up the night sky, creating a brilliant strobe effect on the panoramic view. I finally reached the Ojai Valley Inn and Spa around midnight and stumbled into my room like a zombie.

Just before going to bed, I checked my email. I had received a message from Gary Pitkin, the DOJ representative who took the two first pounds of shrink-wrapped marijuana into evidence during Marino's initial disclosure on January 21.

I had requested an interview with Pitkin for the upcoming article I was writing about Wielsch. Pitkin declined the interview, due to the active status of Wielsch's case, but gave me a very nice compliment in his email.

"I appreciate the amazing work you have done on this matter," Pitkin wrote. "Your work has been accurate and thorough."

The note gave me a sense of relief. The stress of the past few days had been overwhelming, but Pitkin's message reminded me of something very important: I helped instigate the investigation as a concerned citizen, and then did my best to report the story fairly. I had done a good job, and the fact that Carl Marino's true colors were starting to show couldn't change that.

I got into bed and crashed hard until morning.

On September 24, I grabbed a to-go cup of coffee and drove to an elevated spot in the Ojai Valley called Meditation Mount.

I parked in a spot where I could look across the valley, and tuned my satellite radio to a public radio channel for *This American Life*. I was honored to be considered for the show in the first place, then worked hard to help Josh Bearman report the story I was about to hear. But the events of the past few days—specifically Marino's behavior—had significantly curtailed my excitement for the broadcast.

The show began at 10 AM, and within the first minute I heard my voice, talking about how the PR agent had contacted me about the PI Moms. Then came Ira Glass' voice, introducing me to the story: "This is Pete Crooks, a writer and editor for *Diablo* magazine..."

I was a character on *This American Life*. In my geeky world of magazine editors and film critics, this was a big deal.

I sat there on Meditation Mount for the full hour, transfixed by the program. (Like any of the show's superfans, I've been transfixed many, many times by *This American Life*.) Bearman's take on the piece was more screwball comedy than nail-biter, which worked in the retelling. I thought Marino came off well, and there wasn't anything on the show that made me think he would end up in handcuffs.

The hour whizzed by and I breathed a sigh of relief.

The scenic overlook where author Pete Crooks listened to the original broadcast of the *This American Life* episode, "The Incredible Case of the PI Moms." *Photo by Pete Crooks.*

I went back to my hotel room and checked my email, and quickly appreciated the size of the audience that listens to *This American Life*. An old girlfriend had already reached out, as had a former coworker and several other long-lost friends.

There was also a message from a news producer at *48 Hours* and a movie producer from Hollywood.

I got back into bed and slept until late afternoon.

That night, I sat down in front of a large audience to interview with Louise Fletcher, one of my favorite people I've met as an entertainment reporter.

Louise and I talked for more than an hour about the making of *One Flew Over the Cuckoo's Nest*. She shared stories about auditioning for the part and how she embodied the role of Nurse Ratched, one of the most villainous screen characters in Hollywood history. (The American Film Institute ranks Nurse Ratched behind only Hannibal Lecter, Norman Bates, Darth Vader, and the Wicked Witch of the West on its Top Five Villains short list. I wholeheartedly agree—Fletcher is magnificently evil in the film.)

After Fletcher told a story about winning the Academy Award for Best Actress, and giving one of the greatest acceptance speeches in Oscar history—she signed her speech for her deaf parents—the audience gave her a standing ovation. I took Louise and her family out for a nice dinner in the hotel's restaurant. At the end of the evening, her son took me aside and thanked me for putting together such a nice event and treating his mom with such appreciation.

Still a stressed-out emotional wreck, I resisted an urge to collapse into a heap of tears. I was so happy to have gotten my head out of the Chris Butler fifteen-minutes-of-fame vortex for a few hours.

"Thank you," I replied to Louise's son. "I can't think of a place I'd rather be tonight than here, having dinner with the real Nurse Ratched."

When I got back to the *Diablo* office on Monday, my voice mail had blown up with messages from news producers. Representatives from *48 Hours*, *Dateline*, *Nightline*, and *20/20* had all heard *This American Life* during the weekend, and all of them wanted to talk right away about doing a story. Prime time, baby.

I also got calls from several movie producers, the most excited of whom was working on a con artist movie, which would later be titled *American Hustle*. He asked which actor I would want to play me in a movie based on my story.

"Parker Posey," I answered, before giving him the contact information of an agent in Beverly Hills who was representing the *This American Life* team.

I also caught up with Marino, who had temporarily cooled his jets about *Diablo*'s press release. Marino liked the attention the radio show was bringing his way. He didn't get a visit from the DOJ or FBI, but did get calls from the same news programs that had contacted me, and spent quite a bit of time on the phone with each one.

Marino also took a long call with a screenwriter whose credits included *The Smurfs*. Marino said the screenwriter understood that the story was *All About Carl*.

"The *Smurfs* guy really gets it," Marino told me.

Later that week, Marino gave a radio interview on the WLEA 1480 morning show in his hometown of Hornell, New York. He went on a local radio morning show to describe his role in the bust of Butler and Wielsch. Marino's *All About Carl* version highlighted the danger he put himself in to take down the commander of the Central Contra Costa County Narcotics Enforcement Team.

"If [Butler and Wielsch] had found out, they definitely would have killed me," Marino told the morning show hosts, Casey and Colleen. "There's no question about that."

Casey and Colleen ate it up and asked if the story was going be made into a movie. Marino confirmed that it absolutely was.

"There's been a meeting with the Coen brothers," Marino said, telling the Hornell listening audience something that was completely untrue. "It's the perfect type movie for them."

Casey and Colleen asked Marino who was going to play him in the movie. For a few seconds, Marino couldn't come up with an A-lister who could do the part justice, then he remembered to check in with his superego.

"I don't know who could do it better than I could," Marino said. "I'd love the opportunity to play myself. If I don't, I'm definitely going to play someone else in the movie."

The last time I spoke with Marino on the phone was in early October 2011. He wanted to discuss the opportunities to go on one of the national news magazine shows.

"I think I'm going to do *48 Hours*," Marino told me. "They want to do the Carl Marino Story, and that's the real story. The producer told me very specifically that without Carl Marino, there is no story."

"Well, you do what you gotta do, Carl," I told him, not mentioning that I had heard exactly the same about my participation from the same producer. "I'll probably do *48 Hours*, but I need some time to get back on track here on all the work I need to do at *Diablo*. So, I'm still thinking about it."

Marino was flummoxed by my indifference, but said he was still debating doing an interview because of his busy work and travel schedule. I told Marino that I was getting called into a meeting and would have to catch up with him at a later time.

"Wait, wait, wait," Marino said, sounding panicked. "What am I supposed to tell *48 Hours* about you?"

"You can tell them what I just told you," I said. "I'm still thinking about it, and I'm going to need some time to make up my mind."

"All right, but . . .," Marino tried to keep me on the line.

"Good-bye, Carl," I said.

The next day, CBS News producers Greg Fisher and Chuck Stevenson took me to lunch to talk about the story. We went to an Italian restaurant next door to one of the historic movie theaters where I host classic film events. I joked to Fisher and Stevenson that if I did decide to help them put a show together, they had to show the theaters and promote my efforts to bring the community together by watching old movies—something different than the who-killed-who content of their usual program.

We sat down to eat, and the producers dropped a bomb right away.

"We put Carl on tape yesterday," Stevenson told me. "He sat down with our correspondent, Maureen Maher."

I thought about the conversation I had with Marino just after 1 PM the day before, when he told me he was leaning toward doing *48 Hours*, but still not sure. Given that the interview with Maher had taken place in the afternoon, I imagined that Marino had gone straight into makeup after telling me he was weighing his options and needed some time to think before doing an interview.

"The first thing Carl told us when he got to the interview was, 'I got Crooks to agree to do the show,'" Fisher told me.

I shook my head.

"Listen guys, Carl Marino does not speak for me," I said. "I need to make that very clear."

30
Background Check

IN MID-OCTOBER, I made a call to the records department of the prestigious West Point US Military Academy and asked if Carl Earl Marino, born August 26, 1970, was a graduate.

The answer was no.

Obviously, I should have checked with West Point before printing that Marino was a graduate, instead of believing what Marino told me. Funny thing though: In the six months since printing that article, Marino had never mentioned the error. In fact, his initial reaction to the article was extremely positive, and he said that his quotes were all accurate.

I'm certainly not the only person Marino misled about his West Point history: I've seen him comment on Facebook that he has a degree in environmental engineering from West Point. Moreover, stories in western New York's *Evening Tribune* and the Hornell Senior High School alumni newsletter both stated that Marino had a bachelor of science degree from West Point. A 2014 profile of Marino on Examiner.com had also identified Marino as a West Point grad. Marino "liked" the article on Facebook and made no effort to correct the error.

Screenshots of Marino's LinkedIn page, which listed "United States Military Academy at West Point, Environmental Engineering" under his education history, as well as a Facebook comment he made in August 2012, in which he claimed, "I have an engineering degree from West Point," were further evidence that Marino had been intentionally misleading people to believe that he was a West Point graduate.

The West Point receptionist told me that Marino did attend the academy for two years, from 1988 to 1990, and that he left after his sophomore year. If he had started his third year, he would have had at least a two-year service obligation. If he had graduated, it would have been six years.

I was told that cadets at the academy are technically active duty in the Army, so the students can receive a cost of living stipend in addition to having their education paid for. The representative also pointed out that no cadet had been pulled out of school and sent into battle during the past one hundred years.

I wrote a letter to the Army records offices in St. Louis, requesting any information about Marino's service. I received a written reply that there were no records of anyone with that name and birth date having served in the US Army.

Which meant Marino had lied to me about being a Desert Storm vet.

What was truly bizarre was that he had lied to me *after* he had earned my trust by helping the DOJ take down Butler and Wielsch. When he asked me to put him in touch with law enforcement, Marino promised that he had not lied to me and would not lie to me. I felt that lying about serving in a war was inexcusable.

Since Marino had claimed to have been a police officer for seventeen years, I searched for his employment records and found that he had worked for the Monroe County Sheriff's Office in western New York. The response I received from a public information officer was that Marino was never a police officer but a jail deputy—a peace officer position that does not have anywhere near the same responsibilities that police officers uphold.

And why did Marino leave his jail deputy job after seventeen years?

The short answer is that he resigned.

The long answer is considerably more complicated. Interviews with witnesses and documents filed in the federal prosecution of Steve Tanabe, for which Marino was subpoenaed as a possible witness, revealed the following:

In a February 2012 interview with the FBI, Marino admitted that internal affairs investigators had discovered multiple findings of his dishonesty while working for the Monroe County Sheriff's Office.

Each finding of dishonesty followed an ugly domestic incident during Marino's tenure as a correctional officer. The first incident was on or about October 21, 2004, when Marino pled guilty to an internal affairs investigation. Marino was charged with violations of the sheriff's office's rules and regulations regarding reporting arrests and court actions, general conduct, and truthfulness.

There were several incidents in 2005 in which Marino was found to be dishonest by his sheriff's office, and these incidents included Marino submitting two false reports. The most troubling was an incident on or about December 19, 2005, in which Marino reportedly shoved his sister-in-law outside of a restaurant in front of a group of startled witnesses. When someone went to call 9-1-1, Marino told them not to, claiming he was a Monroe County sheriff's deputy. According to a court document, Marino lied to two separate investigating officers and filed a false report about the incident.

Then, in 2007, a witness gave a statement that she pulled up behind Marino's vehicle at a stop sign and watched Marino get out of the driver's seat, walk to the passenger side, pull a struggling woman out of the truck, shove her to the ground into a dark ditch, and drive away.

Finally, in February 2008, a brouhaha involving Marino, his second wife, and another man led to Marino leaving the Monroe County Sheriff's Office for good. There was a violent fight, which led to Marino's arrest on charges of assault and criminal mischief. In March 2008, Marino was suspended without pay by the Monroe County Sheriff's Office because "his continuing presence on the job unduly interfered with the department and/or reflected upon the integrity of the department." Marino was also given a two-year protective order that said he could not possess firearms during that time.

The 2008 incident and subsequent dishonesty findings led to Marino's resignation from the Monroe County Sheriff's Office. He stuck around the Rochester area long enough to get popped driving while alcohol impaired, to which he pled guilty in August 2008.

Not long after his DWAI (driving while ability impaired), Marino moved from New York to California. Within weeks of his arrival, he answered Chris Butler's Craigslist ad. Within weeks of that, he was filmed impersonating a police officer and wearing a firearm during Operation Candyman while making that teenager's false arrest—which was a crime on its own, as well as an assumed violation of his protective order. During the next two years, Marino assisted Butler on numerous stings and setups, some of them criminal, such as the attempt to smear a lieutenant in the Richmond Police Department.

Given his own history with internal affairs investigations, the fact that Marino would create an alias and lie to the chief of police to besmirch a law enforcement officer he had never met says much about Marino's character.

They were quite a match, Chris Butler and Carl Marino.

It's no wonder Butler choked up when he talked to DOJ investigators about the betrayal he felt when Marino turned his ass in.

Butler told investigators that he and Marino were like brothers; Marino told me the same thing on numerous occasions.

I see the relationship a bit differently. I think Butler saw Marino as a better-looking version of himself, a con man lacking conscience who could be used as an agent of exploitation for dirty DUIs and decoy tests. Butler was Marino's Uncle Screwtape, and man, they could have really done big things together—reality shows, an office in Hollywood, money, guns, and glamour.

But then Butler got busted—and all the dreams of celebrity and *The Real Mr. and Mrs. Smith* and franchised PI Moms training centers were obliterated.

On the other side of the fence, Marino saw Butler as a guy who attracted spotlight. Butler's national media coverage and reality show deal were certainly more appealing than the holes Marino had dug for himself back in Monroe County before moving to sunny California. Going along with setups and stings and criminal scams was just a required part of the package needed to get some of that spotlight Butler was promising.

But when the *PI Moms* camera crews arrived, the spotlight didn't shine on Marino. So he burned Butler—and, by extension, the TV show—down. And two pounds of stolen marijuana turned out to be just enough kindling to start the fire.

31
Showdown on Dr. Phil

AS I WORKED WITH *48 Hours* on its episode "Soccer Mom Confidential," I learned that the CBS news folks were crossing their fingers, hoping to get an interview with Dr. Phil McGraw for the show. In exchange, *Dr. Phil* wanted to do a follow-up about the Chris Butler scandal.

I thought it was a great idea to interview Dr. Phil about Chris Butler, especially if Dr. Phil would answer questions about how Butler and the PI Moms got away with so much fakery on his show. In March 2011, I told representatives from *Dr. Phil* about what Butler had done to them, so the *Dr. Phil* folks had had a full year to do their homework.

If they had done their homework, they would have discovered some interesting information about the *PI Moms* episode that aired in June 2010. It was chock-full of bullshit.

For example, one former employee of Butler's told me that she had only been working at the office for a few days when Butler told her to lie on *Dr. Phil* as her very first assignment. Butler told her she would wear a wig and pretend to be a client—Butler wanted to use video footage he had from a cheating-husband sting in Hawaii; he just needed someone to pretend to be married to the guy in the video.

The employee was horrified and refused to go on *Dr. Phil* and lie.

"Nobody's going to see it!" Butler berated his new employee.

"My parents watch *Dr. Phil*!" the employee countered.

Butler lifted his hand to his eye level.

"When you started working here, you were up here," Butler told his new hire, then lowered his hand toward the floor. "Now, you're down here."

In the end, Butler was able to convince his real client, who Dr. Phil identified as "Laura," to come on the show and talk about how Butler set up her husband with decoy Sharon Taylor in Hawaii.

Butler failed to mention to Dr. Phil that the Hawaii video was actually the second time he had set up this husband. The first sting, which was certainly not afternoon TV material, involved Butler conning the guy into having drinks with two women in a hotel restaurant and going upstairs to a room with them for the promise of a three-way. The husband allowed himself to be restrained to the bed and have chocolate sauce drizzled over his bare chest.

The poor horndog thought the two hotties were going to lick the sauce off him. Instead, Butler and another man broke into the room and robbed the man of his wallet and clothes. Then they stung him again in Hawaii (as seen on *Dr. Phil*!).

I tracked down "Laura," and asked her why she went on the show. She told me that Butler had convinced her to play along with my fake ride-along the same way he had convinced Sharon the Client: by telling her that she would be helping women who faced the same issues she was facing. (Which, similar to Sharon the Client, was that her partner spent far too much time chasing other women on the internet.)

If the *Dr. Phil* folks had checked into the *PI Moms* show they aired in June 2010, they also might have discovered that there was some funny business in the segment in which Butler and the Moms send a male decoy into a hotel room to investigate a sensual masseuse. Turns out that the sensual masseuse worked in Butler's illegal massage parlor, and the PI hired her to sting the *Dr. Phil* show as well. Multitasking!

I interviewed the masseuse, who told me that Butler took her to the hotel the same day that the *Dr. Phil* camera crews were supposed to arrive. Butler paid for the room and paid the masseuse to hang out and give his decoy a rub 'n' tug on camera. She did a great job too; the decoy set up the hidden camera briefcase at an awkward angle, and it fell over during the massage. The masseuse got up from the bed and repositioned the briefcase, to make sure that *Dr. Phil* got the money shot.

———

The second *PI Moms* show on *Dr. Phil* aired on February 16, 2012. I didn't have to go to L.A. for the taping earlier that month, because I was able to do my segment via video conference. I had been hesitant to appear on the show at all, after my wife pointed out, "If you go on *Dr. Phil*, you will always be one of those people who went on *Dr. Phil*." But I figured it would at least make for an entertaining chapter in the book, so I agreed to do an interview with the understanding that *Dr. Phil*'s producers knew I would be writing about what happened.

The taping gave Phil McGraw a chance to roll up his sleeves and proverbially punch people in the face for lying to him. Marino took the worst of it, getting knocked back on his heels early on for snickering at something that Dr. Phil didn't think was very funny.

During the show, Marino claimed that he was introduced to Butler's drug dealing before Lifetime started filming the *PI Moms* reality show. Marino also stated that he did not participate in any illegal stings until after he was working undercover as an informant. False and false.

Dr. Phil spent a lot of time complaining that no one told him that he had been duped into airing footage of fake cases. When he got to my segment, Dr. Phil failed to mention that I was the one who had told his producers about the fakery.

Instead, Dr. Phil asked me, "Did you burn your source?" and "Why does Carl say the biggest mistake he made was coming to you?" Marino even threw in a drama-queenish "Pete almost got me killed" complaint when he had a chance.

I did my best to keep it classy, and explained how I felt about being duped on the fake ride-along. I also rebutted Marino's claims that I put him in danger when I contacted law enforcement about Butler and Wielsch's criminal activity during the same week that Marino was aggressively sabotaging the *PI Moms* show.

I sat there, biting my tongue, knowing that Marino lied to me about being a Desert Storm vet and a police officer, and that he was making provably false statements right there on *Dr. Phil*'s set. But I also knew a pissing contest on the *Dr. Phil* show was not the appropriate forum to bring out that information.

Later, I heard from multiple sources that Marino had a full-volume meltdown in *Dr. Phil*'s backstage dressing rooms after the show. Again, I was glad that I didn't make the trip for the taping.

A few days before the *Dr. Phil* taping, I sat down for an interview with Special Agent Dean Johnston, the Department of Justice agent who oversaw Marino's work as a confidential informant during the investigation.

"[Marino] was really worried about not being factual with us," said Johnston, who pointed out that he had checked out every claim Marino made about his background right away. "If he said, 'In my past, I was involved with law enforcement,' that's a broad statement—to me that means he was someone who works a patrolman. Someone who works at a jail, in my mind, that is not someone who works on the street, a detective, or whatever. Even though the jail is a form of corrections, that's not law enforcement in my mind. So when you meet Carl, he tells you, 'I was in law enforcement in New York.' But when you ask him, 'Where did you work and what did you do?'—he actually tells you."

That wasn't the case with me, as Marino repeatedly claimed to have been a full-fledged police officer, with lots of surveillance experience. A review of various modeling résumés showed Marino claiming police officer as previous employment. A prominent Bay Area photographer's website highlighted Marino's engagement photos with the caption, "Carl, an ex-NYPD sergeant turned famous actor." And Marino told the producers of *Homicide Hunter* enough about his policing experience that he started getting a screen credit as "Police Consultant" on the show.

I asked Johnston if he thought Marino's honesty issues and his media campaign could jeopardize the case against Butler and Wielsch. Johnston said no.

"[Marino] wants to say, 'Now I can tell my side of the story.' He was an informant, and then a very involved witness," Johnston said. "[I told him] at the end of it, you're going to look like a liar. Everyone is going to weigh what you said, and they are going to call you a liar."

Johnston made it clear that Marino's primary value was as an informant, and that he knew the DOJ's agents needed to collect evidence and provide witness testimony if the cases did go to trial.

"My job was to make sure that [Marino's] statements [in court] are irrelevant. If I do my job, even if he passes away from a heart attack—it won't matter," Johnston said. "It was hard for him to realize that the evidence speaks for itself. [The prosecutors] could lose him. He was very important to get to where we are at, but now he's not."

I helped *48 Hours* put together an hour-long look at the case, including telling my story on camera, all the while keeping a distance from Marino. I helped bring in interviews with Ryan Romano and Norm Wielsch. PI Mom Ami Wiltz and a former employee of Butler's, Meagan Bernabe, also gave interviews, so the show was able to give a fairly colorful look into Butler's world.

One of the highlights of the show was a *48 Hours* news producer chasing Chris Butler across the parking lot of a Contra Costa courthouse, asking him if he had any other ideas for reality shows.

Marino received quite a bit of screen time from *48 Hours*. The show's final segment showed him meticulously cleaning the Glock 19 that was given to him for free while he was working in Butler's office during the filming of *PI Moms*—in fact, Marino received the gun about three weeks after taking possession of the first pound of stolen marijuana. Marino told *48 Hours* he sleeps with his loaded product-placement pistol under the bed, in case Butler or any other bad guys come after him.

As the airdate for *48 Hours* grew closer, Marino became unhinged, just as he had with *This American Life*. He demanded that the producers tell him how much face time I was going get on the show, because he had expected the hour to be *All About Carl*, with just a little bit of Pete Crooks.

The producers would not tell him anything, because they had discovered that Marino had also given an interview to ABC's *20/20*, and did not want to disclose anything that Marino might go tell to a competitor.

During the broadcast of *48 Hours*, Marino took to its Facebook page to complain about the show's accuracy, writing: "If you want the true story, it will be coming out soon... this is an overhyped warped version of the truth," and "Ask Pete for the true story and how he fumbled and almost got me killed…he has become the new Chris Butler trying to become famous with book and movie deals of other people's stories," and "Watch the upcoming *20/20* if you want the accurate, better story. [The *48 Hours*' anchor] was just very angry that I called her out when she wasn't prepared in my first interview and gave all the things they wanted to [*20/20*'s] Chris Cuomo who is a first class correspondant [*sic*]."

On August 20, 2012, ABC's *20/20* ran its piece about Marino, and it was the *All About Carl* treatment he had always wanted, which was fine by me, as I had promised exclusivity to *48 Hours*. The nine-minute story on *20/20* presented Marino as an actor who had to "play the role of a lifetime" by going into "the teeth of the dragon" to take down Butler and Wielsch. The story started with footage from the February 15 meth buy, showing Butler handing over a burrito-shaped bag of crystal to Marino as Wielsch counted out a stack of bills.

Somehow, *20/20* also obtained the coveted Candyman sting video, but used it only for B-roll shots showing Butler and Wielsch together. It did not show the part of the video in which Marino impersonated a cop with a gun, taking part in the false arrest of a terrified teenager—maybe it did not have the complete video?—but it did throw in a nice plug for *Homicide Hunter* at the end of the segment.

The story was one of five segments in *20/20*'s "Caught on Tape" special, featuring people who got busted because there was a video camera running somewhere. Marino's story was sandwiched between a piece about a shitfaced drunk who got caught trying to have a small child drive him home, and another about a Hooters waitress who kept getting groped.

In addition to burying the Marino story deep into the hour, the episode did not even receive its usual prime-time time slot. The *20/20* show aired its July 20, 2012, "Caught on Tape" special at 9 PM instead of its usual 10 PM slot because the show needed its expected airtime for breaking coverage about a young man named James Holmes.

Holmes dressed as the Joker and went into an Aurora, Colorado, movie theater with a shotgun, a semiautomatic rifle, and a Glock 22, and started shooting people who were watching *The Dark Knight Rises* at a midnight screening. Holmes killed twelve people and injured seventy.

I watched both *20/20* shows that night, then went to bed and had another horrific nightmare about a C-4 explosion in my hometown.

Just before *Dr. Phil* and *48 Hours* aired, Marino emailed a 3,400-word, single-spaced diatribe to my bosses and colleagues at *Diablo* magazine, complaining about all things related to Pete Crooks.

Marino's email claimed he had done a favor for the magazine by letting us know that the ride-along he had helped stage had been a hoax. Then he complained that I put his life in grave danger by safely coordinating a meeting with law enforcement, not mentioning that he sat on the drug evidence for two months before asking me for help and was intentionally sabotaging a case that the reality show was filming while I was putting him in touch with the right people.

Marino claimed that the producers of *48 Hours, This American Life*, and *20/20* all made disparaging comments to him about me being a pushy and crass attention whore—which was simply not possible, as each program had courted me for interviews.

Marino complained that *Diablo* had not done a big feature about him, after all that he went through as a confidential informant. But once again, Marino failed to own up to the criminal activity he had been involved in while working for Butler, or to admit that he had posed as a *Diablo* reporter to set up a man for a DUI.

Buried deep in the body of the email was a line that summed up Marino's biggest problem with the way I covered the story.

Marino wrote: "[Pete Crooks] knows more than anyone, that I was not a character in Pete Crooks' story, Pete Crooks was a character in mine."

32
The Talented Mr. Marino

THE PROBLEM WITH TRYING to tell the Carl Marino Story is that there are so many versions of it. I knew that I would never again be able to trust Marino when I realized that he had been lying to me about being a Desert Storm war veteran, which was the version I had spent months believing.

I had given Marino the benefit of the doubt many times, but pulled the plug on corresponding with him when I realized he had been perpetuating such a disgraceful lie.

And I quickly realized that I wasn't the only one who Marino had been lying to about his military background. In November 2011, just after I broke off contact with Marino, I happened to look at his Facebook page on Veteran's Day.

I noticed numerous messages from Marino's Facebook friends—including one from his wife, Ilona—thanking him for his military service. I screengrabbed the more detailed comments and started reaching out to several people to see if I could find out what Marino had been saying about his bravery in battle.

I was amazed by what his Facebook friends told me about the Carl Marino stories they had heard.

One of my first chats was with an actor who had worked with Marino on *I (Almost) Got Away With It*. I explained why I was calling and the background about how I was taken for a ten-hour ride-along by Butler and the PI Moms.

"You got duped," the actor said, laughing.

I then explained Marino's role in the hoax and gave him credit for his work as an informant with the DOJ. The actor said that he knew Marino and proceeded to tell me that, in their first conversation, Marino claimed to have received two Purple Hearts and a Silver Star for valor during his service in Operation Desert Storm.

"Wow," I said.

"Wait a second," said the actor. "Did I get duped?"

Another person who had heard Marino's "two Purple Hearts" stories was Ted Leonard, a television director who worked with Marino on *Trauma* and *I (Almost) Got Away With It*. Leonard told me that he believed Marino had been wounded in Desert Storm because 1) Marino told him so, and 2) "Carl showed me a gnarly scar on his arm that he said came from a bullet fragment."

Leonard also told me that he remembered Marino telling stories on the set of *Trauma* about working as a paramedic on September 11, and performing triage on victims of the terrorist attacks.

"I guess it proves he's a pretty good actor," said Leonard, "because I believed him."

Marino told me on several occasions about getting his start on *Trauma*. He had repeated this version of his lucky-break story in two 2014 interviews, claiming that he originally agreed to try out for a *Trauma* role as a police officer. "I found out about it on Craigslist. They wanted real police officers to play the fake police officers on the show," Marino said in an interview.

Marino said he was unable to attend the police officer audition because of complications with a Chris Butler case, but was later asked to do some casting work as a background extra, playing a paramedic.

"Turns out it was a show about paramedics, so it was one of the best things that could have happened," Marino said, during an internet-radio interview in early 2014. Marino went on to explain that after spending three or four episodes as an extra, *Trauma*'s producer and director, Jeffrey Reiner, picked him out of the crowd and gave him a speaking role on the show.

"[Reiner] gave me lines on the show," Marino claimed. "Turns out it was a really big deal. Everybody around me—the other background [actors]—was, like, in awe. Then I saw them opening a chair for me next to the [stars], and the director knew my first name, and I went from making eighty dollars for the day to one thousand dollars for the day. They give you a piece of the trailer, you eat in a different line than the rest of the background actors, and I started to realize, 'Yeah, this is kind of a big deal. This is kind of fun.'"

Marino went on to say that Jeffrey Reiner continued to give him lines, episode after episode, launching his career as an actor.

"Jeffrey Reiner is one of those people where, as long as he knows you can do it, he keeps giving them to you," Marino said. "Luckily, I was on his good side. They gave my character a name on the show and made me part of the cast. And that's kind of what got everything going, as far as my acting went."

It was kind of a fantastic big-break story, like Lana Turner getting discovered at a soda fountain. So, I reached out to Jeffrey Reiner to get his side of the story.

After forwarding Marino's interviews about Reiner to the director's manager, I received the following reply: "I spoke to Jeffrey briefly about your questions—he does not know or remember Mr. Marino."

I contacted an L.A. actor who worked with Marino on a few episodes of the first season of *Homicide Hunter: Lieutenant Joe Kenda*.

The actor had written an article for the Sherman Oaks edition of Patch.com, detailing a day in his life on the set of the show. The article caught my eye because it mentioned that Marino was a retired police detective, just like the guy he plays on the show, Joe Kenda. The article also said that Marino is the cousin of Hall of Fame quarterback Dan Marino. (Marino told me he was a "distant relative" of the NFL legend.)

"Did Carl tell you he was a police detective?" I asked the actor.

"He absolutely told me he was a police detective," said the actor, who said that Marino had also claimed to be a decorated war vet and a first responder at 9/11. The lie-trifecta.

I interviewed the real Joe Kenda, the retired Colorado Springs homicide detective who is featured on the cable crime show *Homicide Hunter: Lieutenant Joe Kenda*. Kenda solved more than 350 murders, retired, and became an accidental TV star when Investigation Discovery created a show about his prolific career. The show has been a huge success for Investigation Discovery, thanks to Kenda's no-nonsense persona. The tough-as-nails detective narrates each episode, explaining the grisly details of a specific murder case that he solved.

Marino plays a young version of Kenda in the re-creation sequences. Example: Kenda says, in voice-over narration: "I wanted to check the police report again, so I went back to my office and pulled the file."

Then Marino is shown looking at a manila folder.

After setting up an interview through Investigation Discovery, I asked Kenda what he thought of Marino. Kenda said, "I've talked to him on the phone one time, for about ten minutes. You know what he told me? In the brief call we had, he told me he was a detective back in New York. I thought, 'You're pretty young to be a retired detective,' so I made a couple of calls. Turns out, he was a detention officer in Upstate New York."

Kenda had seen Marino on *48 Hours*, and told me he thought Marino was "lying his ass off" on that show. "What was he even doing [working for Butler], where someone would give him drugs to sell?"

Kenda, who spent forty years interrogating liars, had an interesting take on Marino. "He's Walter Mitty," Kenda said. "He wants you to think he's this other guy, not the guy he really is. And if you say, 'No, you're *not* that guy, you're this guy,' he gets upset."

Sometime after my interview with Kenda, he had a chance to meet Marino in Knoxville, Tennessee, during production of *Homicide Hunter*'s third season. Kenda posed for a few pictures with Marino, and "the two Kendas" filmed a behind-the-scenes video together. Kenda's experience meeting Marino in person was similar to that of retired FBI agent Chuck Latting.

"I met Walter Mitty," Kenda wrote. "He was quiet, nervous, and intimidated."

Kenda noticed that Marino carried a prop to the set to feel important.

"He has purchased a director's chair, hardwood and canvas, looks pricey," Kenda wrote. "He has had a canvas back support made and embossed with his name in white 4" letters on one side, and the other side reads LIEUTENANT JOE KENDA: HOMICIDE HUNTER in blue. Why don't I have such a chair?"

Filmmaker Adam Reeves, who I know from Bay Area film festivals, told me another doozy. Reeves wrote a screenplay for a family-friendly movie called *December Dilemma*, and cast Marino in a small part in the yet-to-be-shot project. Reeves heard that I was going to be on an upcoming episode of *48 Hours* and asked what the story was about.

I tried to give him the quick version of the Chris Butler story, and told him, "You'll be interested to watch the show because one of your *December Dilemma* cast members worked for Butler."

I described the ride-along that Butler and Marino had devised to set me up as a publicity stunt, then explained that Marino had tipped me off about the hoax and eventually became a criminal informant. Reeves seemed concerned that a member of his cast was involved in such shady business.

"So was Carl even in the military?" Reeves asked me.

"What did he tell you about the military?" I asked.

Reeves told me that Marino had claimed to be a war veteran. During a later conversation, Reeves explained that when Marino had come in to audition for *December Dilemma*, Marino told Reeves an elaborate story about being injured while serving overseas. Reeves recalled that Marino described how a teenage Iraqi boy had ambushed him by hiding above a door and jumping onto Marino's back as he entered a room. Marino told Reeves the Iraqi boy stabbed him in the shoulder with a knife, and the war wound still caused him great discomfort all these years later.

"It was a very detailed story," Reeves told me. "And I know that he told it to a number of other people."

That's true—the part about Marino telling the lie to many people. I've heard the story about Marino stabbed in the back by an Iraqi teen from several sources who worked with Marino on the sets of various TV shows. None of the sources knew one another, but each recounted the same details of the story in independent interviews.

I also heard a version of the story from an ex-girlfriend of Marino's, Dana McConnell, who knew Marino during his jail-deputy days in New York.

"Carl had a small scar on his back, and he said it came from hand-to-hand combat in Iraq," McConnell told me.

McConnell told me that Marino courted her when she was in her very early twenties, but failed to mention he was married at the time. "Carl told me a lot of lies when I knew him. He was not a nice person," said McConnell, who also revealed that she was interviewed by the internal affairs department of the sheriff's office where Marino had worked as a jail deputy.

Another source who knew Marino before he moved to California confirmed that Marino does have a scar on his back, and explained that the scar came from an infected cyst that had to be surgically lanced.

Which stung like a bitch, I'm sure.

It's just that having an infected cyst lanced isn't as exciting a story as being stabbed in the back with the rusty knife blade of an Iraqi teen during a war.

Trauma Extra #1, a groomsman in Carl and Ilona Marino's wedding, was startled to hear that Marino had never earned two Purple Hearts and a Silver Star in Iraq, and that he had not been a police officer back in New York, and that he didn't perform triage on victims of terrorist attacks at Ground Zero on September 11.

"Carl didn't just tell me those stories," said *Trauma* Extra #1. "He told everyone on the set of *Trauma* those stories. In fact, I believe that's how he went from being an extra on the show to getting a speaking part."

Trauma Extra #1 said he felt terribly when I told him that the drug dealer role Marino had recruited him to play in the Case of the San Fernando Valley Hot Tub Party and Decoy Test involved stinging a writer to believe the event was a genuine DOJ investigation.

"I had no idea at all," *Trauma* Extra #1 told me. "And I never would have had anything to do with that if I knew there was an actual DOJ agent there. Carl said it was a routine training exercise for his PI boss."

Trauma Extra #1 said that, after Butler and Wielsch were arrested, Marino claimed to have been a deep-cover DOJ agent the whole time he worked for Chris Butler.

"I figured that had to be bullshit," said *Trauma* Extra #1. "I just did not realize that everything Carl ever told me was bullshit."

Finally, I talked to Greg Carlson, a bartender who lives in the same neighborhood as the Marinos in San Francisco. Carlson knew Carl Marino, who was a regular in a local tavern, because Marino had invited him to participate in Chris Butler's reality show. Carlson had some very interesting information to pass along when I reached out to ask him about his involvement with *PI Moms*.

Carlson told me that Marino had recruited him to help the reality show film some decoy tests. Carlson worked on *PI Moms* in late November 2010, after Marino had taken possession of the first pound of marijuana. Marino had always claimed that once he knew about Butler and Wielsch's drug dealing, he did everything he could to keep innocent people away from Butler, yet here he was inviting a friend to come do day work on the show.

"Carl introduced me to the show people, and told me what a great opportunity it was going to be," Carlson said. "He seemed very excited about the reality show."

In addition to being invited by Marino to be a part of the reality show, Carlson was also invited to participate in the setup of the Livermore winemaker in January 2011. Marino tried to get Carlson to pose as a camera operator for ArtistFilm, but Carlson declined the invitation.

When I explained to Carlson the details of that sting, and what Marino was actually inviting him to do—to pose as an employee of an existing production company as a false pretense to hoodwink a businessman who had already been set up for an illegal Dirty DUI arrest, Carlson was stunned.

Our conversation turned to Marino's background. Carlson believed Marino had been a war veteran and a former police officer, because he had heard Marino make those claims many times. Carlson told me a number of stories about Marino, including an incident in which he witnessed Marino claim a sailor in a San Francisco bar was posing as active military to get free drinks during Fleet Week.

Then Carlson dropped a bombshell on me, *Columbo*-style.

"There's one more thing," Carlson told me. "What did Carl tell you about that marijuana that Butler got busted for selling?"

I explained that Marino definitely sat on the drugs for two months before handing them over to the DOJ, but he had given many interviews claiming he intended to turn in Butler and Wielsch from the moment he first saw the drugs in Butler's warehouse.

"Well, you can do whatever you want with this," Carlson said. "Carl tried to sell me that weed."

Carlson continued. "Carl told me he had access to all this weed—he said there were nine pounds of it—and told me that we could make a lot of easy money if I unloaded it to people I knew who smoked weed. I told Carl I wasn't interested."

Carlson said he was startled when he read in the newspaper that Marino's boss had been busted for selling drugs that were stolen out of police evidence. Soon after that, he ran into Marino in the neighborhood bar and listened to Marino spin a tall tale about being a deep-cover agent for the government.

"Carl was claiming that he was working for the government the entire time, and that he took those guys down," Carlson told me. "I said to him, 'Wait a second, you tried to sell me that weed. I could be looking at prison time.' Carl got flustered and said, 'Oh, the DOJ doesn't care about marijuana, they only care about hard drugs. I just thought I would hook you up.'"

Carlson said that he never trusted Marino after that.
I know the feeling.

The last time I spoke with Marino was in October 2011, but I did see him again in early 2013, when I attended the One Hundred Club Crab Feed fundraiser with Cindy Hall. It was the site of Norm Wielsch and Chris Butler's last dinner together before being arrested in 2011, and I wanted to experience the event in person. Carl and Ilona Marino were there. I'm not really sure why, but the Marinos have attended the benefit for fallen police and firefighters each year since the time Carl wore a wire while breaking crab and drinking wine with Wielsch and Butler.

The night I went, Marino and I made eye contact from across the room. He nodded at me, then spun on his heel and walked in the other direction.

Since I stopped communicating with Marino, I did receive a few emails from him, each angrier than the last. The reasons for his messages were always the same: I would notice someone on Facebook thanking him for his military service, or praising his career as a police officer. I'd reach out and ask, "Why did you think Carl was a war veteran or a cop?" and often they would reply (usually with, "Because that's what he told me").

Sometimes, however, the source would contact Marino and let him know I was asking about him. And Marino would respond by sending me threats that he had secretly (and if so, illegally) recorded every conversation he and I had ever had. Each email would end with Marino's demand that I stop harassing his fans and friends.

One of these contacts was with a woman whose nickname on Facebook was "Lizzy." "Lizzy" had posted a comment on Marino's Facebook page, inviting Marino to "try talking to fellow veterans. There are so many of us who came home wounded and are constantly being told we should be thankful we made it back."

Lizzy also posted a Memorial Day message on his Facebook page, thanking him for his service as a soldier and a law enforcement officer.

I contacted Lizzy and asked what she meant when she wrote that Marino should talk with fellow veterans. After a while, Lizzy replied with an email address—"InquisitiveSoldier"—to write to. Feeling that InquisitiveSoldier sounded like one of Marino's aliases, I wrote the same series of questions, both as a Facebook direct message to Lizzy and in an email to InquisitiveSoldier.

Lizzy wrote back on Facebook, saying, "People at all levels of importance lie about their credentials. Ever hear of the lying bastard Obama? Perfect example." At which point, I was pretty much done asking Lizzy questions, as I wasn't interested in theories about birth certificates and socialism and Kenya.

But then I received an email from InquisitiveSoldier, which had a much different tone. The person sending this message wanted to know everything I knew about Carl Marino, and said that Marino had never claimed to be active duty. It was signed, "Respectfully, Lizzie." With *ie* at the end of her name, not a *y*, like the Lizzy I had been corresponding with on Facebook.

Hi, Carl.

I stopped writing back to the InquisitiveSoldier address, as there was nothing more to learn from the "Lizzy" who hated Obama or the "Lizzie" who respectfully wanted to know what I knew about Marino. Neither could provide a believable response to my query about why she thanked Marino for his service as a soldier and a law enforcement officer.

If Lizzie was really Carl, as I suspect, it demonstrates once again what a far cry he is from the person I had originally thought was going to be one of the "good guys" in this book.

I spent most of 2011 thinking Carl was a friend, someone who was thankful for my help exposing Butler and Wielsch for their heinous crimes. I had liked Carl—or Rutherford—the inside informant who had helped me become an accidental investigative journalist.

I thought we had been a crime-busting team for the ages. Too bad.

But hindsight is twenty-twenty. Now I believe that "Lizzie" and "Ronald Rutherford" were both smoke screen aliases, phantom trolls with self-serving agendas.

When I didn't reply to Lizzie's emails, I received another email from Carl's own account, with a remarkable explanation for the various stories I might hear about him from various sources.

Marino wrote:

> You never really asked me about my acting, which I found strange... First and foremost, I am a very strict method actor. Most who are close with me already know that, as difficult as it may be on them to deal with. I actually had the honor to discuss this exact topic with Daniel Day-Lewis at the most recent SAG awards. As you should know, he is one of the most famous method actors and actually became Abraham Lincoln for many months before they even started filming.

I didn't bother reaching out to Daniel Day-Lewis' management on that one, to see if the acclaimed actor remembered having a deep conversation about method preparation with someone who posed for a quick picture with him at the 2013 Screen Actors Guild afterparty.

Marino, who has mentioned in numerous interviews that he has no formal acting training, continued:

> I also create backgrounds and history for my characters and live them thoroughly. I did so for my character on *Trauma* for almost 2 years as I did for my first small role in *Sedona's Rule*. These character backgrounds and histories, while sometimes similar to some of my past, are just that... character backgrounds. If you have ever acted you would see how that is invaluable to getting into character. It is the most helpful tool I have found to be a better actor. Over the past couple of years, when not filming *Homicide Hunter*, I was a full bird Colonel as a lead in a movie project and the sheriff of a small town as the lead on a TV pilot. Both have backgrounds I created that are super complex and fantastic. One very heroic and the other very tragic, and I lived them both at the times as those characters, both when on set and when not. These aren't Carl Marino's background, and I can't be responsible for other people's assumptions or ignorance.

So, that was Marino's explanation for why some people might have believed the detailed stories he told them about being a decorated war hero, a retired police detective, and a 9-11 responder.

He was just acting.

33
The End of the Line

THE BIG-SCREEN Hollywood version of the Chris Butler reality show scandal has yet to be filmed. Hopefully, someone will pick it up and run with it. I think this material could make a great movie, and I would love to show it at my classic film series someday.

Until then, here's what happened to the real figures in the story:

Former PI Moms **Charmagne Peters** and **Denise Antoon** would not comment about the fake ride-along following Chris Butler's arrest. I did not hear from either one again. However, former PI Mom **Ami Wiltz** did get her private investigator's license and is currently running her own PI business, Ami's Investigations, in the Bay Area.

Television producer **Lucas Platt** has worked on several successful series, including *Alaska Wing Men* and *Boston's Finest*, after Lifetime pulled the plug on *PI Moms*. The footage from *PI Moms* has never been shown to the public.

San Ramon police officer **Louis Lombardi** was the first cop in the scandal to plead to charges of selling marijuana and stealing nearly $50,000 in cash, as well as personal property, during searches of suspects' homes. Can't do that, Lou.

On May 4, 2012, Lombardi was sentenced to three years in federal prison.

Former Richmond police officers **Ray Thomas** and **Danny Harris** pleaded guilty in federal court in March 2012. Harris admitted to making false statements in connection with purchasing firearms, and both Harris and Thomas admitted to conspiring to obstruct an official proceeding.

On August 21, 2012, US District Judge Claudia Wilken sentenced Harris to five years of probation and Thomas to three years of probation. Wilken mentioned in court that the big mistake that Harris and Thomas made was getting involved with Chris Butler.

On May 4, 2012, **Chris Butler** pleaded guilty in federal court to seven felony counts, including selling drugs, extortion, robbery, a civil rights violation against the Candyman, and planting illegal wiretaps and listening devices in more than seventy-five automobiles.

I sat in court and watched Butler plead out, remove his belt, and be escorted out of the courtroom and into the piss-yellow fluorescent lights of the hallway to jail. Butler returned to court on September 25, 2012, and was sentenced to eight years in federal prison.

In 2014, Butler received a sentence reduction of one year for cooperating with investigators and prosecutors in the cases against his former friends in the East Bay law enforcement community.

Butler is currently serving in Colorado, where I understand he made acquaintances with Rod Blagojevich, the former governor of Illinois, and Jeffrey Skilling, the former CEO of Enron. Those must be interesting conversations at the cafeteria lunch table.

Butler never responded to my letter requesting a follow-up interview.

After being arrested in February 2011, **Norm Wielsch** worked as a volunteer for the Salvation Army in Antioch, California, and became very involved in a church in Concord, California.

On December 2, 2012, I went to Wielsch's church and watched him say good-bye to the congregation and minister. Wielsch credited the guidance he received from his minister, as well as the support he received form his wife and children, as the reasons he did not commit suicide following his spectacular flameout from his career as a narcotics officer.

On December 5, 2012, Wielsch pleaded guilty to five felony counts of stealing and selling drugs, theft of federal funds, civil rights conspiracy, and robbery. On May 20, 2013, he was sentenced to fourteen years in federal prison.

Wielsch is currently serving his time in Texas, where he is taking ministerial classes and working in the prison's church and hospital.

Former Danville Sheriff's Deputy **Steve Tanabe** was the only police officer implicated in the scandal who challenged his charges in federal court and requested a trial.

While he was awaiting his day in court, Tanabe auditioned for some of the same Bay Area–based true-crime shows that Marino had tried out for. When Tanabe was cast as a detective on an episode of *I (Almost) Got Away With It*, the show's production company and casting director started getting "I'm doing you a favor" emails from someone named Rene Riley. Rene Riley complained that Tanabe should not be cast because of his legal troubles, and falsely accused Tanabe of frightening people on the set of *I (Almost) Got Away With It*.

I have the emails and am quite certain that I know who sent them.

Tanabe's trial went well for the government. On September 3, 2013, Tanabe was convicted on six out of seven felony charges for his role in the dirty DUI arrests of the Martinez businessman and the Livermore winemaker.

The jury acquitted Tanabe on the count that he extorted cocaine as payment, presumably because the only direct evidence the prosecution was able to provide that Tanabe accepted cocaine was the testimony of Chris Butler, who was transferred from federal prison in Colorado for the trial.

While on the stand, Butler admitted to setting people up for DUIs, staging fake cases for the media, planting drugs on people, setting up police officers for internal affairs reviews, making a false arrest on a teenager, running an illegal massage parlor, and a whole shitload of other shady behavior. Butler, wearing his prison pajamas and leg shackles, did not make a likable witness.

Tanabe did have a ray of sunshine in late 2013, when he got his biggest break yet as an actor, playing Drake Manns, a corrupt Oakland cop in an online series called *The Dirty.* Tanabe told me that the show's creators kept his character alive until episode three, at which point Tanabe had to report to prison. After that, the filmmakers had Drake Manns take a bullet to the head, putting him into a long coma. Manns may pull out of the coma after Tanabe's release, so watch for that.

On February 19, 2014, Tanabe was sentenced to fifteen months in federal prison. He self-surrendered on April 15, 2014, in a federal prison in Colorado.

Madame DD was called to testify in the case against Tanabe. She told the jury that she did give cocaine to Chris Butler on two occasions, but did not know what he did with the drugs. There was some question in the courtroom about a previous statement Madame DD had given to a grand jury, in which she claimed she had only given Butler cocaine on one occasion. Madame DD clarified the statement by saying she did provide cocaine to Butler on two occasions, but she hadn't mentioned the second time because she did not want to get a friend in trouble.

Madame DD is currently working in the public sector, thrilled to be away from Chris Butler.

She has been approached by multiple reality shows, but has yet to appear on one.

Mystery Date, aka **Ryan Romano**, continues to nanny, bartend, and party.

Carl Marino was never prosecuted for his role in the illegal arrest of the Candyman, for filing a false complaint against Lieutenant Michael Booker of the Richmond Police Department, or for his role in the dirty DUI setups of the Turkish businessman or the Livermore winemaker.

Marino was never called to testify in the federal trial against Steve Tanabe. Marino did testify in a family law case involving the Turkish businessman he set up for a dirty DUI. On December 13, 2011, Marino testified under oath that 1) he had never participated in any shady setups for Butler before that particular dirty DUI (despite having previously participated in the Candyman takedown, the setup of the Richmond police lieutenant, and numerous "decoy tests"); 2) at the time of the first client meeting about that dirty DUI, Marino was already trying to get in touch with law enforcement about Butler and Wielsch's drug dealing (which Marino did not know about at that time); and 3) Marino had been given immunity from prosecution by the California Department of Justice. However, according to my sources in the California Department of Justice, Marino was never given immunity.

Marino received copious media coverage for his work as an informant. He gave interviews to *20/20*, *Dr. Phil*, *48 Hours*, WLEA radio in New York, NBC11 Bay Area, CBS5 San Francisco, *This American Life*, and the *San Francisco Chronicle*, and used some variation of his mantra, "There's no doubt that Butler and Wielsch would have killed me," in at least seven of those interviews.

Marino also stated in a radio interview that "both the [California] Department of Justice and the FBI completely back me up as to what I did and what my motivations were, and that I did the right thing."

I asked representatives from both law enforcement agencies if Marino's comment was an accurate assessment of their position.

Neither agency would come close to verifying Marino's claim. An FBI representative replied, "I will not be interpreting or speculating on what Carl Marino may or may not have said."

The California Department of Justice sources were less vague in their response. Both Kent Shaw and Dean Johnston told me it was very clear from the moment he turned over those two bags of weed that Marino was upset that he had not been cast on *PI Moms*.

"If Carl had gotten a role on that television show, we may have never heard about that marijuana," Shaw told me.

Ironically, Marino did wind up playing a detective on a cable TV show. He filmed season four of *Homicide Hunter: Lieutenant Joe Kenda* in 2014. The show is a smash for the Investigation Discovery channel, averaging more than 1.7 million viewers per episode in season three. Marino frequently posts comments and interacts with viewers on the Carl Marino Fanpage on Facebook, which has more than four thousand followers from around the world.

Also in 2014, Marino announced via Facebook that he and his wife would be running twenty half-marathons in support of the Wounded Warriors Foundation, a cause Marino claimed was "very close to [his] heart."

"We run for those that can no longer," Marino wrote on his fund-raising page.

Kent Shaw and **Dean Johnston** continue to do outstanding work for California's Department of Justice Bureau of Investigations. In September 2013, Johnston headed an investigation in the Bay Area that led to the arrest of the alleged killer of eight-year-old Alaysha Carradine, who was murdered in Berkeley at a sleepover party.

In July 2014, Shaw was appointed deputy director of the Division of Law Enforcement, a position in charge of all the bureaus of law enforcement within California's Department of Justice. Bad guys, watch out.

Shaw and Johnston, and the Department of Justice investigative team who took down Butler and Wielsch, have my eternal appreciation for their outstanding, expedient work. I am glad I was able to put Ronald Rutherford in touch with the right people.

Assistant United States Attorney **Hartley West** and four other deputy district attorneys were given the 2014 California Lawyer Attorney of the Year Award for their efforts in prosecuting former reality show wannabe and setup enthusiast Chris Butler; disgraced former law enforcement officers Norm Wielsch, Louis Lombardi, Ray Thomas, Danny Harris, and Steve Tanabe; and former family law attorney Mary Nolan, who conspired with Butler to place illegal listening devices in cars.

I sat down for an interview with West in April 2014. We discussed a number of topics, including the concern I had felt when I took the allegations to law enforcement that Chris Butler and Norm Wielsch were selling stolen drugs. I told West that I was thankful that Cindy Hall, Dean Johnston, and Kent Shaw had acted with immediacy and integrity, and that the information about police corruption had not been swept under the rug, which would have caused me to spend the rest of my days paranoid about the lights in my rearview mirror.

"It was a very interesting series of cases to work on," West told me. "And for that, I thank you."

Cindy Hall retired from a distinguished career in law enforcement one year shy of full pension, due to injuries she sustained on the job. She remains a dear friend.

I continue to work at *Diablo* magazine and am currently behind deadline for filing a guide to East Bay jazz. I also host a classic movie night once a month at the historic Orinda Theatre. We recently flew in Jerry Mathers to help me introduce the Alfred Hitchcock gem *The Trouble with Harry.*

Author Pete Crooks poses with Hollywood legend Tippi Hedren after a benefit screening of Alfred Hitchcock's *The Birds. Photo by John Crooks.*

If you're in the Bay Area, you should come check out my film series—especially when we show *Double Indemnity*, or *Thieves' Highway*, or *Ace in the Hole*.

I just love a good noir.

Acknowledgments

THE AUTHOR WOULD LIKE to offer special thanks to Charles Willeford, Elmore Leonard, and Carl Hiaasen, whose work made me want to be a writer long before I got caught up with the creeps, pyschos, and actual cops featured in this book.

I would also like to thank the editors and staff of *Diablo* magazine, past and present. It has been a thrill and a treat to get to work so creatively in a community I care so much about. Thanks also to my literary agent, Katherine Latshaw, for her enthusiasm and dedication to this project. And to the staff at BenBella, including publisher Glenn Yeffeth and my editor, Erin Kelley, thanks for your interest in this book, which has been such a huge part of my life for more than four years now.

My deepest appreciation goes out to Kent Shaw, deputy director of the Division of Law Enforcement for the California Department of Justice for his support of my reporting this complete story. In addition to Shaw, I also must acknowledge Special Agent Dean Johnston and the team he put together for this investigation, not just for their availability for interviews but for their tireless work on behalf of the citizens of California.

Thanks are also due to Lucas Platt and Chris Flitter, whose perspectives were crucial to reporting the inside story of what really went on during the filming of a certain reality show. Other media personalities who deserve a shout-out are Josh Bearman, Ben Calhoun, and Ira Glass from *This American Life*, Greg Fisher, Chuck Stevenson, Peter Shaw, and Maureen Maher from *48 Hours*.

Numerous sources, both named and confidential, deserve thanks for their interviews and revelations during my reporting. Beyond those mentioned in the book, I'd like to thank the dozens of private investigators, law enforcement professionals, news journalists and television producers, West Point graduates and military experts, legal experts, and psychiatric experts who were helpful to my understanding of the characters and events in this book. And I want to thank Joe Kenda, retired homicide detective and subject of *Homicide Hunter: Lieutenant Joe Kenda*. Joe has become a good friend and deserves all the success in the world as a cable TV celebrity.

My parents, John and Shirley, and my sister, Madeline, have my lifelong appreciation for their love and support. Sorry about all the f-bombs, Mom.

My wife, Tamara, deserves my deepest appreciation for her love, her sharpness and savvy, and most of all, her patience. I love you very much. And, I would be remiss not to acknowledge the dedication of our dogs, Henry and Shylo (no longer with us), and Maizy and Maybelline—who have greeted me with enthusiasm and energy on many nights that I have come home dead-tired during this ordeal.

Finally, Cindy Hall deserves my eternal gratitude for being there for me when I came to her in a panic. She also deserves the appreciation of the East Bay community that she helped by getting the ball rolling on a serious criminal investigation, even though she would never expect credit for what she did. In my mind, Cindy is the one truly heroic crime-solving soccer mom in this story.

About the Author

PETE CROOKS is a Bay Area native, fan of crime fiction and film noir, and longtime senior editor and senior writer for *Diablo* magazine. In addition to his work for *Diablo*, Crooks has worked as a film reviewer for KFRC radio and KSAN radio in San Francisco, and has contributed articles about baseball, entertainment, and travel to *Access, Marin, Napa Sonoma, Oakland Athletics, Santa Cruz Style*, and *Via* magazines. Crooks also hosts a monthly classic film series in the Bay Area, and hosts *Get Lit*, a television show featuring interviews with a range of authors and artists. Crooks lives in the East Bay with his wife, Tamara, and four rescue animals.